LIFE AND LETTERS

OF

WASHINGTON IRVING.

THE

LIFE AND LETTERS

OF

WASHINGTON IRVING.

BY HIS NEPHEW

PIERRE M. IRVING.

VOLUME III.

NEW YORK:
G. P. PUTNAM, 441 BROADWAY.
1864.

JOHN F. TROW,
PRINTER AND STEREOTYPER,
50 Greene Street.

CONTENTS

CHAPTER I.

CHAPTER II.

CHAPTER III.

CHAPTER IV.

CHAPTER V.

CHAPTER VI.

CHAPTER VII.

CHAPTER VIII.

CHAPTER IX.

CHAPTER X.

CHAPTER XI.

CHAPTER XII.

CHAPTER XIII.

CHAPTER XIV.

CHAPTER XV.

CHAPTER XVI.

CHAPTER XVII.

CHAPTER XVIII.

CHAPTER XIX.

CHAPTER XX.

CHAPTER XXI.

CHAPTER XXII.

LIFE AND LETTERS

OF

WASHINGTON IRVING.

CHAPTER I.

PETER IRVING IN PARIS—AN AUTOGRAPHICAL SKETCH OF HIMSELF—PUBLICATION OF THE ALHAMBRA—ITS RECEPTION—EXCURSION TO WASHINGTON—THE OLD GENERAL—HENRY CLAY—INVITED TO A PUBLIC DINNER IN PHILADELPHIA—MEETING WITH COOPER, THE TRAGEDIAN—VISIT TO THE HAUNTS OF RIP VAN WINKLE—TOUR TO THE WHITE MOUNTAINS—AT TARRYTOWN—THE BRAMIN—FIRST NOTION OF SUNNYSIDE—SARATOGA SPRINGS—ITALIAN TROUPE—TRENTON FALLS—HOMEBRED DELIGHTS.

THE excitement and exhilaration that followed Mr. Irving's arrival in his native city did not soon subside. "I have been topsy-turvy ever since," he writes to Peter, after a hurried and laborious, though joyous round of visits and congratulations among his friends; friends, at his departure, "clustered in neighboring contiguity in a moderate community, now scattered widely asunder over a splendid metropolis." New York had been advancing rapidly in wealth and population since he left, and at this date numbered more than two hundred thousand inhabitants. "I have repeatedly wished, since my return, that you could be here with me," he writes to Peter, whose prolonged exile from his native land now threatened to be final. "The mode of living, the sources of quiet and social enjoyment, and the sphere of friendly and domestic pleasures, are improved and multiplied to a degree that has delightfully surprised me."

The brother to whom this extract was addressed, now sixty years of age, had made no resolution to spend the remainder of his days in Europe, and in a letter to his friend Beasley, the American consul at Havre, lying before me, expresses "a great desire to return home," but, he adds, "at my time of life, and in my state of health, and with my acquired habits and my aversion to a sea voyage, in which I am accustomed to suffer so much, I do not think a return probable." He was now living in Paris, whither he had withdrawn from Havre for solitude and regimen.

It is in the crowd of a great metropolis (he writes) that I *can most successfully seek seclusion, and live precisely in the* way most suitable to my health. * * * I do not know any city so desirable as a residence as Paris. All the works of science and of art, of curiosity and amusement are so varied and abundant and accessible; and at the same time absolute solitude is so completely within our reach, without becoming an object of remark or supervision. To prevent myself from becoming lonely and hypochondriacal, while the state of my health obliges me to withhold myself from society, I have become *abonné* at one of the theatres. I have selected the Vaudeville, which has the best company, and exhibits the pleasantest pieces, both serious and comic. They have generally three in an evening, and sometimes four, but I never stay to more than two.

In a letter to Washington, a month later in date [August 19], he gives a similar sketch of his life in the great metropolis:

I live so retired in the midst of this great city, in consideration of my health, that I know little of what is passing, and see but few of our many countrymen who resort to it. Society is a vortex, and I am obliged to keep resolutely without the margin, or I should inevitably be engulphed. I therefore avoid dinners and *soirées*, and abstain as far as possible even from visits. By pursuing rigidly this course, I escape the indisposition to which I seem peculiarly liable; and Paris is so full of resource for a literary lounger, in its libraries, its galleries of painting and sculpture, its noble institutions in every department of science, its palaces and gardens, all open to the stranger, and its places of amusement all easy of access, that a man may lead here the life of a hermit, and at the same time a life of luxurious enjoyment. I have also punctual correspondents and supplies of newspapers in the reading room and in my own apartment, through the attention of our friend Beasley, so that I can supervise the operations of the great world as I would overlook a game of chess. We read of anchorites who retired to caves and cells, amid rocks and deserts, when infirmities or other causes rendered them unsuitable to mingle in society, and the world seems to have sanctioned and approved their taste. I feel justified, therefore, in my more cheerful seclusion.

The passages I have quoted from these letters of Peter exhibit the character of the invalid, and the wise and beautiful spirit of philosophy in which, in the midst of his ailments, he contrived to put into life whatever of comfort and enjoyment it could be made to yield.

In another letter, after giving Washington a picture of his being "most snugly and pleasantly established in a little apartment in the Hotel Breteuil," he adds: "You perceive, therefore, that I am getting along very cheerily, the indisposition to which I am rather predisposed being kept completely at arm's length by quiet and moderate living; and when you recollect how principal a part you have performed in procuring me so serene and agreeable a sunset, it cannot but form an addition by reflection to your own happiness."

I am delighted (writes Washington in reply) to find you are passing your time so comfortably and pleasantly at Paris. That old hotel is the very place for you—a kind of Castle of Indolence, where you seem to have various inmates passing in review from time to time before you. Though it would glad my heart and rejoice your friends to have you on this side of the Atlantic, and though there are sources of enjoyment here of which you have no idea from former experience, yet I know the wisdom of being content with *good*, instead of seeking for *better*, and think you are acting wisely in resting satisfied with plain, simple PARIS.

In the first letter written to his brother Washington, after hearing of the safe arrival of the vessel at New York, Peter mentions that a French translation of the Alhambra had been published in two octavo volumes, and the work had received favorable notices in several of the Parisian journals, from which he extracts some paragraphs. It would appear from this that the publication of the Alhambra in England, and possibly its translation in France, preceded its appearance in America, where it was issued by Messrs. Carey & Lea on the 9th of June, three weeks after the author's arrival in his own country. He had expected that its publication would precede his arrival, and it is not easy to see why it did not, as the contract of his agent, Ebenezer Irving, granting to Carey & Lea "a right to print, publish, and vend five thousand five hundred copies," bears date as early as the 17th of March. The time required for disposing of these five thousand five hundred copies was not to exceed the last day of December in the year one thousand eight hundred and thirty-four. After the printing, if the work should be prepared for publication from stereotype plates, the author was to have the privilege of taking the plates at a fair value, if he should elect to do so. The consideration was three thousand dollars, payable in three equal notes, bearing date on the day of publication, in six, nine, and twelve months. The amount paid by Colburn & Bentley for the absolute copyright of the work, as has been before stated, was one thousand guineas, in six, nine, and twelve months.

The Alhambra was published in Philadelphia in two duodecimo volumes. I give two extracts, which may serve as a specimen of the immediate tone of criticism. The first I take from a Baltimore paper of June 16, seven days after the publication:

> The Alhambra displays the characteristic excellencies of Mr. Irving—the easy, natural narrative, the smooth and elegant diction, the pithy humor. The grace and polish of his style are generally considered Mr. Irving's chief merit. A too high value cannot, certainly, be put upon these qualities in a book: the want of them sinks many an otherwise good one. But still, they are secondary. It may even be said, that they cannot exist without the presence of more substantial qualities. You cannot give a high polish to a common substance: an intrinsic fineness of grain is indispensable to this; and hence, the existence of a high degree of polish on the exterior denotes internal excellence of material. Gracefulness, too, is inseparably connected with something internal: it is not an addition, but rather an emanation.
>
> When, therefore, the style of Mr. Irving is made the object of especial commendation, it must be recollected that the qualities of style are dependent upon the qualities of the matter they set forth. The character of the style of an

author is ultimately determined by that of his thoughts and feelings. It is not merely to peculiar cultivation—to the study of good models, however serviceable as auxiliary exercise—that is owing the charm of Mr. Irving's style; but it is to the soundness of his intellect—the correctness of his feelings—to his susceptibility to the beautiful and the touching—his accuracy of observation—to the harmony of his mind with nature and with itself—in short, to those capabilities whose combined action constitutes his individuality as a man, and his superiority as a writer.

Under the light, and sometimes fantastic sketches of the Alhambra, these capabilities are all manifested. Like the slight and airy fabric of a gothic spire, the volumes have a solid basis: their most marvellous fictions rest on a shrewd observation of real life. Beneath the *naif* narration of the wildest dreams of oriental imagination, there flows a current of good sense; behind some of the most comic and grotesque scenes there lurks a latent wisdom.

The next extract I take from the New York *Mirror* of June 23, a weekly periodical edited by George P. Morris, Theodore S. Fay, and Nathaniel P. Willis—names well known in the literary world. After speaking of the serious disadvantage a popular writer has to contend against in the unmeaning and vague expectations elicited by a brilliant fame, and alluding to the Sketch Book and Bracebridge Hall as the greatest enemies his future productions would ever meet, the critic proceeds:

Yet the Tales of the Alhambra are brilliant and striking, told with the most delightful grace of language, and addressed to the imagination of all classes. The preliminary sketches, relating the author's ramblings over Spain, his approach to the palace from which the volumes derive their title, his drawings of character, his minute household observations, his moonlight thoughts on that interesting scene, his reveries from the various points of prospect, are, in our estimation, really delicious. Their very familiar and easy simplicity makes them so. They are impressed in every page, every line, every word, with the reality of truth and the glow of nature. They are evidently no inventions, but transcripts. His scenes stretch away before you; his people move, look, and walk with an individuality and a force only to be produced by the hand of a master. Indeed, these opening pages are full of those delightfully graphic and pleasing delineations peculiar to this author, and worthy of the best parts of the Sketch Book.

This "beautiful Spanish Sketch Book," as it was happily designated by Prescott, the historian, was also very favorably noticed in the *Westminster Review* for July, in an article which, after singling out portions as of great felicity, concludes thus:

The whole is a luxury, but of an extremely refined order. As a work of art, it has few rivals among modern publications. Were a lecture to be given on the structure of the true poetical prose, nowhere would it be possible to find more luculent examples. Many paragraphs, and even chapters, want but the voice to make them discourse most eloquent music.

The *North American Review* for October, which contained, by the way, a review of Wheaton's History of the Northmen, from the pen of Mr. Irving, in an article written by the distinguished Edward Everett, remarks of it: "The subjects are all wrought up with great felicity," "and are among the most finished and elegant specimens of style to be found in the language." I know not whether it was before or after the publication of the Alhambra that the poet Campbell remarked to an American gentleman, from whose brother I have the anecdote: "Washington Irving has added clarity to the English tongue."

The Alhambra was dedicated to David Wilkie, the painter, his companion, as we have seen, in many Spanish scenes, though he did not accompany him to Granada. When it appeared, the author was at Washington, to which city he had repaired a few days after the public dinner which had welcomed his return, to make his bow to the head of the Government, and settle his accounts as *chargé*. He wished also to pass a little time with the McLanes, from whom he had received the most pressing letters of invitation, and who had already prepared a room for him. Mr. McLane was, at this period of great political discord and discontent, Secretary of the Treasury under Andrew Jackson, who was soon to launch his memorable veto at the bill for the renewal of the charter of the Bank of the United States, while glancing ominously at the imperial State of South Carolina, preparing to pass her ordinance of nullification, accompanied with threats of secession, and armed hostility and defiance to the Government.

My journey (he writes to Peter, from Washington, June 16) was rapid but delightful, being for the greater part of the way in splendid steamboats, and at one place for some distance on a railroad. I slept in Philadelphia, and arrived at Washington in the evening of the second day. Here I was received with acclamation by the McLanes, large and small, and have now spent nearly a fortnight with them in the most delightful manner.

* * * * * *

McLane stands the fatigue and annoyance of his station much better than I had anticipated, and seems generally in better tone of spirits than he was at London.

I have been most kindly received by the old general, with whom I am much pleased as well as amused. As his admirers say, he is truly an *old Roman*—to which I would add, *with a little dash of the Greek;* for I suspect he is as *knowing*, as I believe he is *honest.* I took care to put myself promptly on a fair and independent footing with him; for, in expressing warmly and sincerely how much I had been gratified by the unsought, but most seasonable mark of confidence he had shown me, when he hinted something about a disposition to place me elsewhere, I let him know emphatically that I wished for nothing more—that my whole desire was to live among my countrymen, and to follow my usual pursuits. In fact, I am persuaded that my true course is to be master of myself and of my time. Official station cannot add to my happiness or respectability, and certainly would stand in the way of my literary career.

The opinion you express in regard to your future career (writes Peter in reply) accords very much with my own. It is difficult to accept of office without being supposed to attach yourself to a party, and it is then in the nature of things that the opposing factions should presently regard you as an enemy. The great object of ambition is that popularity which constitutes renown. You have fortunately obtained it without any charlatanism, by the quiet operation of your qualities and exertion of your talents. A perseverance in the same course seems to hold out prosperity, respectability, and happiness.

The letter of Washington, from which I broke off to give this passage of Peter's reply, continues:

I have renewed my acquaintance with Clay, who looks much better than I had expected to find him, and very much like his former self. He tells me he has improved greatly in health since he was dismissed from office, and finds that it is good for man as well as beast to be turned out occasionally to grass. Certainly official life in Washington must be harassing and dismal in the extreme.*

I have been offered public dinners at Philadelphia and Baltimore, but have declined them, as I shall all further ceremonials of the kind; but the general manifestation of cordial kindness and good will I have met in all places and at all hands, since my arrival, is deeply gratifying.

* Henry Clay had been Secretary of State under the Presidency of John Quincy Adams. The latter, a veteran statesman, retired from the

The following is the reply of Mr. Irving to the letter of C. C. Biddle, Esq., and numerous other gentlemen, inviting him to a public dinner in Philadelphia:

WASHINGTON, June 9, 1832.

GENTLEMEN:

I cannot feel otherwise than deeply sensible of the distinguished honor you propose to confer on me, in giving me a public dinner on my return to Philadelphia. Associated as your city is with some of the most agreeable recollections of my early life, and endeared as it is to me by many cherished friendships, I know of no city but that of my birth where the proffered testimonial of esteem and kindness would be more acceptable. I have, however, so strong and unfeigned a repugnance to being the object of public distinction of the kind, that, with the exception of the first welcome to my native place, I have made up my mind to decline all invitations but those of a private nature.

Trusting that you will properly appreciate these reasons, and will feel assured of my heartfelt gratitude and perfect respect, I have the honor to be, gentlemen, your very obliged friend and servant,

WASHINGTON IRVING.

In the following letter to his brother Peter, we have an account of his first meeting with his old theatrical friend, Thomas A. Cooper, and Mary Fairlie, his

chair of state, was now serving his country as a member of the House of Representatives. Clay was in the Senate.

wife, the "Sophy Sparkle," as before noted, of Salmagundi:

PHILADELPHIA, *June* 21*st.*—I have only time to write a few hurried lines at long intervals, my time and mind are so much engrossed in my present hurried existence. I left Washington a few days since, and stopped a couple of days at Baltimore, where I was so much pleased that I have determined to pay it a visit of some space in the autumn.

This morning I was seated at breakfast at the public table of the Mansion House, when Cooper entered to take his repast. I recognized him instantly; indeed, he retains much of his shape and look, though the former is a little squarer and heavier. I immediately accosted him. He took his seat beside me, and we had an interesting dish of chat. He was on the point of starting for his home at Bristol, and invited me to pay his wife and family a visit, and return in the afternoon steamboat. So said, so done. I took my seat beside him in a light, open carriage, with a tall stripling in the uniform of a cadet of West Point, whom he introduced as his eldest son, and who had much of his mother's countenance. I found Mary Fairlie in a pretty cottage in the pretty town of Bristol, on the banks of the Delaware. She was pale, and thinner than I had expected to find her, yet still retaining much of her former self. I passed a very agreeable and interesting day there.

* * * * * *

Mary talked much about you, and, like all your old friends, expressed the most longing desire to see you in this country. After dining with them, I got on board a steamboat that was passing at five o'clock, and was whisked up to this city in an hour and a half.

New York, *June 28th.*—Since writing the foregoing, I saw Cooper act a few scenes of Macbeth, before a very thin Philadelphia audience. He acted much as formerly, excepting rather more slowly and heavily. His form is still fine on the stage, but his countenance is muzzy and indistinct. I was engaged for the evening, and could only stay to the end of his dagger and murder scene. I should think his Macbeth equal to any they have at present in England, though this is not saying much. It did not relish with me, however, as in the olden time; but a thin and cold-hearted audience is enough to dampen the spirit of a performer, and to chill the feelings of a spectator.

Charles Joseph Latrobe and the Count de Pourtales, the travelling companions mentioned in the following letter, made the acquaintance of Mr. Irving at Havre previous to his embarcation, and were his fellow passengers across the Atlantic. They also accompanied him, as will be seen hereafter, in his roving expedition to the prairies of the far West. Latrobe afterward wrote a work, entitled "The Rambler in North America," which was published in London in 1835, and inscribed to Washington Irving, "in token of affectionate esteem and remembrance."

[*To Peter Irving, at Paris.*]

New York, July 9, 1832.

My dear Brother:

I received, last evening, your letter from Paris, dated May 18th, and am sorry to find that your headaches continue so bad as to oblige you to fly from Havre. I trust, however, that a respite from the hospitable oppression of friend Beasley has before this restored you to your usual health.

I wrote to you some days since, giving an account of my excursion to Washington. Since then I have been for a few days up the Hudson. I set off in company with James Paulding, Mr. Latrobe, and the Count de Pourtales, whom I have found most agreeable travelling companions. We left New York about seven o'clock, in one of those great steamboats that are like floating hotels, and we arrived at West Point in about *four hours.* Gouverneur Kemble's barge, with an awning, was waiting for us, and conveyed us across the river into a deep cove to his cottage, which is buried among beautiful forest trees. Here we passed three or four hot days most luxuriously, lolling on the grass under the trees, and occasionally bathing in the river. You would be charmed with Gouverneur's little retreat; it is quite a bachelor's Elysium. * * * From thence we took steamboat, and in a few hours were landed at Catskill, where a stage coach was in waiting, and whirled us twelve miles up among the mountains to a fine hotel built on the very brow of a precipice, and commanding one of the finest prospects in the world. We remained here until the next day, visiting the waterfall, glen, &c., that are pointed out as the veritable haunts of Rip Van Winkle.

This was the author's first visit to the scene of his renowned story, published twelve years before. "I have little doubt," writes Peter in reply, "but some curious travellers will yet find some of the bones of his dog, if they can but hit upon the veritable spot of his long sleep." The letter proceeds:

The wild scenery of these mountains outdoes all my conception of it. Leaving the hotel at four o'clock in the afternoon, we took steamboat the same evening, and landed in New York at six o'clock the next morning, after enjoying a comfortable night's sleep. In fact, one appears to be wafted from place to place in this country as if by magic.

It will be borne in mind that Peter had left the country in the beginning of 1809, just after the invention of steamboats, and that it was altogether natural in Washington, in writing to him, to refer constantly to the changes and improvements that had taken place in the country during the lapse of twenty-three years in which he had been away. At the close of the letter which I have quoted in part, he mentions an intended excursion to the White Mountains in New Hampshire, which, says Peter in reply, "are altogether strangers to me."

Three weeks later, when he had just returned to Tarrytown from a visit to Boston and a tour to the White Mountains, he writes to Peter (August 3):

At Boston I passed five days, a great part of which was in company with Newton and his friends. * * * Here I met with Mr. Latrobe and Count Pourtales, and we proceeded on our tour to the White Mountains. The journey through the centre of New Hampshire was delightful—the roads good, the inns good, and the country beautiful beyond expectation. A fine medley of lakes and forests, and bright, pure running streams. At an inn at the head of a fine lake* we paused for

* Lake Winnepisaugee, or Winnipisiogee.

part of two days. On my return to the inn after a ramble, I observed a pleasant face smiling at me from the parlor window. I entered, and who should it be but Mrs. L——, who, with our worthy Paris friend of apple-pie memory, and their children, was making the same tour with myself. I was delighted, as you may suppose, at the rencontre. We kept together through the mountains, when Latrobe and Pourtales left me, and made a tour through Vermont, and I took a seat in L——'s carriage, and proceeded with him down the valley of the Connecticut. We followed the course of that lovely river to Springfield, through a continued succession of enchanting scenes; when I parted from them, and made the best of my way to New York. After passing a day in the city, which is desolate and deserted on account of the cholera, I came off with the Bramin to this place, where a great part of the family forces is collected. Here I am in a little cottage, in which is Mr. Paris's family, and a number of the Bramin's young fry, among which are his two oldest daughters, whom I have now seen for the first time.

"The Bramin" was his brother Ebenezer, whom, by some whimsical fancy, he now styles by this designation, the first written trace of it which I meet. "Brom" and "Captain Greatheart" were the familiar titles by which, in earlier days, he passed among his brothers.

At Tarrytown—"old Tarrytown," as he calls it in one of his letters, from its association with his early days—he was within two miles of Sunnyside, and he seems even at this time to have had some notion of purchasing it. Perhaps his visit to the "bachelor's Elysium" of his friend Kemble, further up the Hudson, from which he had lately returned, may have set him revolving the purpose of a similar "nest." At all events, he writes to his sister, Mrs. Paris, when on his rambles in November:

> I am more and more in the notion of having that little cottage below Oscar's* house, and wish you to tell him to endeavor to get it for me. I am willing to pay a little unreasonably for it, and should like to have it in time to make any alterations that may be advisable, as early as possible in the spring.

Before the purchase was effected, however, or even attempted, he was informed of a serious pecuniary loss, which suspended for the time his project of securing the little retreat.

On the 4th of August he left Tarrytown for Saratoga Springs, where he was joined by Latrobe and Pourtales, who were to accompany him in a tour he was then meditating through the western part of the State of New York, but which was destined to extend to the remote West. Among the visitors to the Springs he found many old friends, with whom he resumed acquaintance. "It quite delights me," he writes to Peter, "to find how soon I fall into the current of old intimacies, and forget the lapse of years."

* Oscar Irving, the third son of his brother William, who owned and occupied the adjoining acres.

From the Springs he proceeded to Trenton Falls, from whence he writes to Peter, August 15 :

This place has risen into notice since your departure from America. The falls are uncommonly beautiful, and are on West Canada Creek, the main branch of the Mohawk, within sixteen miles of Utica.

My tour thus far has been through a continued succession of beautiful scenes; indeed, the natural beauties of the United States strike me infinitely more than they did before my residence in Europe. The accommodations for travellers also have improved in a wonderful degree. In no country out of England have I found such excellent hotels, and such good fare, in places remote from cities. I am now in a clean, airy, well-furnished hotel, on a hill with a broad, beautiful prospect in front, and forests on all the other sides. My travelling companions and myself have the house to ourselves. Our table is excellent, and we are enjoying as pure and delightful breezes as I did in the Alhambra. The murmur of the neighboring falls lulls me to a delicious summer nap, and in the morning and evening I have glorious bathing in the clear waters of the little river. In fact, I return to all the simple enjoyments of old times with the renovated feelings of a schoolboy, and have had more hearty, homebred delights of the kind since my return to the United States, than I have ever had in the same space of time in the whole course of my life.

The cholera—that Asiatic scourge which had crossed the Atlantic, in June, to Quebec—was at this time extending about the country, and spreading great alarm, so that the whole course of business, as well as pleasure, was interrupted. Many of the towns through which he would have to pass would be in the first stage of panic and outbreak. This was then the case with Utica, about sixteen miles from Trenton Falls, where his letter is dated. "I shall leave that place out of my route," he writes, "though hitherto I have never avoided the malady, nor shall I do so in the course of my tour; simply observing such general diet and habits of living as experience has taught me are best calculated to keep my system in healthful tone."

CHAPTER II.

CHANGE OF TRAVELLING PLANS—LETTERS TO MRS. PARIS—TOUR THROUGH OHIO—VOYAGE ON THE OHIO AND MISSISSIPPI—BLACK HAWK—THE PRAIRIES OF THE MISSOURI—A LAUNCH INTO SAVAGE LIFE—LETTER TO PETER—NEW ORLEANS—WILLIAM C. PRESTON—SOJOURN AT WASHINGTON—MISGIVINGS AS TO THE LONG EXISTENCE OF THE GENERAL UNION—LETTER TO JAMES K. PAULDING—LETTERS TO GOUVERNEUR KEMBLE FROM WASHINGTON—RETURN TO NEW YORK—LETTER TO PETER IRVING—AGAIN AT BALTIMORE—LETTER THENCE TO PETER IRVING—GENERAL JACKSON AND LIEUTENANT RANDOLPH—HERMAN KNICKERBOCKER—VISIT TO OLD DUTCH VILLAGES IN THE NEIGHBORHOOD OF THE CATSKILL MOUNTAINS—A KNICKERBOCKER EXCURSION WITH MR. VAN BUREN—ABRIDGMENT OF COLUMBUS RECOMMENDED BY THE LEGISLATURE OF NEW YORK AS A CLASS BOOK FOR THE COMMON SCHOOLS—SANGUINE CALCULATIONS ABOUT IT—THEATRE—ITALIAN OPERA.

WHEN Mr. Irving set out on this journey, he was meditating a tour in the western part of the State of New York, and in Ohio, Kentucky, and Tennessee. In the following letter we find him changing his purpose, and embarking in an extensive expedition into the far West, beyond the bounds of civilization, in company with one of the three Commissioners appointed by the Government to treat with deputations of different tribes of the Indians. The Commissioners were to rendezvous at Fort Gibson, seven hundred miles up the Arkansas. It was an opportunity to see the aborigines of America in their own wild territory, too tempting to be resisted.

[*To Mrs. Paris, at New York.*]

CINCINNATI, Sept. 2, 1832.

MY DEAR SISTER :

You have no doubt heard from our brother E. I. of the alteration, or rather extension of my travelling plans, in consequence of which I shall accompany the Commissioners on their expedition into the territories west of the Mississippi, to visit and hold conferences with the emigrating Indian tribes. The Commissioner, Mr. Ellsworth, who invited me to this journey, and whom I accidentally met on board of a steamboat on Lake Erie, is a very gentlemanly and amiable person, and an excellent travelling companion. I have also my old fellow travellers, Mr. Latrobe and the young Count Pourtales, who are delighted with the idea of travelling on horseback through the forests and prairies, camping in tents at nights, and hunting deer, buffaloes, and wild turkeys. We have made a very interesting tour through Ohio. We landed at Ashtabula, a small place on the shore of Lake Erie. From thence we proceeded along the ridge road parallel to the lake to Cleveland, and thence through the centre of the State to this city, where we arrived last evening. I have been greatly delighted with the magnificent woodland scenery of Ohio, and with the exuberant fertility of the soil, which will eventually render this State a perfect garden spot. When the forests are cleared away, however, the country will be a vast plain, diversified here and there by a tract of rolling hills; and nothing will compensate for the loss of those glorious trees, which now present the sublime of vegetation.

In the course of our journey we diverged from the direct route, to visit one of those stupendous and mysterious Indian antiquities which are among the wonders of the land. Immense ramparts and mounds of earth extending for miles, that must have required the united labors of a vast multitude, and have been intended to protect some important city or some populous region. These works are now in the depths of thick forests, overgrown with trees that are evidently the growth of centuries. Nothing relative to them remains in Indian tradition, nor is the construction of such vast works in any way compatible with the habits and customs of any of our aboriginal tribes. You may imagine what a subject for speculation and reverie the sight of such monuments presents in the silent bosom of the wilderness.

We shall leave Cincinnati very probably the day after tomorrow. Indeed, I remain as brief a time as possible in towns and cities, for the attentions I meet with are often rather irksome and embarrassing than otherwise. I went into the theatre, last evening, to see the acting of Mrs. Drake, with which I was wonderfully delighted, when, to my astonishment and dismay, the manager came out between the acts, and announced that I was in the house. As you partake of the nervous sensibility of the family, you may conceive how I felt on finding all eyes thus suddenly turned upon me. I have since had a note from the manager, requesting me to visit the theatre on Tuesday evening, and to permit him to announce it. I have declined it, of course, and have induced my companions to hasten our departure, that I may escape from all further importunities of the kind.

I hope my countrymen may not think I slight their proffers of kindness and distinction; no one can value their good opinion more highly; but I have a shrinking aversion from being made an object of personal notoriety, that I cannot conquer.

* * * * * *

I hope you will take care of my little man John during my absence. See that he is well clad, well schooled, and well drilled. Keep him with you, if he is useful to you, and let brother E. I. charge to my account all expenses for his maintenance, clothing, &c.

The "little man" alluded to was a German lad of about eleven years of age, who crossed the water with Mr. Irving. The latter conceived a liking for him on shipboard, and took him in his employ. He remained with him for three years, when he went with his father to try his fortunes in Illinois, where, with a loan from Mr. Irving of one hundred dollars, he entered eighty acres of land. Some years afterward he made a visit to Sunnyside, the father of sundry children, and with the hundred dollars advanced to him by Mr. Irving transmuted, by Western alchemy, into seventy thousand.

[*To Mrs. Paris.*]

ST. LOUIS, MO., Sept. 13, 1832.

MY DEAR SISTER:

I wrote to you from Cincinnati, which place I left in a steamboat on the 3d inst., and arrived the next day at Louis ville, Ky. There we embarked in another steamboat, and continued down the Ohio to its confluence with the Mississippi, when we ascended the latter river to this place, where we arrived late last night. Our voyage was prolonged by our repeatedly running aground in the Ohio from the lowness of the water. Twice we remained aground for the greater part of twenty-four hours. The last evening of our voyage we were nearly run down and sent to the bottom by a huge steamboat, the "Yellow Stone," which came surging down the river under the impetus of "high pressure" and a rapid current. Fortunately our pilot managed the helm so as to receive the blow obliquely, which tore away part of a wheel, and staved in all the upper-works of one side of our boat. We made shift to limp through the remainder of our voyage, which was but about twelve miles. I have been charmed with the grand scenery of these two mighty rivers. We have had splendid weather to see them in—golden sunshiny days, and serene moonlight nights. The magnificence of the Western forests is quite beyond my anticipations; such gigantic trees, rising like stupendous columns—and then the abundance of flowers and flowering shrubs.

* * * * * *

I am writing late at night, and with difficulty, for I have unluckily strained the fingers of my right hand a few days since, so that I can scarcely hold a pen. Good night.

Sept. 16th.—Since writing the foregoing, I have been to Fort Jefferson, about nine miles from this, to see the famous Black Hawk, and his fellow chiefs, taken in the recent Indian war. This redoubtable Black Hawk, who makes such a figure in our newspapers, is an old man, upward of seventy, emaciated and enfeebled by the sufferings he has experienced, and by a touch of cholera. He has a small, well-formed head, with an aquiline nose, a good expression of eye, and a physician present, who is given to craniology, perceived the organ of benevolence strongly developed, though I believe the old chieftain stands accused of many cruelties. His brother-in-law, the prophet, is a strong, stout man, and much younger. He is considered the most culpable agent in fomenting the late disturbance; though I find it extremely difficult, even when so near the seat of action, to get at the right story of these feuds between the white and the red men, and my sympathies go strongly with the latter.

[*To Mrs. Paris.*]

INDEPENDENCE, Mo., Sept. 26, 1832.

MY DEAR SISTER.

We arrived at this place the day before yesterday, after nine days' travelling on horseback from St. Louis. Our journey has been a very interesting one, leading us across fine prairies and through noble forests, dotted here and there by farms and log houses, at which we found rough but wholesome and abundant fare, and very civil treatment. Many parts of these prairies of the Missouri are extremely beautiful, resembling cultivated countries, embellished with parks and groves, rather than the savage rudeness of the wilderness.

Yesterday I was out on a deer hunt in the vicinity of this place, which led me through some scenery that only wanted a castle, or a gentleman's seat here and there interspersed, to have equalled some of the most celebrated park scenery of England.

The fertility of all this Western country is truly astonishing. The soil is like that of a garden, and the luxuriance and beauty of the forests exceed any that I have seen. We have gradually been advancing, however, toward rougher and rougher life, and are now at a little straggling frontier village, that has only been five years in existence. From hence, in the course of a day or two, we take our departure southwardly, and shall soon bid adieu to civilization, and encamp at night in our tents. My health is good, though I have been much affected by the change of climate, diet, and water since my arrival in the West. Horse exercise, however, always agrees with me. I enjoy my journey exceedingly, and look for still greater gratification in the part which is now before me, which will present much greater wildness and novelty. The climax will be our expedition with the Osages to their hunting grounds, and the sight of a buffalo hunt.

[*To Mrs. Paris.*]

FORT GIBSON, ARK., Oct 9, 1832.

MY DEAR SISTER:

I arrived here yesterday afternoon in excellent health, after ten or eleven days' travel from Independence, from whence I last wrote to you. Our journey has laid almost entirely through the vast prairies, or open grassy plains which extend over all these frontiers, diversified occasionally by beautiful groves, and deep fertile bottoms along the streams of water. We have encamped almost every night, excepting when we stopped at the Missionary establishments scattered here and there in this vast wilderness. The weather has been beautiful. We have encountered but one rainy night and one thunder storm. I have found sleeping in a tent a very sweet and healthy kind of repose, and have been in fine condition ever since I left Independence. It is now upward of three weeks since I left St. Louis and took to travelling on horseback, and it has agreed with me admirably. On arriving at this post, I found that a mounted body of rangers, nearly a hundred, had set off two days before to make a wide tour to the West and South, through the wild hunting countries, by way of protecting the friendly Indians who have gone to the buffalo hunting, and to overawe the Pawnee Indians, who are the wandering Arabs of the West, and continually on the maraud. Colonel Ellsworth and myself have determined to set off to-morrow morning in the track of this party. We shall be escorted by a dozen or fourteen horsemen, so that we shall have nothing to apprehend from any straggling gang of Pawnees; and we shall have three or four Indians with us as guides and interpreters, besides the servants that have accompanied us hitherto. A couple of Creek Indians have been dispatched by the commander of this fort to overtake the party of rangers, and order them to await our coming up with them, which we expect to effect in the course of three days; and to find them in the buffalo range on the Little Red River. * * * I am in hopes that we may be able to fall in with some wandering band of Pawnees in a friendly manner, as I have a great desire to see some of that warlike and vagrant race. We shall have a Pawnee captive woman with us as an interpreter.

You see, I am completely launched in savage life, and am likely to continue in it for some weeks to come. I am extremely excited and interested by this wild country, and the wild scenes and people by which I am surrounded.

I am uncertain whether Mr. Latrobe and Pourtales will accompany me on this further tour. I left them about forty miles behind, at one of the agencies, and they have not yet arrived here, though they probably will in the course of the day. I am writing in great haste, having all my preparations to make.

Take care that my little man John is warmly clad for the winter, and that he has a comfortable great coat.

[*To Mrs. Paris.*]

GREENPOINT, NEAR THE RED FORK OF THE ARKANSAS, Oct. 18, 1832.

MY DEAR SISTER:

I wrote to you when about to start from Fort Gibson, under an escort, to join the exploring party of rangers. We came up with them, in the course of three or four days, on the banks of the Arkansas. The whole troop crossed that river the day before yesterday, some on rafts, some fording. Our own immediate party have a couple of half-breed Indians as servants, who understand the Indian customs. They constructed a kind of boat or raft out of a buffalo skin, on which Mr. Ellsworth and myself crossed at several times, on the top of about a hundredweight of luggage—an odd way of crossing a river a quarter of a mile wide.

We are now on the borders of the Pawnee country, a region untraversed by white men, except by solitary trappers. We are leading a wild life, depending upon game, such as deer, elk, bear, for food, encamping on the borders of brooks, and sleeping in the open air under trees, with outposts stationed to guard us against any surprise by the Indians.

We shall probably be three weeks longer on this tour. Two or three days bring us into the buffalo range, where we shall have grand sport hunting. We shall also be in the range of wild horses.

I send this letter by a party of the men who have to return to escort two or three sick men, who have the measles and fevers. The rest of the camp is well, and our own party in high spirits. I was never in finer health, or enjoyed myself more, and the idea of exploring a wild country of this magnificent character is very exciting.

I write at the moment of marching. The horses are all saddled, and the bugle sounds for mounting. God bless you. I shall not have another opportunity of writing until I return to the garrison of Fort Gibson. We are far beyond any civilized habitation, or even an Indian village.

Love to all. Your brother,

WASHINGTON IRVING.

[*To Mrs. Paris.*]

MONTGOMERY'S POINT, MOUTH OF THE ARKANSAS,
MISSISSIPPI RIVER, Nov. 16, 1832.

MY DEAR SISTER:

I arrived safe and sound at Fort Gibson about a week since, after thirty-one days' tour in the wilderness west of the Territory. Our tour was a very rough but a very interesting and gratifying one, part of the time through an unexplored country. We led a complete hunter's life, subsisting upon the produce of the chase, camping by streams or pools, and sleeping on skins and blankets in the open air; but we were all in high health; and, indeed, nothing is equal to such a campaign, to put a man in full health and spirits. * * * We got out of flour, salt, sugar, &c., and had to eat our meat without bread or seasoning, and drink our coffee without sweetening. Our horses were tired down by the pasturage bring withered, and by their having been coursed after buffaloes and wild horses. Some of them had to be left behind; and those of us who brought back our horses to the fort, had to walk, and lead them for the greater part of the three or four last days.* The very evening of my arrival at Fort Gibson a steamboat came up the river, and was to return down it the next day. I took advantage of it, and embarked, and have just put my foot on shore at this place this morning. The steamboat proceeds down the Mississippi, in the course of an hour or two, for New Orleans, and I think of continuing on in her; to be governed in my future movements by the reports I shall receive of the health of New Orleans, and the facilities of proceeding from that place on my route homeward, where I am now very anxious to arrive. * * *

He continued down the Mississippi in the steamboat in which he had descended the Arkansas to New Orleans, where, he writes to Peter from Washington,

I passed a few days very pleasantly. It is one of the most motley and amusing places in the United States—a mixture of America and Europe. The French part of the city is a counterpart of some provincial French town; and the levee, or esplanade along the river, presents the most whimsical groups of people of all nations, castes, and colors—French, Spanish, half-breeds, creoles, mulattoes, Kentuckians, &c., &c. I passed a couple of days with Judge M——, Mrs. McLane's

* In a letter to Peter, he mentions that though they had an occasional alarm, they passed through the country without seeing a single Pawnee. "I brought off, however," he adds, "the tongue of a buffalo, of my own shooting, as a trophy of my hunting, and am determined to rest my renown as a hunter upon that exploit, and never to descend to meaner game." The particulars of this feat will be found in his "Tour on the Prairies," published in 1835.

brother, on his sugar plantation, just at the time they were making sugar.

From New Orleans I set off in the mail stage, through Mobile, and proceeded through Alabama, Georgia, South and North Carolina, and Virginia, to this place—a long and rather dreary journey, travelling frequently day and night, and much of the road through pine forests, in the winter season. At Columbia, the capital of South Carolina, I sought our friend Preston, who resides in that place, is a member of the Legislature, and one of the leaders of the nullifiers. * * * I passed a day most cordially with him, talking and laughing over old times, and recalling the scenes and personages of our rambles.

[This was William C. Preston, the brilliant orator, formerly travelling companion of himself and Peter in Scotland and England.]

Preston spoke of you with the most lively regard, and called to mind a host of your pleasantries. I dined with him at Governor Hamilton's, the nullifying Governor, whom I had known when a young man at New York, and who is a perfect gentleman, but a Hotspur in politics. It is really lamentable to see such a fine set of gallant fellows as these leading nullifiers are, so madly in the wrong.

Governor Hamilton had just then transmitted to the Legislature of South Carolina his message, enclosing the nullifying edict of the convention of its people, and invoking the coöperation of the two branches to carry into effect this measure of *peaceable* redress, for he claimed it to be essentially of a pacific character.

When Mr. Irving took leave, the Governor gave him a warm invitation to "come soon" and see him again. "Oh, yes!" was the playful but suggestive reply; "I'll come with *the first troops*."

Mr. Irving arrived in Washington just before the President issued his proclamation of December 10, generally understood to be the production of his distinguished Secretary of State, Edward Livingston, containing an able exposition of the nullifying question, and of the Constitution of the country, and furnishing to South Carolina a significant intimation of the fallacy of any hopes of annulling peaceably within her limits a law of the General Government. He was hastening back from his prolonged tour to pass a Christmas among his family and friends, and had intended to stop but two or three days in Washington; yet he found it such "an interesting place to see public characters," and the "crisis" so "interesting," that he was induced to linger here, with the exception of a brief excursion to Baltimore, during the remaining term of Congress, a period of three months. "I am very pleasantly situated," he writes. "I have a very snug, cheery, cosey room in the immediate neighborhood of McLane's, and take my meals at his house, and, in fact, make it my home. I have thus the advantage of a family circle (and that a delightful one), and the precious comfort of a little bachelor retreat and *sanctum sanctorum*, where I can be as lonely and independent as I please."

I give some letters and passages of letters written during this interval:

[*To Peter Irving.*]

McLane is hard worked by his office, but it is a kind of work that agrees with him, and he is generally in better health, looks, and spirits than he was at London.

I found Gouverneur Kemble here, to my great surprise. He had business at the War Department, being a great contractor for founding cannon, &c. He has been consulted, also, by the Committee of Ways and Means, of which Gulian C. Verplanck is chairman, in the formation of a bill for the reduction of the Tariff. I hope such a bill may be devised and carried as will satisfy the moderate part of the nullifiers; but I confess I see so many elements of sectional prejudice, hostility, and selfishness stirring and increasing in activity and acrimony in this country, that I begin to doubt strongly of the long existence of the general Union.

The following is addressed to his old friend and early literary associate, James K. Paulding, then Navy Agent at New York, whom some were seeking to displace, from his want of due subserviency to the behests of party.

WASHINGTON, Jan. 3, 1833.

MY DEAR PAULDING:

I have just returned from an interview with the President on the subject of the rumor of your removal from office. He assured me it was the first word he had heard on the subject; and had you heard the terms in which he spoke of your official conduct, you would feel not merely secure of your office, but proud of holding it, guaranteed by such sentiments. The more I see of this old cock of the woods, the more I relish his game qualities.

As to rumors, they are as numerous as they are absurd. Gouverneur's particular friend, Bankhead, the British *chargé d'affaires*, has just returned from New York, very gravely charged with one concerning myself; viz., that I was *to marry Miss ——, and receive the appointment of Postmaster of New York!!* Now either the lady or the office would be a sufficient blessing for a marrying or an office-craving man; but God help me! I should be as much bothered with the one as with the other. * * *

With affectionate regards to Gertrude and the family, I am, my dear James, yours ever

WASHINGTON IRVING.

The following is in reply to a letter of Kembie, invoking his aid in inducing Leslie to accept the offer of the Professorship of Design at the Military Academy at West Point:

[*To Gouverneur Kemble.*]

WASHINGTON, Jan. 18, 1833.

MY DEAR KEMBLE:

* * * * * *

I will write to Leslie, and state to him what advantages he will have in fixing himself at West Point; though I shall cautiously refrain from giving any advice or using any persuasion in the matter. It is a delicate and responsible thing to influence a man in a measure that is to change his whole situation and course of life. I think it doubtful whether he will accept. For my own part, few things would give me equal pleasure to having him on this side of the Atlantic, and in my neighborhood.*

* * * * * *

Charles Kemble and his talented daughter are here, turning the heads of young and old. I find they became very sociable with you, and speak of you with great regard.

God bless you, my dear Kemble. I hope to be with you before long.

Yours ever, WASHINGTON IRVING.

A week later he writes to the same correspondent, from Washington:

MY DEAR KEMBLE:

* * * * * *

An attempt is making to bring the subject of the Tariff to a close in the House this week, by night sessions. I feel extremely doubtful, however, of the bill being carried. The braggadocio speeches and proceedings of South Carolina have raised a spirit of indignation among many who would otherwise be inclined to redress the grievances complained of, and this feeling is taken advantage of by those interested for the manufacturers.

I understand that Governor Hayne is making every preparation for warlike measures. I hope and trust that this will all turn out a game of brag; at any rate, the measures taken by the General Government are such as to entangle the nullifiers

* Leslie did accept the position, but only to retain it for the brief period of six months, when he returned to England.

in all kinds of financial and fiscal difficulties, and to make any act of hostility plainly proceed from themselves.

I think I shall remain here a few days longer, to hear the outbreaking which will take place on Monday next, and which must call all the champions of the different creeds into the field, and elevate the standards of the new parties that are to spring out of this great conflict.

I am, my dear Kemble, yours ever,

WASHINGTON IRVING.

The "outbreaking" was to take place on a discussion of certain resolutions offered by John C. Calhoun, of South Carolina, declaratory of the powers of the Government and the States, and involving the question whether a single State had power to annul the laws enacted by a whole nation. How deeply it interested him, we find from the following letter to his brother Peter, written after his return to his native city, from which he had been absent more than seven months, seeing, during that period, more of his own country and its prominent characters, than most persons would see in a lifetime.

[*To Peter Irving.*]

NEW YORK, April 1, 1833.

MY DEAR BROTHER:

I am shocked, when I look back upon the long time I have suffered to elapse without writing to you; but, indeed, indeed I could not help it. I have been so completely bewildered by the variety of scenes, circumstances, and persons crowding upon my attention, that for months past I have lost all command of my time or my thoughts. The period that has passed since my arrival in this country has been one of the greatest and most delightful excitement I have ever experienced, and the excitement still continues, and unfits me for any calm application. Wherever I go, too, I am received with a cordiality, I may say an affection, that keeps my heart full and running over.

My sojourn in Washington prolonged itself through the whole session. I became so deeply interested in the debates of Congress, that I almost lived in the capitol. The grand debate in the Senate occupied my mind as intensely for three weeks, as did ever a dramatic representation. I heard almost every speech, good and bad, and did not lose a word of any of the best. I think my close attendance on the legislative halls has given me an acquaintance with the nature and operation of our institutions, and the character and concerns of the various parts of the Union, that I could not have learned from books for years.

After leaving Washington, I got detained most delightfully at Baltimore for three weeks by the extreme hospitality of the inhabitants.

It was during this visit to Baltimore that he made the acquaintance of John P. Kennedy, who had lately risen into fame as the author of "Swallow Barn," and with whom his acquaintance soon ripened into lasting intimacy.

On the 15th of April, two or three weeks after his return to New York, he writes to Peter:

Since my return, I have been going the rounds of dinners,

&c., until I am as jaded as I was in London. * * * Time and mind are cut up with me like chopped hay, and I am good for nothing, and shall be good for nothing for some time to come, so much am I harassed by the claims of society.

Soon after the date of this extract he set off on an excursion to the South, to visit the upper part of Virginia, accompanied by his nephew, John T. Irving, Jr. At Washington they heard of the assault of Lieutenant Randolph upon the nation's chief magistrate—an indignity perpetrated on board of the steamboat as she stopped at Alexandria on her way to Fredericksburg, where the President was proceeding to lay the corner stone of a monument about to be erected to the mother of Washington. Mr. Irving arrived at Fredericksburg in the afternoon, after the ceremony of laying the corner stone had been concluded.

I saw a good deal of the President that evening, and the next morning [he writes to Peter, from Baltimore, May 17]. The old gentleman was still highly exasperated at the recent outrage offered him by Lieutenant Randolph, of which, ere this reaches you, you will have heard and read, *usque ad nauseam*.

It is a brutal transaction, which I cannot think of without indignation, mingled with a feeling of almost despair, that our national character should receive such crippling wounds from the hands of our own citizens.

From Fredericksburg he proceeded to Charlottesville, where he visited the Jefferson University, and had to fight off from an invitation to a public dinner on the part of the students. Pursuing his journey, he crossed the Blue Ridge, but unfortunately, at this interesting point of his tour, the weather changed, and he traversed the mountain in a heavy rain, that shut up the whole prospect, and harassed him with small intermission during his continuance in the valley. He returned to New York in time to be present on the arrival of President Jackson on his Northern tour.

The reception of the President, yesterday [he writes to Peter from New York, June 13], was one of the finest spectacles I ever witnessed. I accompanied the Corporation, and a large body of the citizens, in a superb steamboat to Brunswick, to meet him. The ceremonials you will see in the papers; but you can hardly form an idea of the increased splendor given to spectacles of the kind by our steamboats, and the increased population and beauty of our city.

On the 31st of July he is about leaving his "quarters at Oscar's very pretty country box, about two miles below Tarrytown," to go to Saratoga Springs for a few days to take the waters, being still a little out of order from a late accident, in being thrown from his gig. After a fortnight's visit to the Springs, where he met with many old friends, and formed several very agreeable acquaintances, he made an excursion to Schaghticoke, and visited Herman Knickerbocker, whom he had known at Washington about twenty years before, when he was Congressman, and with whom the name still formed a bond of fellowship. "I found him with a houseful of children," he writes to Peter, "living hospitably, and filling various stations—a judge, a farmer, a miller, a manufacturer, a politician, &c., &c. He received me with open arms, and I only escaped from his hospitality by promising to come another time, and spend a day or two with him."

He afterward proceeded down the river to Kingston, where he passed a day in looking about the neighborhood, and visiting the old Dutch villages on the skirts of the Catskill Mountains—scenes in his story of Rip Van Winkle now explored for the first time.

It is an amusing fact in this connection, that not long before his death, Mr. Irving received a letter of inquiry from a young lad at Catskill, informing him that he had "lately been engaged in arguing with a very old gentleman" whether, in his "beautiful tale of Rip Van Winkle," he referred "to the village of Catskill or Kingston," and appealing to him as the only adequate authority to settle the disputed question. "He little dreamt," said Mr. Irving, in exhibiting the letter, "when I wrote the story, I had never been on the Catskills." I think the reader will enjoy the concealed humor of his reply, though I fear it must have been somewhat perplexing to the ingenuous lad, whose "desire for knowledge" had prompted the inquiry.

SUNNYSIDE, Feb. 5, 1858.

DEAR SIR:

I can give you no other information concerning the localities of the story of Rip Van Winkle, than is to be gathered from the manuscript of Mr. Knickerbocker, published in the Sketch Book. Perhaps he left them purposely in doubt. I would advise you to defer to the opinion of the "very old gentleman" with whom you say you had an argument on the subject. I think it probable he is as accurately informed as any one on the matter.

Respectfully, your obedient servant,

WASHINGTON IRVING.

Mr. Irving had been so much in motion since his return to his native country, that he had little opportunity to resume his long-interrupted literary occupations. It might seem, from the tone of the following reply, that his brother Ebenezer was becoming a little anxious that he should get to work again with his pen, made the more necessary, no doubt, in his view, that he had recently suffered to a serious extent from pecuniary losses. His brother felt increased anxiety, also, that the Legislature of New York had recently recommended his Abridgment of Columbus as a class book for the common schools—a measure which he thought likely to produce him an ample revenue out of that single work, if proper arrangements were made to have the recommendation acted upon.

The reply is dated from Washington, whither he had gone to combat a disposition of his friend, McLane, to resign his seat in the Cabinet.

[*To Ebenezer Irving.*]

WASHINGTON, Oct. 7, 1833.

MY DEAR BROTHER:

* * * I want to get to work as much as you can wish me to do so, but God knows my mind and time are so cut up and engrossed, that I am almost in despair of ever getting quiet again. I hope the Abridgment may turn out in any degree profitable; but it has to work its way, I apprehend, through a world of trickery and counter management.

I am sorry, but not surprised, to hear of brother John's ill health. I have said everything that I could say to him on the subject of his wilful slavery. He will keep on until he gets some stroke of ill health that will shatter his constitution completely, and then he will gather together the fragments, and employ the residue of his life in nursing them. It is useless to talk any further with him on the topic. He might make his office a source of rational and interesting employment, by no means incompatible with either health or happiness; but he has a propensity to overwork himself.

John, the brother here alluded to, held the position of First Judge of the Court of Common Pleas for the City and County of New York, and was applying himself to its duties with a conscientious devotion, that was undermining his health. He had acquired an independent fortune by the practice of his profession, and Washington would have preferred his withdrawing to a life of more leisure and ease, knowing that the law was never a congenial employment.

The following is written to Peter, after his mind

had been disturbed by a knowledge of Washington's losses, which the latter had carefully refrained from mentioning in his correspondence. The first part glances at another Knickerbocker excursion with Mr. Van Buren:

[*To Peter Irving.*]

NEW YORK, Oct. 28, 1833.

MY DEAR BROTHER:

I have received several letters from you of late, which, in consequence of my interrupted and irregular life, have not been punctually answered. I have been moving about almost incessantly during the summer and autumn, visiting old scenes about the Hudson. I made a delightful journey with Mr. Van Buren in an open carriage from Kinderhook to Poughkeepsie, then crossing the river to the country about the foot of the Catskill Mountains, and so from Esopus, by Goshen, Haverstraw, Tappan, Hackensack, to Communipaw—an expedition which took two weeks to complete, in the course of which we visited curious old Dutch places and Dutch families. I then made a rapid move to Washington to be with Mr. McLane during a crisis of the Cabinet, when he was much disposed to resign—a measure which would have been very injurious to his interests and happiness.

* * * * * *

The losses that have fallen upon me will be soon filled up by the regular produce of my copyright property; but I shall, before long, be in the way of adding largely to my capital. I am, as you know, dammed up by the necessity (or fancied necessity) of producing a work upon American subjects, before I can give vent to the other materials that have been accumulating upon me. I am now getting at home upon American themes, and the scenes and characters I have noticed since my return begin to assume a proper tone and form and grouping in my mind, and to take a tinge from my imagination.

Ten days later, November 8, he writes to the same brother:

* * * I told you, in my last, that you must not pester your mind about the loss I have lately sustained. It is not material as to comfort or enjoyment. I have abundant means remaining, if I should never make another farthing; but my prospects of further gain are excellent. I am busy with my pen, and feel that I shall work a great deal, and produce much new matter, besides setting loose much manuscript that has lain for some time by me, in a manner bound up.

When I get all my copyrights in my hands again, which will be in about a year, they will be a new source of profit. Independent of all this, I now begin to feel confidence that my Abridgment is going to be, of itself, a steady and *handsome* revenue.

These sanguine anticipations of profit from the Abridgment of Columbus were not destined to be realized. The Carvills, in consideration of four hundred dollars, had, in the previous April, released his agent, Ebenezer Irving, from the conditions of their agreement for the unexpired time, which extended to June 30, 1834; but the difficulties of getting it into complete circulation, from the rivalships of other school books, made the recommendation of the Legislature to some extent a nullity.

November 24th, he writes to Peter:

I am in a course of regular literary occupation, and am getting on very satisfactorily. I am pleasantly situated at Ebenezer's, where, with the addition of sister Catherine and her family, we have a large and delightful domestic circle, and I manage to keep clear of all evening engagements, and to go out but sparingly to dinner parties; so that I shall be able to turn this winter to great advantage in a literary point of view.

* * * * * *

We had a benefit here, lately, for Cooper and his family, which netted nearly four thousand dollars. He made two thousand dollars by a benefit at Philadelphia, and will have very productive benefits at Boston and New Orleans, so that there is every prospect of a fund being accumulated sufficient, with proper economy, to keep the wolf from the door. * * *

The city overflows with strangers, more than any city of the same size in the world. The theatre is constantly crowded, and is a perfect gold mine.

The Italian Opera house has opened here very brilliantly. It is altogether one of the prettiest and politest-looking theatres I have ever seen. The troupe is very fair. We have a *prima donna* (Fanti) that would just suit you—young, pleasing in countenance and person, amiable in her manner, expressive, graceful, and affecting in her acting, and with a pure, sweet, touching voice. She will become quite a pet here.

CHAPTER III.

THE AUTHOR'S FIRST NOTION OF ASTORIA—LETTERS ON THE SUBJECT TO PIERRE MUNRO IRVING—A NOMINATION TO CONGRESS OFFERED AND DECLINED—HIS DISTASTE FOR POLITICS—THE CRAYON MISCELLANIES—PUBLICATION AND RECEPTION OF THE TOUR ON THE PRAIRIES—AMERICAN AND ENGLISH PREFACE—FARMS OUT HIS PRIOR WORKS TO CAREY, LEA & CO. FOR A TERM OF SEVEN YEARS—NO. II. OF THE CRAYON MISCELLANY—ABBOTSFORD AND NEWSTEAD—PURCHASE OF TEN ACRES—SUNNYSIDE IN EMBRYO—NO. III. OF THE CRAYON MISCELLANY—THE LEGENDS OF THE CONQUEST OF SPAIN—ITS PUBLICATION—QUARTERED AT HELLGATE WITH MR. ASTOR, AND AT WORK ON HIS GREAT ENTERPRISE—THE WORKMEN BUSY UPON HIS COTTAGE—THE PLAN EXTENDING AS HE BUILT—THE GREAT FIRE IN NEW YORK.

I PASS over the first portion of this year, which was spent in the bosom of the domestic circle at No. 3 Bridge street, the residence of his brother Ebenezer, with the exception of a flying visit to Philadelphia in June, in the course of which he picked up his material for Ralph Ringwood, and a few summer excursions, and come at once to the following letters to myself, in which he broaches the subject of Astoria—the work which he gave to the public in 1836, and which was to link his name with the region beyond the Rocky Mountains, "where rolls the Oregon."

These letters were addressed to me at Jacksonville, Ill., to which place I had gone from my native city, New York, the preceding year. At the date of the first I had been meditating a visit to New York, though not with the intention of remaining, as the letter supposes.

[*To Pierre Munro Irving.*]

NEW YORK, Sept. 15, 1834.

MY DEAR PIERRE:

* * * John Jacob Astor is extremely desirous of having a work written on the subject of his settlement of Astoria, at the mouth of Columbia River; something that might take with the reading world, and secure to him the reputation of having originated the enterprise and founded the colony that are likely to have such important results in the history of commerce and colonization.

The old gentleman has applied to me repeatedly in the matter, offering to furnish abundance of materials in letters, journals, and verbal narratives, and to pay liberally for time and trouble. I have felt aware that a work might be written on the subject, full of curious and entertaining matter, comprising adventurous expeditions by sea and land, scenes beyond the Rocky Mountains, incidents and scenes illustrative of Indian character, and of that singular and but little known class, the traders and voyageurs of the Fur Companies. Still I am so much engrossed with other plans, that I have not time for the examination of papers, the digesting of various materials, &c., and have stood aloof from the undertaking, though still keeping the matter open.

Since I have heard of your inclination to return to New York, however, it has occurred to me that you might be disposed to take this subject in hand; to collate the various documents, collect verbal information, and reduce the whole to such form that I might be able to dress it up advantageously, and with little labor, for the press.

In an interview which I had with Mr. Astor, a day or two since, in which he laid before me a variety of documents, I accordingly stated to him my inability at present to give the subject the labor that would be requisite, but the possibility that you might aid me in the way I have mentioned; in which case I should have no objection to putting the finishing hand to the work. The old gentleman caught at the idea, and begged me to write to you immediately. He said he would be willing to pay you whatever might be deemed proper for your services, and that, if any profit resulted from the sale of the work, it would belong, of course, to the authors.

I lay this matter before you, to be considered in contrast or connection with your other plans. If you take it in hand, it will furnish you with employment for at least a year, and I shall take care to secure your being well paid for your current time and labor; the ultimate profits of the work may be a matter of after arrangement between us.

Mr. Astor is a strong-minded man, and one from whose conversation much curious information is to be derived. He feels the want of occupation and amusement, and thinks he may find something of both in the progress of this work. You would find him very kindly disposed, for he was an early friend of your father, for whose memory he entertains great regard; and he has always been on terms of intimacy with your uncle Peter and myself, besides knowing more or less of others of our family. Halleck, the poet, resides a great deal with him at present, having a handsome salary for conducting his affairs

When you have thought over this matter, and made up

your mind, let me hear from you. If you determine in favor of it, the sooner you come on the better. I have entertained the matter thus far for your sake, having no care about it for myself; decide, therefore, as you think fit, or as your inclination prompts. * * *

To this letter I replied, that I should think favorably of the enterprise, if my share of the work could be performed in the period specified, and I could be assured of two thousand dollars for my coöperation, rejecting all idea of advantage or remuneration from the sale of the work itself.

To this Mr. Irving responded as follows:

NEW YORK, Oct. 29, 1834.

MY DEAR PIERRE:

I received, a few days since, your letter of Oct. 5th, which gives me to suppose that you would undertake the task proposed to you, provided you could be sure of a compensation of two thousand dollars. I have since had a definite conversation with Mr. Astor, and fixed your compensation at *three thousand* dollars.

Now for the nature of the work, and the aid that will be required of you. My present idea is to call the work by the general name of *Astoria*—the name of the settlement made by Mr. Astor at the mouth of Columbia River: under this head to give not merely a history of his great colonial and commercial enterprise, and of the fortunes of his colony, but a body of information concerning the whole region beyond the Rocky Mountains, on the borders of Columbia River, comprising the adventures, by sea and land, of traders, trappers, Indian warriors, hunters, &c.; their habits, characters, persons, costumes, &c.; descriptions of natural scenery, animals, plants, &c., &c. I think, in this way, a rich and varied work may be formed, both entertaining and instructive, and laying open scenes in the wild life of that adventurous region which would possess the charm of freshness and novelty. You would be required to look over the various papers, letters, and journals in the possession of Mr. Astor, written by various persons who have been in his employ, to draw anecdotes and descriptions from him, and from Northwest traders who occasionally visit him; to forage among various works in French and English that have been published relative to these regions, and thus to draw together and arrange into some kind of form a great body of facts. In all this I may be able to render you much assistance. When the work is thus crudely prepared, I will take it in hand, and prepare it for the press, as it is a *sine qua non* with Mr. Astor that my name should be to the work. You now have a general idea of what will be your task. I think you may find it a very interesting and agreeable one, and may accomplish it within the space of a year.

Should you determine to undertake the work, you must come on immediately. Mr. Astor has his mind set upon the matter, and, in fact, looks forward to it as a source of pleasant occupation for the winter. He has taken a house in town for his winter residence, and, if you undertake the task, would wish you to reside with him, as long as you may find it agreeable, and has likewise invited Halleck [the poet] to be his guest. The latter you will find a very pleasant companion.

Mr. Astor has his papers all arranged, so that you would be able to get to work immediately. Let me hear from you on the receipt of this. If you determine to come, you had better put your portmanteau in the first stage coach, and come on as promptly as possible.

Your affectionate uncle, W. I.

I arrived in New York, to perform my share of this literary undertaking, not long after a closely contested election, which had been conducted with great bitterness, and in which the Jackson party had wished to hold Mr. Irving up for Congress. He had declined, however, mingling in any way in the feuds of party, not even giving a vote. A short time previous he had written to Peter:

You are right in your conjectures that I keep myself aloof from politics. The more I see of political life here, the more I am disgusted with it. * * * There is such coarseness and vulgarity and dirty trick mingled with the rough-and-tumble contest. I want no part or parcel in such warfare.

He had at this time completed his Tour on the Prairies, as will be seen from the following extract of a letter to his brother Peter, dated Nov. 24, 1834:

For my own literary occupations I cannot speak so confidently as you would wish. I have written a little narrative of my tour from Fort Gibson on the Pawnee hunting grounds. It makes about three hundred and fifty pages of my usual writing; but I feel reluctant to let it go before the public. So much has been said in the papers about my tour to the West, and the work I was preparing on the subject, that I dread the expectations formed, especially as what I have written is extremely simple, and by no means striking in its details.

In the letters which follow, we have some further glimpse of his literary plans and purposes—"literary babblings," as he terms them:

[*To Peter Irving.*]

NEW YORK, Jan. 8, 1835.

MY DEAR BROTHER:

* * * I have at length resolved to break the ice, and begin to publish. I have been delayed in this by the expectation manifested that I would publish something about this country, and the difficulty I found in preparing anything, under whip and spur, that would satisfy myself. I have now resolved to come out in a series of volumes, published from time to time, under the general title of "Miscellanies," by the author of the Sketch Book, No. I, II, &c., with a second title giving the particular contents of the volume. In this way I mean to clear off all the manuscripts I have on hand, and to throw off casual lucubrations concerning home scenes, &c. I have sent off the MS. for the first volume to Colonel Aspinwall. The title of the volume will be, "A Tour on the Prairies," by the author of the Sketch Book, and will comprise merely my expedition with the rangers from Fort Gibson to the Pawnee hunting grounds. The volume will be about the size of a volume of the Sketch Book.

* * * * * *

In the course of the volumes I will include my writings relative to Spain, &c., so that the series will form a kind of gallery of varied works. This plan enables me to throw off single volumes which would not be of sufficient importance to stand by themselves, and which would otherwise lie dormant in my trunk, as they have already done. When once launched, I shall keep going.

Three months later (April 11), he writes to the same correspondent:

My "Tour on the Prairies" has just been published here, though it has been out for upward of a month in London. The second volume of my Miscellany is nearly stereotyped, and will be ready for publication in a month or six weeks. I am glad to be once more in dealings with Murray, and am well satisfied with the terms of sale of my volume about the Prairies—£400, in a bill at four months. The price is not so high as I used to get, but there has been a great change in the bookselling trade of late years. The inundation of cheap publications, penny magazines, &c., has brought down the market. The market here, in the mean time, has immensely extended, so that, between the two, I fancy I shall be as well off as before. At any rate, I am content, and feel no further solicitude in money matters, excepting to acquire the means of benefiting others.

The Tour on the Prairies received a highly commendatory notice in the *North American Review*, in which the accomplished critic, Edward Everett, after dwelling on the peculiar merits of Mr. Irving's style, and the wide range of his topics—"the humors of contemporary politics and every-day life in America—the traditionary peculiarities of the Dutch founders of New York—the nicest shades of the school of English manners of the last century—the chivalry of the Middle Ages in Spain—the glittering visions of Moorish romance—and, lastly, the whole unhackneyed freshness of the West--life beyond the border—a camp outside the frontier—a hunt on buffalo ground"—proceeds:

To what class of compositions the present work belongs, we are hardly able to say. It can scarcely be called a book of travels, for there is too much painting of manners and scenery, and too little statistics;—it is not a novel, for there is no story; and it is not a romance, for it is all true. It is a sort of sentimental journey, a romantic excursion, in which nearly all the elements of several different kinds of writing are beautifully and gayly blended into a production almost *sui generis*. * * * We are proud of Mr. Irving's sketches of English life, proud of the gorgeous canvas upon which he has gathered in so much of the glowing imagery of Moorish times. We behold with delight his easy and triumphant march over these beaten fields; but we glow with rapture as we see him coming back, laden with the poetical treasures of the primitive wilderness, rich with spoil from the uninhabited desert. We thank him for turning these poor barbarous *steppes* into classical land, and joining his inspiration to that of Cooper in breathing life and fire into a circle of imagery, which was not known before to exist, for the purposes of the imagination.

For the right of publishing and vending five thousand copies of the Tour on the Prairies, from the stereotype plates furnished by the author, Messrs. Carey, Lea & Blanchard, of Philadelphia, gave fifteen hundred dollars, in three equal notes, dated April 14, at six, nine, and twelve months, and three hundred dollars for every additional thousand. I find that on the

10th November, 1835, they gave their note at nine months ($300) for the eighth thousand.

The American edition of the Tour on the Prairies, published more than a month after the English, contained an Introduction, not retained in subsequent editions. Only that part of the Preface which had relation to the volume was given in the English edition, or will now be found in the collective edition of the author's works published by Mr. George P. Putnam. This portion of the Introduction was so purely personal, temporary, and local in its interest, that any intelligent reader will readily understand why it was neither embraced in the English copy nor retained in later American editions. It will be seen, however, in a future chapter, that this difference between the English and American Preface received a harsh and illiberal construction, and was sought to be turned to the author's prejudice.

I give some further extracts from his letters to his brother Peter, which furnish, at this period, a sort of connected biography of him. Peter had now removed from Paris to Havre, where he was comfortably situated in the mansion of his friend Beasley, the American Consul, vainly hoping to get the better of a malady with which he had recently been attacked, and which, he feared, would throw increased difficulty in the way of his return to America.

[*To Peter Irving.*]

April 17*th.*—The first volume of the Crayon Miscellany is doing well, both in England and the United States. The second volume will go to press here within a fortnight. I have farmed out all my back works (excepting the Abridgment of Columbus) to Carey & Lea, for another term of seven years, at a yearly allowance [eleven hundred and fifty dollars]. The Abridgment goes on steadily increasing in circulation. The funds invested in stock produce handsomely; so that I look forward to have easy times in pecuniary matters for the rest of my life.

Theodore's work* is in the press at Philadelphia, and will soon be published, when I will forward you a copy. Murray has agreed to publish it in London. Treat's "Indian Sketches" † will soon be put to press, so that the family will figure in print this year.

Pierre Munro is busily engaged gathering together materials for the work about old Mr. Astor's grand commercial, or rather colonial enterprise. I have not taken hold of the subject yet, but have no doubt I shall be able to make it a rich piece of mosaic. * * *

[*To the Same.*]

May 16*th.*—* * * Brevoort arrived a few days since. * * * From what he says of your inclinations, and from passages in your letters, I indulge the hope that we shall yet

* De Soto's Conquest of Florida, by Theodore Irving, in 2 vols. 12mo. (Republished in 1851, in one volume.)

† Indian Sketches, taken during an Expedition to the Pawnee Tribes, by John T. Irving, Jr.

have you among us. When your health is better established, it may be worth the ordeal of a sea voyage, and I would come out to accompany you. Indeed, I should come out to you at once, were I not mixed up, just now, with so many matters that concern the interests of others, as well as of myself. These I shall, in the course of a little while, be able to arrange so as to leave me more at liberty. Among other things, I have lately become a bank director! This was for the sake and at the solicitation of Mr. McLane, who has taken the presidency of the Morris Canal and Banking Company, with a salary of six thousand dollars.

* * * My second number of the Crayon Miscellany, containing Abbotsford and Newstead Abbey, will be out in a few days. My next number, I think, will be the Conquest of Spain, which is fairly copied out, and has been so for a long time. I am now engaged in the work on the subject of Mr. Astor's great enterprise; and I am much mistaken if I do not make it a very rich, curious, and unique work. Pierre Munro makes an admirable pioneer.

[*To Peter Irving.*]

NEW YORK, May 25, 1835.

MY DEAR BROTHER:

I have just received a letter from Colonel Aspinwall, dated London, April 14, stating the terms he has made with Murray for the second volume of my Miscellany.* It is a light volume, not quite as full as a volume of the Sketch Book. The following is an extract from the Colonel's letter:

"I have agreed with him for £600, payable in the follow-

* Abbotsford and Newstead Abbey.

ing manner, viz.: £400 at six and nine months after the day of publication, and £200 at six and nine months after the day of publication of a second edition—the first edition to consist of three thousand copies. These were the best terms that I could obtain, and I feel a strong persuasion that the popular character of the work will make them more profitable than the five hundred guineas named by you as your price."

I am highly satisfied with the Colonel's arrangement; indeed, considering the times in England, where the political crisis absorbs all thought, and leaves polite literature nearly stagnant, and considering the quantities of cheap publications that inundate the reading world, the prices obtained for my two light volumes have been very liberal. I shall be well content to go on at such a rate; and, indeed, my pecuniary circumstances are now in such an easy and regular train, that I no longer feel solicitous about making keen bargains for any particular work.

* * * I talk thus much about myself and my concerns, from having no other subject just now to talk about, and because I know you take an interest in my literary prospects and pursuits.

Brevoort is regaining his good looks and good condition rapidly.

We are all well at home. With affectionate regards to friend Beasley, yours ever, my dear brother, W. I.

The price obtained from the American publishers, Carey, Lea & Blanchard, was the same as for No. I of the Crayon Miscellany—fifteen hundred dollars for an edition of five thousand, payable in three equal notes, dated June 1, at six, nine, and twelve months. No. II was published May 1, in London, and May 30 in America.

Aspinwall writes: "Murray says Abbotsford delights everybody, especially the Lockharts."

[*To Peter Irving, Havre.*]

NEW YORK, June 10, 1835.

MY DEAR BROTHER:

I have yours of the 24th April, and regret to find that your distressing malady still continues. I had hoped, from the representations of Captain Funck, that you were gradually recovering from every inconvenience. He seems to think you are much inclined to venture upon a sea voyage, and return to New York. I shall look with some solicitude to hear from you in reply to what I have already written on this subject, and if I find you think of returning soon, I will come out at once to convoy you home. At any rate, I shall push to put all my literary and other affairs here in such train as to permit me to rejoin you. At present I am so committed in various matters, that I cannot leave here without a sacrifice not merely of my own interests, but of those of others. I want to get the Astor work into the rough. Pierre M. has acted as an excellent pioneer, and, in the course of two or three months, will have gathered together all the materials. I have commenced, and have rough-cast several of the chapters, and have no doubt I shall make a rich and taking work of it.

* * * * * *

I am just now putting the finishing touches to the Legends of the Conquest of Spain, which will make the next volume of my Miscellany. I shall send you, by this ship, the second number of the Miscellany, containing "Abbotsford and Newstead Abbey." It takes with the public; indeed, the two numbers of the Miscellany are doing admirably, and give promise that the plan of a series of similar light volumes will be very popular and profitable.

The Hive has sent forth its swarms for the summer.

* * * Our nephew Treat's work (Indian Sketches) is nearly printed. He sets off for Europe about the beginning of next month; and I think it very probable brother John T. will set off at the same time, to be absent eight months or a year, intending to visit England, France, Italy, &c. He can well do it, having an assistant judge in his court, who will take the whole business in his hands during his absence—and being opulent in circumstances. * * *

In the following letter to Peter Irving, at Havre, we have the first mention of his purchase of Sunnyside, which had taken place as early as April, though the deed bears date on the 7th of June:

New York, July 8, 1835.

My dear Brother:

* * * * * *

The valiant little Funck has departed, with the full persuasion that he will be able to induce you to come out with him in the Erie, on her return voyage. I am not so sanguine on the subject, or I should have broken through every plan and occupation, to come out and take charge of you.

It is a matter on which I never wish to press or persuade you; but should you feel at any time strong enough in health, and inclined to attempt the voyage, I will insure you pleasant and comfortable quarters here, both in town and country. It is, at any rate, my intention to come out to you as soon as I can get all the materials in order for my work on the subject of Columbia River: this, however, will probably take me some few months, as I have been interrupted by the publication of my Miscellany, and I shall require, after I have worked upon the materials collected for me by Pierre M. Irving, and possessed myself generally with the subject, to have conversations with various individuals who have been engaged in the enterprises by sea and land connected with the settlement.

I have nearly stereotyped the third volume of my Miscellany, and shall send proof sheets to London for publication; but shall not publish the work here until September or October, so as to give the London publishers full time. The title, I think, will be, "Legends of the Conquest of Spain." It will contain "The Legend of Don Roderick," "The Legend of the Subjugation of Spain," "The Legend of Pelayo," * and "The Legend of the Family of Count Julian." I have preferred giving these writings in this form, rather than giving them the more pretending name of History or Chronicle. It enables me to indulge with less reserve or disquiet in those apocryphal details which are so improbable, yet so picturesque and romantic. Did I claim for these wild medleys of truth and fiction the dignity and credence of history, I should throw a discredit upon my regular historical works. It is this scruple that has lain in the way of the publication of these writings, while I contemplated publishing them under a more imposing form.

The two preceding volumes of my Miscellany have succeeded far beyond my expectations, on both sides of the water;

* It did not contain the Legend of Pelayo, which he withheld.

and I look forward now with confidence, of being able to keep up the series from time to time, with ease to myself, and with much advantage in every respect.

* * * You have been told, no doubt, of a purchase I have made of ten acres, lying at the foot of Oscar's farm, on the river bank. It is a beautiful spot, capable of being made a little paradise. There is a small stone Dutch cottage on it, built about a century since, and inhabited by one of the Van Tassels. I have had an architect up there, and shall build upon the old mansion this summer. My idea is to make a little nookery somewhat in the Dutch style, quaint, but unpretending. It will be of stone. The cost will not be much. I do not intend to set up any establishment there, but to put some simple furniture in it, and keep it as a nest, to which I can resort when in the mood. In fact, it is more with a view of furnishing the worthy little Bramin a retreat for himself and his girls, where they can go to ruralize during the pleasant season of the year. The little man has a great love for the country, and is never so happy as when he can get away for a few days from his multifarious concerns, and refresh himself in the green fields; and since I have purchased this little retreat, the very idea of it has haunted his mind with dreams of "rural felicity."

* * * As soon as I have stereotyped my present volume, which will be in the course of a week, I shall abandon the town altogether, and go to work diligently with my pen in the quiet of the country.

To the same brother he writes, eight days later:

I wrote to you by the last packet, since when I have been to Wilmington, Del., to visit the McLane family, who are waiting until McLane can find a good house for their residence in New York. * * *

I stopped at Carey & Lea's, at Philadelphia, and had prosperous accounts of the success of the two numbers of the Miscellany, which have a great circulation. I send by the packet Hibernia, for Liverpool this day, proof sheets of the third number, containing Legends of the Conquest of Spain. It is all stereotyped, but I shall not publish it here until in September, to give time for the London publisher.

The proof sheets of the Legends of the Conquest of Spain, being No. III of the Crayon Miscellany, were sent to Murray, July 16, who, it appears by a letter to Peter, Feb. 16, 1836, declined publishing them at the price asked by Mr. Irving, but put an edition to press on the author's account, which resulted in a payment of £100. It was published by Messrs. Carey & Lea, of Philadelphia, in October, they giving fifteen hundred dollars for five thousand copies, in their notes, dated October 10, at six, nine, and twelve months. The volume contained the Legend of Don Roderick, the Legend of the Subjugation of Spain, and the Legend of Count Julian and his Family, all of which had been partially finished in the Alhambra —the first entirely so.

This volume was not afterward included in the collective edition of his works, published by Mr. Putnam in 1848, having been kept back, I judge, to accompany an intended publication of the Legend of Don Pelayo, and other Spanish and Moorish themes, at which I have previously glanced. It may be proper, also, to state, that, in consequence of an unlucky hiatus in forwarding the proof sheets to London, the work was not published in that city until the middle of December, two months after its appearance on this side of the water—a circumstance which, with the condition of the times, no doubt had its effect on its English circulation.

In the following extracts we get some further "literary babblings," and a glimpse at the progress he was making in reconstructing the little Dutch cottage he had so lately bought

[*To Peter Irving.*]

NEW YORK, *August 24th.*— * * * I am working away at the Astor enterprise, and hope to get the narrative in frame in the course of the autumn; after which I shall have nothing to do but enrich it. The workmen are busy upon my cottage, which I think will be a snug little Dutch nookery when finished. It will be of stone, so as to be cool in summer and warm in winter. The expense will be but moderate, as I have it built in the simplest manner, depending upon its quaintness rather than its costliness.

While incurring this moderate expense, however, he was locking up several thousand dollars in distant landed investments, into which, like the rest of the world, he was seduced by the prospect of a great and rapid advance in the value of such property.

[*To Peter Irving.*]

NEW YORK, *Sept.* 26, 1835.— * * * For upward of a month past I have been quartered at Hellgate, with Mr. Astor, and I have not had so quiet and delightful a nest since I have been in America. He has a spacious and well-built house, with a lawn in front of it, and a garden in rear. The lawn sweeps down to the water edge, and full in front of the house is the little strait of Hellgate, which forms a constantly moving picture. Here the old gentleman keeps a kind of bachelor hall. Halleck, the poet, lives with him, but goes to town every morning, and comes out to dinner. The only other member of his family is one of his grandchildren, a very fine boy of fourteen years of age.* Pierre Munro Irving has been a guest for several weeks past, but has recently returned to New York. I cannot tell you how sweet and delightful I have found this retreat; pure air, agreeable scenery, a spacious house, profound quiet, and perfect command of my time and self. The consequence is, that I have written more since I have been here than I have ever done in the same space of time. Within the last month I have written more than a volume, and have got within half a dozen chapters of the end of my work—an achievement which I did not expect to do for months. Of course there will be much to be done afterward in extending some parts, touching up others, enriching and embellishing. It will make two good volumes—probably octavo; and Pierre Munro thinks it will be more liked than anything I have lately written.

* Charles Astor Bristed.

Two weeks later (Oct. 8), he writes to the same brother:

I finished my first draught of the Astor work about a week since, very much to my own surprise, not having anticipated such a long and successful fit of writing. I have yet much to do to it, but it will be merely in the way of enriching it by personal anecdotes, &c., to be gathered from individuals, actors in the scenes narrated. I feel sanguine as to the work proving interesting to the general reader. I have promised old Mr. Astor to return to his rural retreat at Hellgate, and shall go out there to-day.

I have just returned from a visit of two or three days to Tarrytown, to take a look at my cottage, which is in a considerable state of forwardness, and will soon be under cover. It has risen from the foundation since my previous visit (about six weeks since), and promises to be a quaint, picturesque little pile. I intend to write a legend or two about it and its vicinity, by way of making it pay for itself.

[*To Ebenezer Irving, New York.*]

TARRYTOWN, Oct. 16, 1835.

MY DEAR BROTHER:

The porch is carried up, and the workmen are in want of the inscription stone, previous to removing the scaffold. I wish you would try to send it up by the Friday sloop or Saturday morning steamboat.

The Dutch for architect is Boumeester. I presume it may be abbreviated Bou^{mr}, or engraved in smaller letters (Geo. Harvey, Boumeester), whichever will be most convenient.

Your affectionate brother, W. I.

George Harvey, the architect mentioned in the foregoing letter, was an English artist, living a few miles south of the cottage, who had interested himself very much in its construction, and whom Mr. Irving frequently consulted for designs and drafts. The inscription stone of the porch still bears his name, with the adjunct of Bou^{mr}.

[*To Peter Irving, Havre.*]

NEW YORK, Nov. 24, 1835.

MY DEAR BROTHER:

* * * I am just from Tarrytown, where I have been endeavoring to hasten the building of my cottage; but though the weather has been uncommonly fine and mild for the season, and there has been no obstruction to the progress of the work, yet a snowstorm has come upon us before the house was completely enclosed. The weather is again bright and mild, and I hope yet to complete all the external work before the rigors of winter. The interior can be finished during the winter, being warmed by stoves, and I hope to have the mansion complete by the time the spring is sufficiently advanced to render a country residence agreeable. Like all meddlings with stone and mortar, the plan has extended as I built, until it has ended in a complete, though moderate-sized family residence. It is solidly built of stone, so that it will last for generations; and I think, when finished, it will be both picturesque and convenient. It is a tenement in which a man of very moderate means may live, and which yet may form an elegant little snuggery for a rich man. It is quite a hobby of the Bramin, and I really think will contribute greatly to his enjoyment for the rest of his life.

I have lately resumed the Astor MS., and hope to complete it in the course of a few weeks.

He had suspended his labors, in expectation of the arrival of a person who had been a principal actor in the enterprise of Astoria, and from whom he was to get many personal anecdotes for the enriching of his work.

The letter to Peter I now give touches upon the great fire in New York, and is written soon after his brother John had returned from a tour in Europe, in which he had visited his long-absent brother, whose residence abroad had now extended to upward of twenty-six years.

NEW YORK, Dec. 25, 1835.

MY DEAR BROTHER:

In consequence of being out at Mr. Astor's, at Hellgate, I miss the run of the packets, and have suffered two to go off without writing a line; and this, too, at a juncture when you may be suffering uneasiness of mind from receiving news of our late calamitous fire. I find, however, that brother E. I. has written to you punctually, and given you particulars. It was fortunate for the Bramin that he removed last spring, by which means he escaped being burnt out. The fire, however, has singed almost everybody. Those who had no houses or goods burnt, suffered through the insurance companies, in which the funds of so many were invested. Poor Brevoort has lost about fifty thousand dollars, and feels a little sore at the loss, but, I trust, will soon get over it, as he has an ample fortune left. Brother John estimates his loss at forty-one thousand dollars—that is to say, he has insurance stock to that amount. Some of the companies in which he holds, however, will not be bankrupt. His son Gabriel thinks his father will not really lose much above half that amount; but brother John is rather tenacious on that point, and we allow him to have the full merit of his misfortune. As his fortune is estimated at some three or four hundred thousand dollars at least, his case is not considered desperate.

I lost three thousand dollars, invested in the Guardian Insurance Company. Fortunately, I am consoled at the very same moment by the rise of another kind of stock in which I hold shares, and which will more than make up the loss. E. I. held twenty-five hundred dollars in the same insurance company. He likewise has been successful in some other quarters, which cover his loss.

Your letter by brother John has diffused a general joy through the family, by the hope it holds out of your attempting the home voyage in the spring. I have been extremely worried at the thoughts of not having been able to come out to you last autumn, and have endeavored to push matters so as to pay you a visit in the course of the winter. Brother John, however, tells me that you and Beasley think you will feel perfectly safe under the guardianship of our worthy friend, Captain Funck. I shall, therefore, relinquish the idea, and turn all my attention to prepare matters for your reception. My cottage is not yet finished, but I shall drive at it as soon as the opening of spring will permit; and I trust, by the time of your arrival, to have a delightful little nest for you on the banks of the Hudson. It will be fitted to defy both hot weather and cold. There is a lovely prospect from its windows, and a sweet green bank in front, shaded by locust trees, up which the summer breeze creeps delightfully. It is one of the most delicious banks in the world for reading and dozing and dreaming during the heats of summer, and there are no mosquitos in the neighborhood. Here you shall have a room to yourself that shall be a *sanctum sanctorum.* You may have your meals in it, if you please, and be as much alone as you desire. You shall also have a room prepared for you in town, where you will be equally master of your time and yourself, and free from all intrusion; while at both places you will have those at hand who love and honor you, and who will be ready to do anything that may contribute to your comfort.

If you can meet with a good servant to take care of you in the voyage, and to remain with you here, you had better engage him. Such a one would be valuable at the cottage. I think you ought to have a trusty servant, accustomed to your ways, and who understands all your wants.

I am still at Hellgate with Mr. Astor, who is detained in the country in consequence of his new house in town not being finished. Pierre M. Irving is here likewise, and we pass our time most pleasantly and profitably. In fact, Mr. Astor does everything in his power to render our residence with him agreeable, and to detain us with him; or rather, he takes the true way, by leaving us complete masters of ourselves and our time. In consequence of having so much leisure and quiet, I have been able to get on famously with my new work, and hope to finish it in the course of a few weeks.

I am writing this from the Hive, where we are all assembled to keep a merry Christmas. I wish to God you were here with us; you would see a happy and charming group around you, comprising three generations; for we have with us a daughter of Pierre P. Irving, a beautiful and delightful little girl about four years old, the pet of the house. She and her little aunt Charlotte are perfectly happy this morning, Santa Claus having filled their stockings with presents last night.

Wishing you a merry Christmas, my dear brother, and sending the most affectionate regards to our worthy friend Beasley, I am ever affectionately your brother,

W. I.

CHAPTER IV.

PETER IRVING ABOUT TO RETURN—EXTRACTS FROM THE LAST LETTER OF WASHINGTON TO HIM PRIOR TO HIS EMBARCATION—JOHN JACOB ASTOR—INVESTMENTS IN LAND—SLOWER AFFAIRS THAN HE ANTICIPATED—RETURN OF PETER—COMPLETION OF THE COTTAGE—COMMENCES HOUSEKEEPING—PUBLICATION OF ASTORIA—PETER AN INMATE OF THE COTTAGE—LETTER FROM "THE ROOST"—ENGAGED UPON THE ADVENTURES OF CAPTAIN BONNEVILLE—THE NEW PIG.

THE year 1836 opens upon the author in "that admirable place for literary occupation," Mr. Astor's country retreat, opposite Hellgate, where he was still sojourning, and working upon various parts of the Astorian manuscript which afforded room for enrichment. He was looking forward impatiently "to the completion of the cottage" in time to render it a "nest" for his brother Peter, who still continued in the purpose to attempt the voyage in April. "Now that you have made up your mind to cross the Atlantic," writes Washington to his brother, January 10, "I am all alive to the manner. I never adverted to it while I thought you would not be disposed to adventure. It is hard for one like myself, who never suffer from sea-sickness, to realize the horrors that it must present to the mind of one subjected to it. I am in hopes that, by regimen and cautious management, you may neutralize its severest inflictions; and if you can but get across the sea, *even in pieces*, we will gather you up and put you together, and make you feel like another being, when we have you once among us."

The infirmities which beset Peter at Washington's departure for this country had increased with the lapse of time, and taken a more painful form; yet he had determined to embark on the 24th of April, with Captain Funck, "his early and excellent friend, who would take as much care of him as he could expect from a near relation." "As the term approaches," he writes to Washington, March 8th, "I feel increasing desire to be united to the family. The affectionate welcome they are disposed to give me, dissipates the hesitation I have felt to become an encumbrance to them. To you, my dear brother, I know not what to say, and will make no effort. I hope, that if our fortunes in life had been reversed, I should have acted with some degree of the same generous affection."

The following extracts are from the last letter addressed by Washington to Peter before his embarcation, from which it will be seen that, in addition to the three thousand dollars stipulated by Mr. Astor, I received a special compensation from Mr. Irving for my literary jobwork in lightening the labor before him; yet the imputation was afterward made that Mr. Astor gave the author five thousand dollars to take up his manuscripts.

I would premise, also, in this place, that during Mr. Irving's long acquaintance with Mr. Astor, commencing when he was a young man, and ending only with his death, he never came under a pecuniary obligation to him of any kind. The only moneyed transaction that ever took place between them, is alluded to in the following letter—the purchase of a share in a town he was founding in Green Bay, for which he paid the cash, though Mr. Astor wished the amount to stand on mortgage. The land was not sold when it had advanced in value; and long after it had declined, when Mr. Irving was in Spain, Mr. Astor, of his own free will, took back the share, and repaid the original purchase money. "He was too proverbially rich a man," says Mr. Irving, in a letter which appeared in the *Literary World* of Nov. 22, 1851, "for me to permit the shadow of a pecuniary favor to rest on our intercourse."

The other investment in Indian lands, alluded to in the letter, in which he embarked five thousand dollars directly, and four thousand dollars in a loan to a friend to enable him to engage in it, turned out almost a total loss, but a small fragment of the loan or the outlay ever coming back to him. A time of public pressure was approaching, which made these investments in wild lands a source of embarrassment. Indeed, almost every attempt he made of this kind to enlarge his means, only resulted in impairing them.

[*To Peter.*]

February 16, 1836.

MY DEAR BROTHER:

* * * Your return will be a perfect jubilee to us all, and I am sure you will feel happy yourself, in seeing how happy you make all around you.

I am giving my last handling to the Astor work. It is this handling which, like the touching and toning of a picture, gives the richest effects. I am interested and pleased with the work, and feel that the labor I am now bestowing upon it will contribute greatly to its success.

Pierre has received three thousand dollars from Mr. Astor for his services in the work. I have given him one thousand dollars. He sets off to-morrow for Toledo, a new town at the head of Lake Erie, where he has the offer of a share in a land purchase, which, it is thought, will turn out very profitable. Real estate, and especially lots in the vicinity of new towns at great commercial points in the interior, are great objects of attention at present, and fortunes are rapidly made. The canals, railroads, and other modes of communication opening in every direction, is one great cause of the sudden rise in the value of various places.

The Bramin and myself, with Mr. ———, and our friend ———, are concerned in a purchase of Indian land in Mississippi. Mr. ———'s brother-in-law, ———, a very correct, amiable man, is the agent. The purchase has been made with great judgment: the formalities with Government have all been complied with, and orders have been sent from Washington to the land agent to deliver the titles. The lands so bought can at this moment be sold for a profit of at least one hundred per cent.; and it is our intention to sell enough to realize our investments, and then to sell the rest from time to time, waiting for higher prices.

Mr. Astor has likewise let me have a share in the town of Astor, at Green Bay, Lake Michigan, for which I pay four thousand dollars, but which is already at an advance of fifty per cent. I think this town is going to equal Chicago in its sudden rise and prosperity.

I have just received a letter from Murray. He had declined purchasing my last work, "Legends of Spain," at the price I asked, and had put an edition to press on my account. I find the success of the work is beyond his expectations, as he has had already to print a second edition. Murray is not his own master in these matters. In consequence of the embarrassments in which he was involved about the time I left England, his affairs are in the hands of trustees, whom he has to consult as to all his undertakings. My dealings with him are perfectly secure as to money matters, and in other respects I have always found him a gentlemanlike person to deal with.

I am, my dear brother, yours affectionately,

W. I.

In less than four months after the date of these extracts, Peter found himself a member of "the family hive" in Bridge street, waiting until the cottage could be rendered habitable, to take up his quarters in that little retreat. Meanwhile, the changes in his native city, after an absence of twenty-seven years, presented a constant subject of interest and curiosity.

There is always "a world of finishing that one never calculates" in most buildings, and the cottage did not prove an exception. Washington had expected it to be habitable some time in June; but at the close of that month, and some five or six weeks after he had sent the first chapters of Astoria to press, he writes to me, then absent at Toledo, Ohio: "I am printing my book and completing my cottage slowly, and hope the former will contribute toward defraying the accumulated expenses of the latter." A month before, he had written me: "The cottage is slowly approaching to a finish, but will take a few weeks yet. For such a small edifice it has a prodigious swallow, and reminds me of those little fairy changelings called Killcrops, which eat and eat, and are never the fatter." The few weeks, however, lengthened out into months, and, though opened on the 1st of September, it was not until October that the little edifice became fully habitable. On the 15th of that month, Washington writes to his brother Ebenezer, from the cottage: "Brother Peter's room shall be put in order the moment the furniture arrives, and I shall come down the beginning of the week to convoy him up. I wish he was here at present to enjoy this delightful autumnal weather."

Astoria, which was going through the press at the close of June, was published in October. He received from Bentley, in London, £500, and from Carey & Lea, for the right of printing five thousand copies, four thousand dollars, in three equal notes, at four months.

In the following letter to myself, we have an interesting allusion to its reception. To render its opening passages intelligible, I must preface it with the statement that in the latter part of March, not long after I had taken up my quarters at Toledo, at the head of Lake Erie, I had been authorized by Mr. Irving to invest, on joint account for himself and his brother Ebenezer, the sum of twenty thousand dollars in the purchase of lots or lands at that infant city—an investment which, like the other speculations in wild lands into which he had been drawn, failed to yield the prompt advantages he had expected.

[*To Pierre M. Irving, at Toledo.*]

TARRYTOWN, Dec. 12, 1836.

MY DEAR PIERRE:

A thousand things have prevented an earlier reply to your letter of Nov. 6th, which gave me great satisfaction. As to Toledo, I hope the Governor's prediction may be verified, and that it may grow to be a mighty city like Babylon of old. I am so accustomed, however, to find *swans* turn out mere *geese*, that I have made up my mind not to be grieved if that should prove to be the case in the present instance. I only hope that our goose may be tolerably plump and well feathered. My confidence in quick returns from land speculations slackened early last summer, or rather in the spring, when I saw how wildly everybody was rushing into them; and I have ever since made my calculations to "weather along," as the sailors say, for some time to come, without any of the funds I have so invested. It takes down some of my towering plans, and may induce me to burn the candle only at one end; but I will make up for it by a perfect illumination, should things really turn out rightly, and I come to a great fortune! Luckily, my cottage was built and furniture bought before this frost set in to chill my prospects. It has only nipped one weathercock, which I shall not mount until more propitious days; fortunately, I have three secure (having received the Vanderheyden one magnificently gilt), and with these I shall endeavor to make out for the present.

Seriously, I am living most cosily and delightfully in this dear, bright little home, which I have fitted up to my own humor. Everything goes on cheerily in my little household, and I would not exchange the cottage for any chateau in Christendom. I am working, too, with almost as much industry and rapidity as I did at Hellgate, and, I think, will more than pay for my nest, from the greater number of eggs I shall be able to hatch there.

Astoria succeeds equal to your anticipations, and far beyond my own. It is highly spoken of in two English reviews which I have read. One pronounces it my *chef d'œuvre*. I am glad he thinks so, though I don't. Old Mr. Astor appears to be greatly gratified, which is very satisfactory to me. William Astor also expresses himself in the most gratifying terms, and seems surprised that the subject should have been made so interesting and entertaining. In fact, I have heard more talk about this work, considering the short time it has been launched, than about any other that I have published for some time past.

Old Mr. Astor most unexpectedly paid me a visit at the cottage about a month since. * * * He landed at Tarrytown, and hired a vehicle, which brought him to the cottage door. He spent two days here, and promised to repeat his visit as soon as there shall be good sleighing.

I follow this letter with a few extracts from one of the reviews of Astoria, to which Mr. Irving alludes—the *London Spectator* for the week ending October 22, 1836, which opens as follows:

We have been agreeably surprised by these volumes. Instead of a novel, which the title, on its first announcement, seemed to propose, *Astoria* is the history of as grand and comprehensive a commercial enterprise as ever was planned with any well-grounded prospect of success, and which was prosecuted among scenes as vast and nations as wild, gave rise to incidents as ludicrous, as interesting, as appalling, and developed characters and manners as marked and striking as anything on record respecting the adventurous explorers of the Middle Ages, or the hardy discoverers of more modern days.

Then, after giving a sketch of the large scheme of Mr. Astor, and the main narratives of the original voyage to Astoria, "full of pleasant humor," and the land journey across the continent, "of a more interesting and massy nature," and glancing at the principal sources from which the materials of the volumes are drawn, the reviewer sums up as follows:

The result is the production of the most finished narrative of such a series of adventures that ever was written, whether with regard to plan or execution. The arrangement has all the art of a fiction, yet without any apparent sacrifice of truth or exactness. The composition we are inclined to rate as the *chef d'œuvre* of Washington Irving. * * * The book, in its better parts, does not appear like a reproduction from other writings, but as a creation of genius from the original observation of things themselves. The author, with a peculiar felicity, has retained the raciness of his authorities. He displays the acuteness, distinctness, and reality of men of business and action, without their necessary minuteness and tedious expansion. He has extracted the spirit from the Astorian archives, and thrown off their dregs and dry matter.

On the 10th of December, 1836, after Peter had become an inmate of the cottage, we have the following amusingly characteristic epistle from Washington, addressed to the daughter of his sister Catherine from the "Roost," as he at first christened his new home:

[*To Miss Sarah Paris.*]

THE ROOST, Dec. 10, 1836.

MY DEAR SARAH:

I was most agreeably surprised, this afternoon, when the worthy and all-provident Mr. Lawrence, on his return from one of his foraging expeditions to Tarrytown, brought home with him, besides many creature comforts, a "bonnie little epistle" from you. It is true, my pleasure was a little dampened on finding that I was not to have you back at the cottage so soon as I had anticipated; but I cannot expect to monopolize you, and beg you to protract your stay in New York as long as business or pleasure may dictate.

I cannot tell you how happy I was to get back again to my own dear, bright little home, and leave behind me the hurry and worry and flurry of the city. I found all things going on well. Your uncle Peter had passed his time comfortably, and was altogether better in health and spirits than when we left him, notwithstanding that he was without the superintending care of that "lively lady," your mother. He continues to improve. He says he is free from headache, and the touch of influenza is over. He is enabled, therefore, to enjoy the cosey comforts of the cottage; takes his meals regularly with me, is cheerful and conversable, and occupies himself with writing long letters to his correspondents—a sure sign that he is in good trim. Tell all this to your mother, and tell her he receives Benjamin's portion of everything, just as faithfully as if she had the dealing out.

Alice accomplished her return voyage successfully, and with but one blunder (which was doing amazing well for an Irishwoman). She landed at Tarrytown, instead of Dobbs' Ferry. As it was late and dark, she was at first at what she calls a *nonplish;* but fortunately she discovered the little mansion of Mrs. Bowman, who gave her quarter for the night. The next morning she reached the cottage in safety, to the great joy of honest John, who welcomed her with a smile of at least a quarter of a yard in width.

The goose war is happily terminated; Mr. Jones'* squadron has left my waters, and my feathered navy now plows the Tappan Sea in triumph. I cannot but attribute this great victory to the valor and good conduct of the enterprising and ambitious little duck, who seems to enjoy great power and popularity among both geese and ganders, and absolutely to be admiral of the fleet.

I am happy to inform you, that, among the many other blessings brought to the cottage by the good Mr. Lawrence,†

* George Jones had purchased the land adjoining his, in September, just after he had commenced his housekeeping.

† Silas Lawrence.

is a pig of first rate stock and lineage. It has been duly put in possession of the palace in the rear of the barn, where it is shown to every visitor with as much pride as if it was the youngest child of a family. As it is of the fair sex, and, in the opinion of the best judges, a pig of peerless beauty, I have named it "Fanny." I know it is a name which, with Kate and you, has a romantic charm, and, about the cottage, everything, as old Mrs. Martling says, must be romance.

[His two nieces, with the rest of the world, had been running mad over the acting of *Fanny* Kemble.]

Imp, finding me abandoned by my womankind, has taken compassion on me, and gives me her company nearly all day long; sometimes clambering on my lap as I sit writing, at other times fondling about my feet, or stretching herself before the fire, clawing the carpet, and purring with perfect enjoyment. As brother John said of his mocking bird, I expect to have great comfort in that cat—"if it should be spared."

I have been writing almost incessantly since my return to the cottage, so that I have scarcely been out of doors, though the weather, a part of the time, has been lovely. I wanted a companion to tempt me to long walks about the hills. Alice and John take good care of us, so that we want for nothing in the way of household comforts; but, old bachelor though I be, I cannot do without womankind about me; so come back, my darling girl, as soon as you are tired of New York, and bring whom you please with you; but Kate must at all events be here in the holidays.

It is Saturday evening. I hear a solemn though rather nasal strain of melody from my kitchen. It is the good ———, setting his mind in tune for the morrow. Thank Heaven, I have brimstoned my cider according to Uncle

Natt's receipt; it would stand poor chance, otherwise, against such melody.

Give my love to all. Your affectionate uncle,

WASHINGTON IRVING.

A few days later, he writes to his brother Ebenezer:

All goes on well at the Roost. Brother Peter is getting quite in good feather again, and begins to crow!

You must contrive to come up soon, if it is only to see my new pig, which is a darling.

CHAPTER V.

NEWSPAPER ATTACKS ON MR. IRVING—JOSEPH SEAWELL JONES—WILLIAM LEGGETT—THE BOOKSELLERS' FESTIVAL—HALLECK AND ROGERS—LETTER TO EBENEZER IRVING—PUBLICATION OF THE ADVENTURES OF CAPTAIN BONNEVILLE—LOUIS NAPOLEON AT "THE ROOST"—PETER NO LONGER AN INMATE—LETTER TO EDWARD EVERETT—LETTERS TO GOUVERNEUR KEMBLE—DEATH OF JOHN—THE TAMMANY PEOPLE PROPOSE TO RUN HIM FOR MAYOR—DECLINES—PRESIDENT VAN BUREN OFFERS HIM THE SECRETARYSHIP OF THE NAVY—DECLINES.

THE month of January, 1837, found Mr. Irving in his little cottage dressed off in Christmas greens, with only Peter for a housemate, who was now completely settled in it, and apparently much to his taste and humor. "We have a brilliant frosty prospect from our windows," writes Mr. Irving to me, who had expressed some fears that he was passing a solitary winter; "Tappan Bay covered with sparkling ice, and the opposite hills with snow; but everything is warm and cosey within doors." In these winter quarters, which he found "anything but gloomy," he was exercising his pen, and "getting on briskly" with the Adventures of Captain Bonneville, which he was intending to launch in the spring. Meanwhile, he is gladdened with the news of the further sale of a Toledo lot. "I am glad," he writes, "to find Toledo is doing so well in these hard times, and begin to think I shall yet be able to afford another weathercock to my cottage."

While thus enjoying himself in the quiet of the country, he is called upon most unexpectedly to notice two gratuitous newspaper attacks. The first censor was Mr. Joseph Seawell Jones, who had written a history of North Carolina, and had got into a controversy respecting the mutual and contested claims of Virginia and North Carolina to be the original depository of the peculiarities characteristic of the days of Sir Walter Raleigh and his Virgin Queen. In the course of the discussion, which was carried on in the columns of the *New York American*, at that time edited by Charles King, now President of Columbia College, one of the parties brought forward, in support of his views, a quotation from a little comic sketch of Mr. Irving's, called "The Creole Village," lately contributed to an annual (the *Magnolia**); and Mr. Jones thereupon—with what propriety I need not say—indulged in some coarse personal allusions toward his innocent and unsuspecting offender. Mr. Irving, in order that there might be no misapprehension of the circumstances under which his name had been introduced into this controversy, addressed the following letter to Mr. King:

* The *Magnolia* was edited by that brilliant but unfortunate English writer, Henry Herbert. Besides the Creole Village, Mr. Irving contributed to this annual another piece—The Happy Man. Both were afterward incorporated in "Wolfert's Roost," the latter under the title of The Contented Man."

To the Editor of the New York American:

SIR: I perceive a prolonged and angry discussion in the papers, with which my name has been strangely mingled. The manner in which I have become implicated is this: In a trifling sketch of a French Creole village, inserted in one of the latest annuals, I observed, incidentally, that the Virginians retain peculiarities characteristic of the times of Queen Elizabeth and Sir Walter Raleigh. By this remark, I have drawn upon me some very ungracious language from a writer of North Carolina, who charges me with a gross violation of the truth of history, and implies that I have committed an intentional wrong on his native State. Conscious of no intention to controvert any point of history; free from all disposition to do wrong or to give offence either to communities or individuals; and accustomed to observe, and to experience, the most courteous conduct in all dealings with my literary contemporaries, I was at a loss to what to attribute so indecorous an attack. I have since, however, understood that the feelings of the writer in question had previously become sore and irritable, in the course of a contest in the papers between himself and some Virginian writers, as to the claims of their respective States to certain historical associations with the names of Queen Elizabeth and Sir Walter Raleigh; and that my innocently intended paragraph aforesaid, being quoted by one of his opponents, had drawn upon me his undiscriminating ire.

I have too great commiseration for any person laboring under a state of mental irritability, to seek to exasperate his malady; and feel nothing but regret that any casual remark of mine should have fallen upon this sore spot in the mind of your correspondent

As, however, the writer's misconception has been reiterated in the newspapers, and as some readers may imagine that I really stand convicted of a deliberate outrage upon historical truth, and hostility to the claims of North Carolina, I beg leave simply to put on record, that I have neither part nor interest in the claims of either of the belligerent parties. The opinion expressed in my unlucky paragraph, had no sinister view with respect to North Carolina. It merely expressed a general notion as to the manners of the Virginians, and an idea that they had taken their original stamp from colonists who had lived in England in the time of Queen Elizabeth and Sir Walter Raleigh, and had brought with them the habitudes and manners characteristic of that period.

If I am wrong in this idea, I plead ignorance, rather than submit to the imputation of wilfully misstating facts; but I believe that the most accurate researches will establish the correctness of the casual remark which has brought upon me so much ire. As to the people of North Carolina, they have always partaken of that general feeling which I have toward the people of the South, which is anything but one of coldness or disrespect.

If, after this explanation, any disputatious writer should think fit to persist in resenting an imaginary offence, I shall leave him to the singular caprice of fighting shadows, and will only pray for his speedy restoration to a happier state of mind and greater courtesy of language.

Very respectfully yours,

WASHINGTON IRVING.

GREENBURG,* Jan. 4, 1837.

* Greenburg, from which the letter bears date, is the name of the township in which the cottage is situated.

Mr. Irving had hardly answered this attack, before he was assailed in the *Plaindealer* of January 14th. William Leggett, who conducted that able but short-lived weekly, has been described, by one who knew him, as taking a sort of pleasure in bearding public opinion. He had been for several years employed as one of the editors of the *Evening Post*, and remained with the paper till December, 1836. During the absence, in Europe, of his editorial associate, William C. Bryant, from 1834 to 1836, the paper suffered in its finances from its extreme political course, and, soon after the poet's return to resume the position of a journalist, Mr. Leggett withdrew from the *Post*, and commenced the *Plaindealer*, the first number of which appeared December 3, 1836. In the seventh number, in an article on "Mutilating Books," the editor remarks: "Whatever be the motive, it is an unwarrantable liberty, particularly when the title page or preface gives no intimation that the work has undergone emendation or mutilation;" and afterward adds: "Liberties of this kind, taken with an author, are bad at best; and they become contemptible, when they result from that unmanly timidity which is afraid to let the public see the truth. Our respect for Washington Irving underwent a sensible diminution, when we perceived that, in supervising the republication of Bryant's Poems in London, he changed a passage in the piece called "Marion's Men":

"And the British foeman trembles
When Marion's name is heard,"

in order to substitute something that might be more soothing to [English] ears than the mention of the effect which the mode of warfare practised by the Southern partisan leader had on the British soldiers. When Mr. Irving, in publishing a book of his own, prepares one preface for his countrymen, full of *amor patriæ* and professions of American feeling, and another for the London market, in which all such professions are studiously omitted, he does what he has an undoubted right to do, whatever we may say of its spirit. But when, at the suggestion of a species of literary pusillanimity, he changes the language of poems, every word of which, as written by the author, will live long after even Bracebridge Hall and Knickerbocker are forgotten, he shows a deficiency of manliness not calculated to raise him in our opinion, to say the least of it."

Mr. Irving first saw or heard of this article in coming to the city to attend the funeral of his old law preceptor, Judge Josiah Ogden Hoffman, who had died on the 24th of January. An attack so unmannerly—as it has been truly characterized by Mr. Evert A. Duyckinck, a fair-minded and elevated critic—and so unjust, took him entirely by surprise; and as it seemed to derive weight from the known friendship of Mr. Leggett and Mr. Bryant, and their long association as editors, he lost no time in addressing the following reply to the editor of the *Plaindealer*, which I find in that paper of January 28 :

To the Editor of the Plaindealer:

SIR: Living, at present, in the country, and out of the way of the current literature of the day, it was not until this morning that I saw your paper of the 14th of January, or knew anything of your animadversions on my conduct and character therein contained. Though I have generally abstained from noticing any attack upon myself in the public papers, the present is one which I cannot suffer to pass in silence.

In the first place, you have censured me strongly for having altered a paragraph in the London edition of Mr. Bryant's poems; and the remarks and comparisons in which you have indulged on the occasion, would seem to imply that I have a literary hostility to Mr. Bryant, and a disposition to detract from the measure of his well-merited reputation.

The relation in which you stand to that gentleman, as his particular friend and literary associate, gives these animadversions the greater weight, and calls for a real statement of the case.

When I was last in London (I think in 1832), I received a copy of the American edition of Mr. Bryant's Poems from some friend (I now forget from whom), who expressed a wish that it might be republished in England. I had not, at that time, the pleasure of a personal acquaintance with Mr. Bryant, but I felt the same admiration for his Poems that you have expressed, and was desirous that writings so honorable to American literature should be known to the British public, and take their merited rank in the literature of the language. I exerted myself, therefore, to get them republished by some London bookseller, but met with unexpected difficulties, poetry being declared quite unsalable since the death of Lord Byron.

At length a bookseller was induced to undertake an edition, by my engaging, gratuitously, to edit the work, and to write something that might call public attention to it. I accordingly prefixed to the volume a dedicatory letter, addressed to Mr. Samuel Rogers, in which, while I expressed my own opinion of the Poems, I took occasion to allude to the still more valuable approbation which I had heard expressed by that distinguished author; thus bringing the work before the British public with the high sanction of one of the most refined critics of the day. While the work was going through the press, an objection was started to the passage in the poem of "Marion's Men":

> "And the British foeman trembles,
> When Marion's name is heard."

It was considered as peculiarly calculated to shock the feelings of British readers on the most sensitive point, seeming to call in question the courage of the nation. It was urged that common decorum required the softening of such a passage in an edition exclusively intended for the British public; and I was asked what would be the feelings of American readers, if such an imputation on the courage of their countrymen were inserted in a work presented for their approbation. These objections were urged in a spirit of friendship to Mr. Bryant, and with a view to his success, for it was suggested that this passage might be felt as a taunt or bravado, and might awaken a prejudice against the work, before its merits could be appreciated.

I doubt whether these objections would have occurred to me, had they not been thus set forth; but, when thus urged, I yielded to them, and softened the passage in question, by omitting the adjective *British*, and substituting one of a more general signification. If this evinced "timidity of spirit," it was a timidity felt entirely on behalf of Mr. Bryant. I was not to be harmed by the insertion of the paragraph as it originally stood. I freely confess, however, that I have at all times almost as strong a repugnance to tell a painful or humiliating truth, *unnecessarily*, as I have to tell an untruth, under any circumstances. To speak the truth on all occasions, is the indispensable attribute of man; to refrain from uttering disagreeable truths, *unnecessarily*, belongs, I think, to the character of a gentleman; neither, sir, do I think it incompatible with fair dealing, however little it may square with your notions of plain dealing.

The foregoing statement will show how I stand with regard to Mr. Bryant. I trust his fame has suffered nothing by my republication of his works in London; at any rate, he has expressed his thanks to me by letter, since my return to this country. I was, therefore, I confess, but little prepared to receive a stab from his bosom friend.

Another part of your animadversions is of a much graver nature, for it implies a charge of hypocrisy and double dealing, which I indignantly repel as incompatible with my nature. You intimate, that "in publishing a book of my own, I prepare one preface for my countrymen, full of *amor patriæ* and professions of home feeling, and another for the London market, in which such professions are studiously omitted." Your inference is that these professions are hollow, and intended to gain favor with my countrymen, and that they are omitted in the London edition through fear of offending English readers. Were I indeed chargeable with such baseness, I should well merit the contempt you invoke upon my head. As I give you credit, sir, for probity, I was at a loss to think on what you could ground such an imputation, until it occurred to me that some circumstances attending the publication of my "Tour on the Prairies" might have given rise to a misconception in your mind.

It may seem strange to those intimately acquainted with my character, that I should think it necessary to defend myself from a charge of *duplicity;* but as many of your readers may know me as little as you appear to do, I must again be excused in a detail of facts.

When my Tour on the Prairies was ready for the press, I sent a manuscript copy to England for publication, and, at the same time, put a copy in the press at New York. As this was my first appearance before the American public since my return, I was induced, while the work was printing, to modify the introduction so as to express my sense of the unexpected warmth with which I had been welcomed to my native place, and my general feelings on finding myself once more at home, and among my friends. These feelings, sir, were genuine, and were not expressed with half the warmth with which they were entertained. Circumstances alluded to in that introduction had made the reception I met with from my countrymen doubly dear and touching to me, and had filled my heart with affectionate gratitude for their unlooked-for kindness. In fact, misconstructions of my conduct, and misconceptions of my character, somewhat similar to those I am at present endeavoring to rebut, had appeared in the public press, and, as I erroneously supposed, had prejudiced the mind of my countrymen against me. The professions, therefore, to which you have alluded, were uttered, not to obviate such prejudices, or to win my way to the good will of my countrymen, but to express my feelings after their good will had been unequivocally manifested. While I thought they doubted me, I remained silent; when I found they believed in me, I spoke. I have never been in the habit of beguiling them by fulsome professions of patriotism, those cheap passports to public favor; and I think I might for once have been indulged in briefly touching a chord on which others have harped to so much advantage.

Now, sir, even granting I had "studiously omitted" all those professions in the introduction intended for the London market, instead of giving utterance to them after that article had been sent off, where, I would ask, would have been the impropriety of the act? What had the British public to do with those home greetings, and those assurances of gratitude and affection which related exclusively to my countrymen, and grew out of my actual position with regard to them? There was nothing in them at which the British reader could possibly take offence; the omitting of them, therefore, could not have argued "timidity," but would have been merely a matter of good taste; for they would have been as much out of place repeated to English readers, as would have been my greetings and salutations to my family circle, if repeated out of the window, for the benefit of the passers-by in the street.

I have no intention, sir, of imputing to you any malevolent feeling in the unlooked-for attack you have made upon me: I can see no motive you have for such hostility. I rather think you have acted from honest feelings, hastily excited by a misapprehension of facts; and that you have been a little too eager to give an instance of that "plain dealing" which you have recently adopted as your war cry. Plain dealing, sir, is a great merit, when accompanied by magnanimity, and exercised with a just and generous spirit; but if pushed too far, and made the excuse for indulging every impulse of passion or prejudice, it may render a man, especially in your situation, a very offensive, if not a very mischievous member of the community. Such I sincerely hope and trust may not be your case; but this hint, given in a spirit of caution, not of accusation, may not be of disservice to you.

In the present instance, I have only to ask that you will give this article an insertion in your paper, being intended not so much for yourself, as for those of your readers who may have been prejudiced against me by your animadversions. Your editorial position of course gives you an opportunity of commenting upon it according to the current of your feelings; and, whatever may be your comments, it is not probable that they will draw any further reply from me. Recrimination is a miserable kind of redress, in which I never indulge, and I have no relish for the warfare of the pen.

Very respectfully, your obedient servant,

WASHINGTON IRVING.

The editor of the *Plaindealer*, in introducing Mr. Irving's dignified reply to his strictures, accompanied the letter with "the most explicit exoneration of Mr. Bryant from any lot or part, directly or indirectly, in the remarks" he made concerning "what seemed to him a piece of literary pusillanimity on the part of Mr. Irving," and added, that "candor required him to state, that on various occasions he had heard Mr. Bryant express the kindest sentiments toward Mr. Irving for the interest he took in the publication of a London edition of his Poems, and for the complimentary terms in which he introduced them to the British public."

Mr. Bryant himself, however, to leave no doubt of the editor's sincerity in this exoneration, took occasion, in the succeeding number of the *Plaindealer*, to state explicitly that, though he would not have made the alteration, he had never complained of it, and had no doubt it was done with the kindest intentions: expressing, at the same time, with some feeling, his surprise at one or two unguarded passages in Mr. Irving's letter, as if levelled at himself. To this Mr. Irving replied through the columns of the *New York American*, in a letter addressed to Mr. Bryant, expressing his deep regret that any passages in his letter to Mr. Leggett should have seemed susceptible of a construction unfavorable to him, and disavowing emphatically any suspicion or the remotest intention to insinuate that he had the least participation in the attack recently made on his character. The letter closed as follows:

> As to the alteration of a word in the London edition of your Poems, which others have sought to nurture into a root of bitterness between us, I have already stated my motives for it, and the embarrassment in which I was placed. I regret extremely that it should not have met with your approbation, and sincerely apologize to you for the liberty I was persuaded to take: a liberty I freely acknowledge the least excusable with writings like yours, in which it is difficult to alter a word without marring a beauty.

The two letters of Mr. Bryant, written after he had received a copy of the London edition of his Poems, forwarded by Mr. Irving, in which he expresses his thanks to him for the kind interest he had taken in procuring the publication of his Poems in England, have already been given in a preceding volume.

It is evident, from the tone of the *Plaindealer* in this attack, that its editor was infected with a notion that Mr. Irving had been too much inclined to pay court to England. It is not necessary to vindicate him from this false impression at the present day, but the question is so fully met, and the analysis of Mr. Irving's character in this particular so admirably and truly given by Mr. Bryant, in the beautiful address delivered on occasion of his death, that I cannot deny myself the pleasure of quoting from it in this connection.

After alluding to the author's agreeable pictures of English life in the Sketch Book, Bracebridge Hall, and the Tales of a Traveller, "seen under favorable lights, and sketched with a friendly pencil," he remarks:

Let me say here, that it was not to pay court to the English that he thus described them and their country; it was because he could not describe them otherwise. It was the instinct of his mind to attach itself to the contemplation of the good and the beautiful, wherever he found them, and to turn away from the sight of what was evil, misshapen, and hateful. His was not a nature to pry for faults, or disabuse the world of good-natured mistakes; he looked for virtue, love, and truth among men, and thanked God that he found them in such large measure. If there are touches of satire in his writings, he is the best-natured and most amiable of satirists, amiable beyond

Horace; and in his irony—for there is a vein of playful irony running through many of his works—there is no tinge of bitterness.

I rejoice, for my part, that we have had such a writer as Irving to bridge over the chasm between the two great nations—that an illustrious American lived so long in England, and was so much beloved there, and sought so earnestly to bring the people of the two countries to a better understanding with each other, and to wean them from the animosities of narrow minds. I am sure that there is not a large-minded and large-hearted man in all our country, who can read over the Sketch Book, and the other writings of Irving, and disown one of the magnanimous sentiments they express with regard to England, or desire to abate the glow of one of his warm and cheerful pictures of English life. Occasions will arise, no doubt, for saying some things in a less accommodating spirit, and there are men enough on both sides of the Atlantic who can say them; but Irving was not sent into the world on that errand. A different work was assigned him in the very structure of his mind and the endowments of his heart—a work of peace and brotherhood; and I will say for him, that he nobly performed it.

I now go back a little, to give the following letter of Washington to his brother Ebenezer, dated January 10, 1837, four days prior to the rude assault of the *Plaindealer:*

All is going on well at the cottage. Peter is in good condition and good spirits.

I have looked over the account current, and find, on computing my expenses since I began housekeeping on the 1st of

September, that I can keep on at the rate at which I have been living without any danger of *running aground.* This is very satisfactory; for so many fears were expressed on my account, that I almost began to doubt, myself, whether I were not playing the part of the prodigal son, and wasting my substance in riotous living. I question, after all, whether the cottage will not prove, in the end, the best of all my speculations.

Let me hear, by mail, about the maps.

The maps in question were designed for the work he was about to publish, entitled "The Adventures of Captain Bonneville, U. S. A., in the Rocky Mountains of the Far West. Digested from his Journal, and illustrated from various other sources."

A few weeks later, we find this work going through the press. Peter writes from the cottage, on the 6th of March:

Washington is in New York, superintending the printing of a new work, which will be supplementary to Astoria, as it treats of expeditions in the same regions since that date, with an ample account of the Indian tribes and the white trappers, with details of their peculiar characters and adventurous lives beyond the Rocky Mountains. It is a picture of a singular class of people midway between the savage state and civilization, who will soon cease to exist, and be only known in such records, which will form a department of great interest in the history of our country.

The "leading theme" of these pages, however, was the expeditions and adventures of Captain Bonneville, of the United States army, "who, in a rambling kind of enterprise, had strangely ingrafted the trapper and hunter upon the soldier." Mr. Irving had first met this gentleman in the autumn of 1835, at the country seat of Mr. Astor. Coming upon him afterward, in the following winter, at Washington, and finding him engaged in rewriting and extending his travelling notes, and making maps of the regions he had explored, he purchased this mass of manuscripts from him for one thousand dollars, and undertook to fit it for publication, and bring it before the world. That manuscript, which was full of interesting details of life among the mountains, and of the singular castes of races, both white and red men, among whom he had sojourned, formed the staple of the work, though other facts and details were interwoven, gathered from other sources, especially from the conversations and journals of some of the captain's contemporaries, who were actors in the scenes he describes; while to the whole he gave a tone and coloring drawn from his own observation during his tour on the prairies.

Mr. Irving obtained for the work, from his American publishers, Carey, Lea & Co., three thousand dollars, and from Bentley, in London, £900.

It was while this work was going through the press, that Mr. Irving attended a complimentary entertainment, given by the booksellers of New York to authors and other literary and distinguished men, at which Chancellor Kent, James K. Paulding, William Cullen

Bryant, Fitz-Greene Halleck, Rev. Orville Dewey, Judge Irving, and others were present. In the absence of Thomas Swords, the oldest bookseller in New York, occasioned by ill health, Mr. David Felt presided. Mr. George P. Putnam, then a youthful member of the trade, was one of the committee of arrangements and a reporter in part of the proceedings. I take from the report of the future publisher, in the *New York American*, the following notice of Mr. Irving's brief remarks, which derive their chief interest from the pleasant allusion to Rogers and Halleck:

Mr. Washington Irving, being called upon for a toast, observed that he meant to propose the health of an individual whom he was sure all present would delight to honor—of Samuel Rogers, the poet. Mr. Irving observed, that in a long intimacy with Mr. Rogers, he had ever found him an enlightened and liberal friend of America and Americans. Possessing great influence in the world of literature and the fine arts in Great Britain, from his acknowledged soundness of judgment and refinement of taste, he had often exerted it in the kindest and most gracious manner in fostering, encouraging, and bringing into notice the talents of youthful American artists. He had also manifested, on all occasions, the warmest sympathy in the success of American writers, and the promptest disposition to acknowledge and point out their merits. I am led to these remarks, added Mr. Irving, by a letter received yesterday from Mr. Rogers, acknowledging the receipt of a volume of Halleck's Poems which I had sent him, and expressing his opinion of their merits. Mr. Irving here read the following extract from the letter:

"With Mr. Halleck's Poems I was already acquainted, particularly with the two first in the volume, and I cannot say how much I admired them always. They are better than anything we can do just now on our side the Atlantic [Hear, hear]. I hope he will not be idle, but continue long to delight us. When he comes here again, he must not content himself with looking on the outside of my house, as I am told he did once, but knock and ring, and ask for me as for an old acquaintance [Cheers]. I should say, indeed, if I am here to be found; for if he or you, my dear friend, delay your coming much longer, I shall have no hope of seeing either of you on this side the grave."

Mr. Irving concluded by giving as a toast: Samuel Rogers—the friend of American genius.

The company all rose, and drank the health standing, with the greatest enthusiasm.

Notwithstanding the boding allusion to his declining years in Rogers' letter—for he was then seventy-five—it was the fortune of Mr. Irving to meet again the venerable bard "on this side the grave" more than once.

Among the memorable events of this season at the cottage, was a visit from the present Emperor of France, then simple Louis Napoleon, who, after having been a prisoner of state for some months on board of a French man-of-war, was set at liberty on our shores at Norfolk, early in the spring of 1837. From Norfolk he came immediately to New York, where he remained about two months, and then returned to Europe. It was during this interval that he made his visit to the "Roost," accompanied by a young French count, and escorted by a neighbor, Mr. Anthony Constant, with whom he had been passing a day or two, and who had previously announced to Mr. Irving his intention of bringing him to breakfast. Mr. Irving enjoyed the visit, and was much interested in the peculiar position of his somewhat quiet guest, though little anticipating the dazzling career which awaited him.

At this time Peter had resumed his place in "the family hive" in New York, preferring, in his invalid state, to reconnoitre the world from a nearer and more populous point than the cottage. During the remaining fourteen months of his life he continued in the city, which furnished so much more for amusement and observation.

In the following letter to Edward Everett, Mr. Irving declines an invitation to deliver a public address:

GREENBURG, July 12, 1837.

DEAR SIR:

I have to acknowledge the receipt of your favor of the 24th ult., informing me that the government of the Boston Lyceum had done me the honor to invite me to deliver the introductory address at the opening of their course for next winter. The official communication to which you advert has not come to hand, probably owing to the irregularity with which my letters are forwarded me from town. I trust, therefore, that a reply to you as President of the Institution will be sufficient. I have delayed replying earlier, in the hope that I might prevail upon myself to accept so very flattering and gratifying an invitation; but I regret to say that a shrinking repugnance to everything calculated to bring me personally before the public eye, has, by unwise indulgence, grown upon me to such a degree as to be, I fear, absolutely insurmountable. There is no gift I more envy and admire than that which enables the possessor to bring his mind to act directly upon an intelligent audience, and to arouse and delight his auditors. Did I possess this great and glorious gift, I should feel a triumph in exerting it before such an audience as that of the Lyceum; but feeling and deploring my incapacity, I can only, through you, convey to that institution my most sincere and grateful acknowledgments for the high proof they have given me of their esteem.

Accept for yourself, my dear sir, my kindest thanks for the repeated marks of friendly consideration which I have experienced from you from time to time, and believe me, with the highest respect and regard,

Very faithfully yours,

WASHINGTON IRVING.

Hon. EDWARD EVERETT, &c., &c., &c.

The little domain of the Roost, originally of ten acres, afterward swelled to eighteen, now consisted of about fifteen acres—eight acres, added in the spring of 1836, having been exchanged by the author for a neighboring lot, the property of his nephew, Oscar Irving. In the succeeding year he bought fourteen additional acres, of which he soon after parted with six for the cost of the fourteen—the only fortunate speculation, as he used to say, he ever made, though the purchase of Michigan lands, in which he went shares with his friend Kemble, humorously hinted at in the following letter, must certainly claim exemption from his unlucky ventures. The letter is addressed to his old friend, then a member of the House of Representatives at Washington, from the residence of Mr. John Jacob Astor, in the city, where he was then on a visit, and contains something like a profession of political faith—as near, perhaps, as he ever came to one; for though always keenly alive to everything that affected the interest or honor of his country, he had no party prejudices or strongly marked political opinions.

[*To Gouverneur Kemble.*]

NEW YORK, Jan. 10, 1838.

MY DEAR KEMBLE:

On coming to town, I found yours of the 3d inst. waiting for me. Arrange with Godfrey as you think best about the payment of the land. The late hardships of the times have moderated all my towering notions. I am now perfectly resigned to fifty per cent. profit, and seven per cent. interest until paid. Nothing teaches a man better philosophy than a little experience in "castle building."

My brother E. I., who, you know, is a wary man of business, suggests that the mortgage we are to receive should be signed by the wives of the opposite parties, if they have any, and that the buildings on the land mortgaged should be insured, and the policies assigned to us.

As to Van Buren's insinuation that I have *cut* him, I repel the monstrous charge. What! cut a President?—turn my back upon a friend when at the height of power? What the plague does he take me for? I always suspected he had no very high idea of my merit as a politician, but I never imagined he could think me capable of so gross a departure from the ways of the political world.

Seriously, however, I have not corresponded with Van Buren, because I did not relish some points of his policy, nor believe in the wisdom and honesty of some of his elbow counsellors; yet had too great diffidence of my own judgment and experience in political matters to intrude upon him my opinions. I have for him the most hearty and sincere regard, and, if I had the arm of a Hercules, I would lift him out of the mire in which I think others are plunging him, and would place him upon firm ground; but, with my feeble and uncertain means, I should only bother where I might seek to aid.

As far as I know my own mind, I am thoroughly a republican, and attached, from complete conviction, to the institutions of my country; but I am a republican without gall, and have no bitterness in my creed. I have no relish for puritans either in religion or politics, who are for pushing principles to an extreme, and for overturning everything that stands in the way of their own zealous career. I have, therefore, felt a strong distaste for some of those loco-foco luminaries who of late have been urging strong and sweeping measures, subversive of the interests of great classes of the community. Their doctrines may be excellent in theory, but, if enforced in violent and uncompromising opposition to all our habitudes, may produce the most distressing effects. The best of remedies must be cautiously applied, and suited to the state and constitution of the patient; otherwise, what is intended to cure, may produce convulsion. The late elections have shown that the measures proposed by Government are repugnant to the feelings and habitudes, or disastrous to the interests of great portions of our fellow citizens. They should not then be forced home with rigor. Ours is a Government of compromise. We have several great and distinct interests bound up together, which, if not separately consulted and severally accommodated, may harass and impair each other. A stern, inflexible, and uniform policy may do for a small, compact republic, like one of those of ancient Greece, where there is a unity of character, habits, and interests; but a more accommodating, discriminating, and variable policy must be observed in a vast republic like ours, formed of a variety of States widely differing in habits, pursuits, characters, and climes, and banded together by a few general ties.

I always distrust the soundness of political councils that are accompanied by acrimonious and disparaging attacks upon any great class of our fellow citizens. Such are those urged to the disadvantage of the great trading and financial classes of our country. You yourself know, from education and experience, how important these classes are to the prosperous conduct of the complicated affairs of this immense empire. You yourself know, in spite of all the commonplace cant and obloquy that has been cast upon them by political spouters and scribblers, what general good faith and fair dealing prevails throughout these classes. Knaves and swindlers there are doubtless among them, as there are among all great classes of men; but I declare that I looked with pride and admiration at the manner in which the great body of our commercial and financial men have struggled on through the tremendous trials which have of late overwhelmed them, and have endeavored, at every pecuniary sacrifice, to fulfil their engagements. Europe, after an interval of panic and distrust, is beginning to do them justice; and the faith of an American merchant, and of American moneyed institutions, is likely to take a still higher rank in foreign estimation, from the recent trials it has sustained.

As to the excessive expansions of commerce, and the extravagant land speculations, which excited such vehement censure, I look upon them as incident to that spirit of enterprise natural to a young country in a state of rapid and prosperous development; a spirit which, with all its occasional excesses, has given our nation an immense impulse in its onward career, and promises to carry it ahead of all the nations of the globe. There are moral as well as physical phenomena incident to every state of things, which may at first appear evils, but which are devised by an all-seeing Providence for some beneficent purpose. Such is the spirit of speculative enterprise which now and then rises to an extravagant height, and sweeps throughout the land. It grows out of the very state of our country and its institutions, and, though sometimes productive of temporary mischief, yet leaves behind it lasting benefits. The late land speculations, so much deprecated, though ruinous to many engaged in them, have forced agriculture and civilization into the depths of the wilderness; have laid open the recesses of primeval forests; made us acquainted with the most available points of our immense interior; have cast the germs of future towns and cities and busy marts in the heart of savage solitudes, and studded our vast rivers and internal seas with ports that will soon give activity to a vast internal commerce. Millions of acres which might otherwise have remained idle and impracticable wastes, have been brought under the dominion of the plough, and hundreds of thousands of industrious yeomen have been carried into the rich but remote depths of our immense empire, to multiply and spread out in every direction, and give solidity and strength to our great confederacy.

All this has in a great measure been effected by the extravagant schemes of land speculators. I am, therefore, inclined to look upon them with a more indulgent eye than they are considered by those violent politicians who are prescribing violent checks and counter measures, and who seem to have something vindictive in their policy.

But enough of all this scribble scrabble. I shall be heartily glad if Mr. Van Buren, by his sub-treasury scheme, or any other measure, can extricate both the Government and the country from the present state of financial perplexity. For my own part, I cannot but think a national bank, properly restrained and guarded (especially as it respects dealing in foreign exchange), will, after all, be the measure most likely to suit the circumstances of the country, and restore the prosperous action of its trade. It would be a salutary check upon all minor banks, and would curb the power of Mr. Biddle, who is now getting a complete financial sway.

And now, my dear Kemble, let me have done with this "mortal coil," and thank you for your kind invitation to Washington. I should like much a visit there, if I could lounge about, a quiet and idle spectator; but I have a love of ease and tranquillity growing upon me, that makes even the bustle of gay society irksome, and which quite incapacitates me for the turmoil and excitement of a great political metropolis in a high state of fermentation. I am now in the city, on a visit to old Mr. Astor, with whom I shall probably remain for two or three weeks, and then return to my little retreat in the country, where I play the hermit without the least shadow of gloom, and from whence I peep forth upon the world without the slightest tinge of misanthropy or spleen.

Give my kindest regards to Mr. Van Buren, and tell him, that though I refrain from "bestowing my tediousness" upon him in the way of advice, yet I like him just as well as if I scribbled to him by the ream; and that though I may appear to cut him now in the day of his power, yet, whenever he may retire from the Presidential chair, he shall be welcome to the easiest chair in my cottage.

With kind remembrances to your sister Mary,

Yours ever, my dear Kemble,

WASHINGTON IRVING.

The following is also addressed to the same correspondent, in reply to some query respecting a rumor which had reached him:

NEW YORK, March 12, 1838.

MY DEAR KEMBLE:

Absence from town has prevented my answering sooner your letter of the 4th inst. There is no truth in the rumor of my having consented to become a candidate for the Mayoralty. I have not even been applied to on the subject; but, if I had been, nothing could induce me to undertake an office for which I feel myself so little fitted. Besides, I value my peace of mind too highly to suffer myself to be drawn into the vortex of New York politics; which, not to speak profanely, is a perfect political Hellgate.

* * * With kindest remembrances to your sister, I am, my dear Kemble, yours ever,

WASHINGTON IRVING.

P. S.—How stands the Godfrey affair? Are we likely to have any more money this spring? I wish to know, that I may make my calculations for the ways and meant for the current year.

So large a portion of Mr. Irving's funds had now been locked up in unproductive land purchases, that it was a subject of anxious interest with him to know from what quarter he would derive an income to meet the current expenses of the cottage.

At the date of the foregoing extract, Washington was in the city, attending at the bedside of John, who was soon after removed from him by death. This brother, about whom he had long before expressed his fears that his health would give way under the exhausting duties of his official position, was now sinking into the grave, a martyr to an overtasked mind. He expired on the 15th of March, in the fifty-eighth year of his age, after having filled with honor the position of First Judge of the Court of Common Pleas for the City and County of New York for twenty years. He was a man of perfect uprightness and great refinement of character, and enjoyed, through life, the high respect of the community. In his earlier days he had something of a literary turn, which, however, was soon quenched under the dry details of the law, and the resolute fidelity with which he gave himself up to the claims of his profession.

Some time after this, we find Mr. Irving again in his little country home, whence he writes to his sister, Mrs. Paris:

My return to the cottage was a return to peace and tranquillity of mind. I laid awake early this morning, with the little birds singing before the window, and all my thoughts and plans were pleasant. I am convinced, now, that I can carry on this little establishment much more economically than heretofore, and full as pleasantly. When the housekeeping at Bridge street is broken up, the girls *must hail from the cottage as a homestead*, and must consider it such.

* * * * * *

Yesterday I had a full deputation from Tammany Hall at the cottage, informing me that I had been unanimously and vociferously nominated as Mayor, and hoping that I would consent to be a candidate. Of course I declined.

Mr. Irving had scarcely declined this proffered nomination for an incongruous post, when he received a letter from President Van Buren, informing him of the intention of the existing Secretary of the Navy to retire, and tendering him the appointment as his successor.

I believe you to possess [writes Mr. Van Buren, with whom he had maintained intimate and friendly personal relations] in an eminent degree those peculiar qualities which should distinguish the head of that Department, and the successful and efficient employment of which is so important to this branch of the public service. This opinion has been confirmed by a full and confidential conversation with your friends Paulding and Kemble, whose judgment and sincerity I highly respect, and the former of whom is more particularly informed in regard to the services to be rendered.

Mr. Irving, however, was not to be tempted by the offer of so honorable a post in the Cabinet of the President.

Mature reflection [he writes in reply] and self-examination have served to confirm my first impulse, which was to decline your most kind and flattering offer. It is not so much the duties of the post that I fear, as I take a delight in full occupation, and the concerns of the Navy Department would be peculiarly interesting to me; but I shrink from the harsh cares and turmoils of public and political life at Washington, and feel that I am too sensitive to endure the bitter personal hostility, and the slanders and misrepresentations of the press, which beset high station in this country. This argues, I confess, a weakness of spirit and a want of true philosophy; but I speak of myself as I am, not as I ought to be. Perhaps, had my ambition been directed toward official distinction, I might have become enured to the struggle; but it has lain in a different and more secluded path, and has nurtured in me habits of quiet and a love of peace of mind that daily unfit me more and more for the collisions of the world. I really believe it would take but a short career of public life at Washington to render me mentally and physically a perfect wreck, and to hurry me prematurely into old age.

CHAPTER VI.

LETTER TO PIERRE M. IRVING—DEATH OF PETER—LETTER TO MRS. VAN WART ON THE SUBJECT—FURTHER EXTRACTS FROM LETTERS TO MRS. VAN WART, GIVING GOSSIPINGS ABOUT THE COTTAGE—HIS INVESTMENTS IN LAND UNPRODUCTIVE OF REVENUE—GETS HIS PEN IN MOTION—ENGAGES UPON THE CONQUEST OF MEXICO—SURRENDERS THE THEME TO PRESCOTT—CORRESPONDENCE ON THE SUBJECT—EXTRACT FROM LETTER TO PIERRE M. IRVING AFTER RECEIPT OF PRESCOTT'S HISTORY OF THE CONQUEST OF MEXICO.

THE letter which follows shows the anxiety of Mr. Irving to turn some of his unproductive real estate into the means of income, as his cottage, from being a bachelor nest, had assumed the character of a family mansion, and made proportionate demands upon his purse. It had been decided that Ebenezer should give up the house in town, and his family, heretofore fluctuating inmates of the Roost, were now to make it their permanent home. Ebenezer and Peter still retained apartments in the city, while Washington, to quote from one of the last letters Peter was ever to write, addressed to Mrs. Irving at Toledo, "was vibrating between town and country like the pendulum of a clock." The letter is addressed to me at Toledo, at which place I remained until the following autumn, when I resumed my residence in New York.

[*To Pierre M. Irving, Toledo, Ohio.*]

WOLFERT'S ROOST, May 18, 1838.

MY DEAR PIERRE:

I am more and more convinced that the very best thing to be done with the Toledo lots, is to put up small buildings on some of them as speedily as possible; by this means we may soon be in the receipt of a full interest on the whole amount invested there; and, for my own part, I should be well contented to let it remain thus invested. I have urged your uncle E. I. to write to you on the subject, but as he is apt to take a long time to load his piece regularly, I have thought proper to give you this random shot.

* * * We are all cosily quartered at the Roost, and very comfortable. The season is coming out in all its beauty, and we are in the midst of birds and blossoms and flowers. I look forward with pleasure to the prospect of seeing you and Helen at the cottage in the course of the summer, and showing you what a capital florist and horticulturist and agriculturist I am becoming. I beat all the gentleman farmers in my neighborhood, for I can manage to raise my vegetables and fruits at very little more than twice the market price.

With my best love to my dear Helen,

Yours ever affectionately,

WASHINGTON IRVING

On the 27th of the following month, Washington was called to meet one of the severest blows of his life in the death of his cherished brother Peter. His danger was considered imminent but a very few days. How deeply he felt this great bereavement, following so soon after the death of his brother John, the following extract from a letter to his sister, Mrs. Van Wart, dated nearly three months after, will show:

Every day, every hour I feel how completely Peter and myself were intertwined together in the whole course of our existence. Indeed, the very circumstance of our both having never been married, bound us more closely together. The rest of the family were married, and had families of their own to engross or divide their sympathies, and to weaken the fraternal tie; but we stood in the original, unimpaired relation to each other, and, in proportion as others were weaned away by circumstances, we grew more and more together. I was not conscious how much this was the case while he was living, but, now that he is gone, I feel how all-important he was to me. A dreary feeling of loneliness comes on me at times, that I reason against in vain; for, though surrounded by affectionate relatives, I feel that none can be what he was to me; none can take so thorough an interest in my concerns; to none can I so confidingly lay open my every thought and feeling, and expose every fault and foible, certain of such perfect toleration and indulgence. Since our dear mother's death, I have had no one who could so patiently and tenderly bear with all my weaknesses and infirmities, and throw over every error the mantle of affection. I have been trying, of late, to resume my pen, and, by engaging my mind in some intellectual task, to keep it from brooding over these melancholy themes; but I find it almost impossible. My literary pursuits have been so often carried on by his side, and under his eye—I have been so accustomed to talk over every plan with him, and, as it were, to think aloud when in his presence, that I cannot open a book, or take up a paper, or recall a past vein of thought, without having him instantly before me, and finding myself completely overcome. I hope and trust that, as the autumn advances, and the weather becomes cool and bracing, I shall regain something of my usual vigor of body, and with it a healthier tone of mind; at any rate, I will not trouble you again with such sad lamentations

This extract is dated September 22d. October 24th he writes to the same sister:

My little cottage is well stocked. I have Ebenezer's five girls, and himself also, whenever he can be spared from town —sister Catherine and her daughter—Mr. Paris occasionally—with casual visits from all the rest of our family connection. The cottage, therefore, is never lonely. It is now the beautiful autumnal season, and the weather this year is extremely fine. The summer has extended far into autumn; we have had no sharp frosts, and it is but recently that we have made fires. The foliage has its rich and variegated autumnal tints, and the wide landscape has that prevailing golden hue that gives such sober magnificence to the decline of the year. The girls live very much in the open air. The retired situation of the cottage, with its secluded walks, quiet glens, and sheltering groves, enables them to rove about without fear or restraint.

December 1st he writes again to Mrs. Van Wart, giving her this glimpse into his domestic and literary concerns:

You are urgent with me, my dear sister, to pay you a visit in the spring. You have no idea how completely I am rooted here. I cannot afford any more to travel. A considerable part of my means is invested in land, which at the present moment is unproductive of revenue, and I have to economize on various points, to keep from going too much behindhand. I cannot, as formerly, carry my home with me, and limit my expenses to my personal expenditure. Wherever I go, my cottage must be kept up; so that my travelling expenditures would be an additional drain on my purse. What has made me feel rather poor of late, and cautious as to extra expenses, is the circumstance that for a long time past I have been unable to exercise my pen; until at length I became despondent, and thought the vein had entirely deserted me. This, of course, would dry up my usual source of support, and throw me entirely on the income to be derived from my actual capital, which, as I have already observed, is in a great measure invested in unproductive property. Happily, within the last month, I have been once more enabled to get my pen into motion; and the effect has been most salutary on my spirits, as well as cheering to my prospects. * * * The bracing weather of autumn has been quite a restorative to me, and I feel myself recovering from that wretched depression of spirits, and prostration of all physical and mental energy, into which I sank for a time last summer. I begin to hope there is yet some stuff in me unworked, and which I may be able to work out successfully. If so, life will still have its occupation and motive, and I may continue to live to some purpose.

* * * I had intended to write Marianne a letter the week before last, but I got into a vein of literary occupation—the first I had had for a long time—and it was too important an event to be trifled with; so I nursed the mood along, to get it completely under way, and had to give up all letter writing.

Mr. Irving was now busy upon the History of the Conquest of Mexico, and it was upon this theme that he was exercising that "vein of literary occupation" alluded to at the close of the foregoing letter. He had not only commenced the work, but had made a rough draft to form the groundwork of the first volume, when he went to New York to procure or consult some books on the subject. He was engaged in "The City Library," as it is commonly designated, though its official style is "The New York Society Library," then temporarily in Chambers street, when he was accosted by Mr. Joseph G. Cogswell, the eminent scholar, afterward so long and honorably connected with the Astor Library. It was from this gentleman that Mr. Irving first learned that Mr. Prescott, who had a few months before gained a proud name on both sides of the Atlantic by his History of Ferdinand and Isabella, now had the work in contemplation upon which he had actually commenced. Cogswell first sounded him on the part of Mr. Prescott, to know what subject he was occupied upon, as he did not wish to come again across the same ground with him. Mr. Irving asked: "Is Mr. Prescott engaged upon an American subject?" "He is," was the reply. "What is it? Is it the Conquest of Mexico?" Mr. Irving rapidly asked. "It is," answered Cogswell. "Well, then," said Mr. Irving, "I *am* engaged upon that subject, but tell Mr. Prescott I abandon it to him, and I am happy to have this opportunity of testifying my high esteem for his talents, and my sense of the very courteous manner in which he has spoken of myself and my writings in his Ferdinand and Isabella, though they interfered with a part of the subject of his history."

In a subsequent conversation, Mr. Irving learned from Mr. Cogswell that Mr. Prescott had not commenced the work, but had merely collected materials for it. He did not, however, revoke what he had said, but threw by his pen, and gave up the task on which he had been occupied during the autumn and winter.

It was not, however, without a pang that he surrendered so glorious a theme; and I think that on the same day in which he told me what I have related above, he mentioned to me that he had been looking over some papers in the morning, and had come across his commencement of the Conquest of Mexico; that he read over what he had written, and, in a fit of vexation at having lost the magnificent theme, destroyed the manuscript.

With this preface, I introduce the following correspondence between him and Mr. Prescott, alike honorable to both parties. The first letter is from Mr. Prescott:

BOSTON, Dec. 31, 1838.

MY DEAR SIR:

—If you will allow one to address you so familiarly, who has not the pleasure of your personal acquaintance, though he feels as if he had known you for a long time. Our friend, Mr. Cogswell, who is here on a short visit, mentioned to me a conversation which he had with you respecting the design I had formed of giving an account of the Conquest of Mexico and Peru. I hope you will excuse me, if I tell you how the matter stands with me.

Soon after I had despatched their Catholic Highnesses, Ferdinand and Isabella, I found the want of my old companions in the long hours of an idle man's life; and as I looked around for something else, the history of Cortes and Pizarro struck me as the best subject, from its growing out of the period I had become familiar with, as well as from its relation to our own country. I found, too, I had peculiar facilities for getting such books and MSS. as I needed from Madrid, through the kindness of Mr. Calderon, whom you know. The only doubts on the subject I had, were respecting your designs in the same way, since you had already written the adventures of the earlier discoverers. I thought of writing you, to learn from you your intentions; but I was afraid it would seem impertinent in a stranger to pry into your affairs. I made inquiries, however, of several of your friends, and could not learn that you had any purpose of occupying yourself with the subject. And as you had never made any public intimation of the sort, I believe, and several years had elapsed since your last publication of the kind, during which your attention had been directed in another channel, I concluded that you had abandoned the intention, if you had ever formed it. I therefore made up my mind to go on with it; and as I proposed to give a pretty thorough preliminary view of the state of civilization in Mexico and Peru previous to the Conquest, I determined to spare no pains or expense in collecting materials. I have remitted £300 to Madrid for the purchase and copying of books and MSS., and have also sent for Lord Kingsborough's and such other works relating to Mexico as I can get from London. I have also obtained letters to individuals in Mexico, for the purpose of collecting what may be of importance to me there. Some of the works from London have arrived, and the drafts from Madrid show that my orders are executing there. Such works as can be got here, in a pretty good collection in the College Library, I have already examined, and wait only for my books from Spain. This is the state of affairs, now that I have learned from Mr. C. that you had originally proposed to treat this same subject, and that you requested him to say to me that you should relinquish it in my favor. I cannot sufficiently express to you my sense of your courtesy, which I can very well appreciate, as I know the mortification it would have occasioned me, if, contrary to my expectations, I had found you on the ground; for I am but a dull sailer from the embarrassments I labor under, and should have found but sorry gleanings in the field which you had once thoroughly burnt over, as they say in the West. I fear the public will not feel so well pleased as myself by this liberal conduct on your part, and am not sure that I should have a right, in their eyes, to avail myself of it. But I trust you will think differently, when I accept your proffered courtesy in the same cordial spirit in which it was given. It will be conferring a still further favor on me, if you will allow me occasionally, when I may find the want of it, to ask your advice in the progress of the work. There are few persons among us who have paid much attention to these studies, and no one, here or elsewhere, so familiar as yourself with the track of Spanish adventure in the New World, and so well qualified, certainly, to give advice to a comparatively new hand. Do not fear that this will expose you to a troublesome correspondent. I have never been addicted to much letter writing, though, from the specimen before you, I am afraid you will think those I do write are somewhat of the longest.

Believe me, dear sir, with great respect, your obliged and obedient servant.

WM. H. PRESCOTT.

WASHINGTON IRVING, Esq.

P. S.—Will you permit me to add, that if you have any materials in your own library, bearing on this subject, that cannot be got here, and that you have no occasion for yourself, it will be a great favor if you will dispose of them to me.

Mr. Irving responded as follows:

NEW YORK, Jan. 18, 1839.

MY DEAR SIR:

Your letter met with some delay in reaching me, and, since the receipt of it, I have been hovering between town and country, so as to have no quiet leisure for an earlier reply.

I had always intended to write an account of the Conquest of Mexico, as a suite to my Columbus, but left Spain without making the requisite researches. The unsettled life I subsequently led for some years, and the interruptions to my literary plans by other occupations, made me defer the undertaking from year to year. Indeed, the more I considered the subject, the more I became aware of the necessity of devoting to it great labor, patient research, and watchful discrimination, to get at the truth and to dispel the magnificent *mirage* with which it is enveloped; for, unless this were done, a work, however well executed in point of literary merit, would be liable to be subverted and superseded by subsequent works founded on those documentary evidences that might (be) dug out of the chaotic archives of Spain. These considerations loomed into great obstacles in my mind, and, amid the hurry of other matters, delayed me in putting my hand to the enterprise. About three years since I made an attempt at it, and set one of my nephews to act as pioneer, and get together materials under my direction; but his own concerns called him elsewhere, and the matter was again postponed. Last autumn, after a fit of deep depression, feeling the want of something to arouse and exercise my mind, I again recurred to this subject, fearing that, if I waited to collect materials, I should never take hold of the theme; and, knowing my own temperament and habits of mind, I determined to dash into it at once, sketch out a narrative of the whole enterprise, using Solis, Herrera, and Bernal Dias as my guide books, and, having thus acquainted myself with the whole ground, and kindled myself into a heat by exercise of drafting the story, to endeavor to strengthen, correct, enrich, and authenticate my work, by materials from every source within my reach. I accordingly set to work, and had made it my daily occupation for about three months, and sketched out the groundwork for the first volume, when I learned from Mr. Cogswell that you had undertaken the same enterprise. I at once felt how much more justice the subject would receive at your hands. Ever since I had been meddling with the theme, its grandeur and magnificence had been growing upon me, and I had felt more and more doubtful whether I should be able to treat it *conscientiously*—that is to say, with the extensive research and thorough investigation which it merited. The history of Mexico prior to the discovery and conquest, and the actual state of its civilization at the time of the Spanish invasion, are questions in the highest degree curious and interesting, yet difficult to be ascertained clearly, from the false lights thrown upon them. Even the writings of Padre Sahagun perplex me as to the degree of faith to be placed in them. These themes are connected with the grand enigma that rests upon the primitive population and civilization of the American continents, and of which the singular monuments and remains scattered throughout the wilderness serve but as tantalizing indications. The manner in which you have executed your noble history of Ferdinand and Isabella gave me at once an assurance that you were the man to undertake this subject; your letter shows that I was not wrong in the conviction, and that you have already set to work on the requisite preparations. In at once yielding up the theme to you, I feel that I am but doing my duty in leaving one of the most magnificent themes in American history to be treated by one who will build up from it an enduring monument in the literature of our country. I only hope that I may live to see your work executed, and to read in it an authentic account of that conquest, and a satisfactory discussion of the various questions connected with Mexico and the Mexicans, which since my boyhood have been full of romantic charm to me, but which, while they excited my imagination, have ever perplexed my judgment.

I am sorry that I have no works to offer you that you have not in the Boston libraries. I have mentioned the authors I was making use of; they are to be found in the Boston Athenæum, though I doubt not you have them in your own possession. While in Madrid, I had a few chapters of Padre Sahagun copied out for me, relating merely to some points of the Spanish invasion. His work you will find in Lord Kingsborough's collection; it professes to give a complete account of Mexico prior to the Conquest—its public institutions, trades, callings, customs, &c., &c. Should I find among my books any that may be likely to be of service, I will send them to you. In the mean time, do not hesitate to command my services in any way you may think proper.

I am scrawling this letter in great haste, as you will doubtless perceive, but beg you will take it as a proof of the sincere and very high respect and esteem with which I am your friend and servant,

WASHINGTON IRVING.

WM. H. PRESCOTT, Esq.

Mr. Prescott rejoins:

BOSTON, Jan. 25, 1839.

MY DEAR SIR:

You will be alarmed at again seeing an epistle from me so soon; but I cannot refrain from replying to your very kind communication. I have read your letter with much interest, and, I may truly say, that part of it which animadverts on the importance of the theme, as illustrating the Mexican antiquities, with some dismay. I fear you will be sadly disappointed if you expect to see a solution, by me, of those vexed questions which have bewildered the brains of so many professed antiquaries. My fingers are too clumsy to unravel such a snarl. All I propose to do in this part of the subject, therefore, is to present to the reader such a view of the institutions and civilization of the conquered people, as will interest him in their fortunes. To do this, it will not be necessary, I hope, to involve myself in those misty speculations, which require better sight than mine to penetrate; but only to state facts, as far as they can be gathered from authentic story. For this part of the subject I have not attempted, therefore, to collect MSS., of which I suppose there is a great number in the libraries of Mexico—at least there was in Clavigero's time; but I shall content myself with the examination of such works as have been before the public, including, indeed, the compilation of Lord Kingsborough, and the great French work, "Antiquités Mexicaines," since published; the chief value of both which, I suspect, excepting the Chronicle of Sahagun in the former, consists in their pictorial illustrations. My chief object is the Conquest; and the materials I am endeavoring to collect are with the view to the exhibition of this in the most authentic light. It will give you satisfaction to learn that my efforts in Spain promise to be attended with perfect success. I received letters, last week, from Madrid, informing me that the Academy of History, at the instance of Señor Navarrete, had granted my application to have copies taken of any and all MSS. in their possession, having relation to the conquests of Mexico and Peru, and had appointed one of their body to carry this into effect. This person is a German, named Lembke, the author of a work on the early history of Spain, which one of the English journals, I remember, rapped me over the knuckles for not having seen. This learned Theban happens to be in Madrid for the nonce, pursuing some investigations of his own, and he has taken charge of mine, like a true German, inspecting everything, and selecting just what has reference to my subject. In this way he has been employed with four copyists, as he writes me, since July, and has amassed a quantity of unpublished original documents illustrative of the Mexican Conquest, which, he writes me, will place the expedition in a new and authentic light. He has already sent off two boxes of these MSS. for me to Cadiz, and is now employed in hunting up the materials relating to Peru, in which, he says, the library appears to be equally rich. I wish he may not be too sanguine, and that the MSS. may not fall into the hands of Carlists or Christinos, who would probably work them up into musket waddings in much less time than they were copying. The specification of MSS. furnished me by Dr. Lembke makes me feel nearly independent of Mexico, with which the communications are now even more obstructed than with Spain. I have endeavored to open them, however, through Mr. Poinsett, and through the Barings, and cannot but hope I shall succeed through one or the other channel.

I had no idea of your having looked into the subject so closely yourself, still less that you had so far broken ground on it. I regret, now, that I had not communicated with you earlier, in a direct way, as it might have saved both, or rather one of us, some previous preparation; for, during the summer and autumn, I have been occupied with the investigation of the early Mexican history, having explored all the sources within my reach here, and being stopped by the want of them. Now that I have gone on so far with my preparations, I can only acknowledge your great courtesy toward me, with my hearty thanks; for I know well, that whatever advantages I might have acquired on the score of materials, would have been far, very far outweighed by the superiority, in all other respects, of whatever might fall from your pen. And your relinquishing the ground seems to impose on me an additional responsibility to try to make your place good, from which a stouter heart than mine may well shrink. I trust, however, in you I shall find a generous critic; and allow me to add, with sincerity, that the kind words you have said of the only child of my brain, have gratified and touched me more deeply than anything that has yet reached me from my countrymen.

Believe me, my dear sir, with sincere respect, your friend and servant, WM. H. PRESCOTT.

WASHINGTON IRVING, Esq.

It was about five years after this correspondence, that Mr. Irving, then in Madrid, received from Mr. Prescott a copy of his History of the Conquest of Mexico, in the Preface to which he makes his public acknowledgments to him for his surrender of the subject. "I need not say," writes Mr. Irving to me, in noticing its receipt, "how much I am delighted with the work. It well sustains the high reputation acquired by the History of Ferdinand and Isabella." Then, adverting to the terms of Mr. Prescott's handsome acknowledgment in the Preface, to which I had called his attention, he adds:

I doubt whether Mr. Prescott was aware of the extent of the sacrifice I made. This was a favorite subject, which had delighted my imagination ever since I was a boy. I had brought home books from Spain to aid me in it, and looked upon it as the pendent to my Columbus. When I gave it up to him, I in a manner gave him up my bread, for I depended upon the profit of it to recruit my waning finances. I had no other subject at hand to supply its place. I was dismounted from my *cheval de bataille*, and have never been completely mounted since. Had I accomplished that work, my whole pecuniary situation would have been altered. * * * When I made the sacrifice, it was not with a view to compliments or thanks, but from a warm and sudden impulse. I am not sorry for having made it. Mr. Prescott has justified the opinion I expressed at the time, that he would treat the subject with more close and ample research than I should probably do, and would produce a work more thoroughly worthy of the theme. He has produced a work that does honor to himself and his country, and I wish him the full enjoyment of his laurels.

The plan I had intended to pursue was different from that which he has adopted. I should not have had any preliminary dissertation on the history, civilization, &c., of the natives, as I find such dissertations hurried over, if not skipped entirely, by a great class of readers, who are eager for narrative and action. I should have carried on the reader with the discoverers and conquerors, letting the newly explored countries break upon him as it did upon them; describing objects, places, customs, as they awakened curiosity and interest, and required to be explained for the conduct of the story. The reader should first have an idea of the superior civilization of the people from the great buildings and temples of stone and lime that brightened along the coast, and "shone like silver." He should have had vague accounts of Mexico from the people on the seaboard; from the messengers of Montezuma. His interest concerning it should have increased as he went on, deriving ideas of its grandeur, power, riches, &c., from the Tlascalans, &c. Every step, as he accompanied the conquerors on their march, would have been a step developing some striking fact, yet the distance would still have been full of magnificent mystery. He should next have seen Mexico from the mountains, far below him, shining with its vast edifices, its glassy lakes, its far-stretching causeways, its sunny plain, surrounded by snow-topped volcanoes. Still it would have been vague in its magnificence. At length he should have marched in with the conquerors, full of curiosity and wonder, on every side beholding objects of novelty, indicating a mighty people, distinct in manners, arts, and civilization from all the races of the Old World. During the residence in the capital, all these matters would have been fully described and explained in connection with the incidents of the story. In this way the reader, like the conquerors, would have become gradually acquainted with Mexico and the Mexicans; and by the time the conquest was achieved, he would have been familiar with the country, without having been detained by long dissertations, so repulsive to the more indolent class of readers.

My intention also was, to study the different characters of the *dramatis personæ*, so as to bring them out in strong relief, and to have kept them, as much as possible, in view throughout the work. It is surprising how quickly distinctive characteristics may be caught from a few incidental words in old documents, letters, &c., and how the development of them and the putting them in action gives life and reality to a narrative. Most of the traits that give individuality to Columbus, in my biography of him, were gathered from slightly mentioned facts in his journals, letters, &c., which had remained almost unnoticed by former writers on the subject.

However, I am running on into idle "scribble scrabble" about a matter now passed away, and which I would not utter to any one but yourself, who are becoming in a manner my father confessor. My plan might have had an advantage in some respects; it might have thrown a more poetical interest over the work; but the plan of Mr. Prescott is superior in other respects; and I feel I never should have wrought out a work so "worthy of all acceptation," as that which he has given to the public.

The letter from which I take this extract is dated Madrid, March 24, 1844, and is marked (Private); but, now that both are gone, I have felt at liberty to give this interesting portion of its contents.

CHAPTER VII.

ENGAGES TO CONTRIBUTE MONTHLY TO THE KNICKERBOCKER MAGAZINE—HIS POSITION RESPECTING AN INTERNATIONAL COPYRIGHT LAW, IN A LETTER TO THE EDITOR—PRESCOTT'S VIEW—OLD AND NEW TARRYTOWN—PICTURE OF HIS NEIGHBORHOOD—BIOGRAPHICAL SKETCH OF GOLDSMITH FOR HARPER'S FAMILY LIBRARY—EBENEZER IRVING—BIOGRAPHY OF MARGARET DAVIDSON—ANECDOTE OF CLARK AND GEOFFREY CRAYON.

HAVING surrendered the theme of the Conquest of Mexico, as we have seen at the close of the last chapter, Mr. Irving was induced to enter into an engagement with the proprietors of the *Knickerbocker*, a magazine published in the city of New York, to contribute monthly to its pages; they agreeing upon stated payments at the rate of two thousand dollars per annum. In the March number of 1839, in which he introduces himself to the public, he holds the following language to its editor, Louis Gaylord Clark, so long associated with its fortunes:

SIR:

I have observed, as a man advances in life, he is subject to a kind of plethora of the mind, doubtless occasioned by the vast accumulation of wisdom and experience upon the brain. Hence he is apt to become narrative and admonitory—that is to say, fond of telling long stories and of doling out advice, to the small profit and great annoyance of his friends. As I have a great horror of becoming the oracle, or, more technically speaking, the "bore" of the domestic circle, and would much rather bestow my wisdom and tediousness upon the world at large, I have always sought to ease off this surcharge of the intellect by means of my pen, and hence have inflicted divers gossiping volumes upon the patience of the public. I am tired, however, of writing volumes: they do not afford exactly the relief I require; there is too much preparation, arrangement, and parade in this set form of coming before the public. I am growing too indolent and unambitious for anything that requires labor or display. I have thought, therefore, of securing to myself a snug corner in some periodical work, where I might, as it were, loll at my ease in my elbow chair, and chat sociably with the public, as with an old friend, on any chance subject that might pop into my brain.

Few would imagine, from the tone of this extract, at what expense of feeling he had just given up the task of "writing volumes," and bound himself to the irksome obligations of periodical labor. To have to draw upon a capricious fancy once a month for an article, was not a position he would have sought, but for the necessity pressing upon him for additional income. Irksome as the task was, however, and notwithstanding the returns were less prompt than he had anticipated, his good will to the magazine induced him to continue his connection with it for two years. He brought it to an end in March, 1841, with the article of "Don Juan: a Spectral Research." A majority of his contributions to the *Knickerbocker*, including this article, were long afterward collected by him, and incorporated in a little volume, published in 1855, entitled "Wolfert's Roost," the extraordinary sale of which made ample amends for any shortcomings of the magazine.

The most felicitous, perhaps, of all his contributions to this periodical, was "The Birds of Spring," in the May number of 1839, containing the exquisite sketch of "The Boblink," which was extracted into almost every paper in the Union.

In January, 1840, Mr. Irving addressed the following letter to the editor of the *Knickerbocker*, in which he defines his position on the subject of an international copyright law, so long and so ineffectually pressed upon Congress.

To the Editor of the Knickerbocker:

SIR: Having seen it stated more than once, in the public papers, that I declined subscribing my name to the petition, presented to Congress during a former session, for an act of international copyright, I beg leave, through your pages, to say, in explanation, that I declined, not from any hostility or indifference to the object of the petition, in favor of which my sentiments have always been openly expressed, but merely because I did not relish the phraseology of the petition, and because I expected to see the measure pressed from another quarter. I wrote about the same time, however, to members of Congress in support of the application.

As no other petition has been sent to me for signature, and as silence on my part may be misconstrued, I now, as far as my name may be thought of any value, enroll it among those who pray most earnestly to Congress for this act of international equity. I consider it due, not merely to foreign authors, to whose lucubrations we are so deeply indebted for constant instruction and delight, but to our own native authors, who are implicated in the effects of the wrong done by our present laws.

For myself, my literary career, as an author, is drawing to a close, and cannot be much affected by any disposition of this question; but we have a young literature springing up, and daily unfolding itself with wonderful energy and luxuriance, which, as it promises to shed a grace and lustre upon the nation, deserves all its fostering care. How much this growing literature may be retarded by the present state of our copyright law, I had recently an instance, in the cavalier treatment of a work of merit, written by an American, who had not yet established a commanding name in the literary market. I undertook, as a friend, to dispose of it for him, but found it impossible to get an offer from any of our principal publishers. They even declined to publish it at the author's cost, alleging that it was not worth their while to trouble themselves about native works, of doubtful success, while they could pick and choose among the successful works daily poured out by the British press, *for which they had nothing to pay for copyright.* This simple fact spoke volumes to me, as I trust it will do to all who peruse these lines. I do not mean to enter into the discussion of a subject that has already been treated so voluminously. I will barely observe, that I have seen few arguments advanced against the proposed act, that ought to weigh with intelligent and high-minded men; while I have noticed some that have been urged, so sordid and selfish in their nature, and so narrow in the scope of their policy, as almost to be insulting to those to whom they are addressed.

I trust that, whenever this question comes before Congress, it will at once receive an action prompt and decided, and will be carried by an overwhelming, if not unanimous vote, worthy of an enlightened, a just, and a generous nation.

Your obedient servant,

WASHINGTON IRVING.

Not a month before the publication of this letter, in which Mr. Irving commits himself so decidedly to the justice of an international copyright law, as due alike to foreign and native authors, Mr. Prescott had written to him from Boston that, if anything was to be done in the matter, he was the one who, from his literary position in the country, should take the lead in it. In this letter the historian, in reference to a projected copyright bill to be brought in by Mr. Clay at that session of Congress, says:

Whether anything effectual can be done, seems to me very doubtful. Such a law is certainly demanded by every principle of justice. But I suspect it is rather late in the day to talk of justice to statesmen. At all events, one of those newspapers, which they are now turning out every week here, and which contain an octavo volume each, of the new publications, at sixpence apiece, will, I am afraid, be too cogent an argument in favor of the present state of things, to be refuted by the best memorial ever drafted.

In the letter from which I take the above extract,

Mr. Prescott informs Mr. Irving that he was the possessor of a copy of the Sketch Book which had been owned by Sir James Mackintosh, and had his pencillings in the margin.

In April, 1840, Mr. Irving writes me, on renewing his yearly arrangement with the *Knickerbocker*, then behindhand in its payments: "I am convinced that, by exercising my pen in my former independent way, and taking my time to collect my writings into volumes, I should make much more money eventually, and escape a monthly recurring task."

It is worthy of mention, in connection with this allusion to the *Knickerbocker*, that he had just given to the magazine his skilful contribution, entitled, "A Time of Unexampled Prosperity: The Great Mississippi Bubble," afterward published in "Wolfert's Roost." He had written feelingly on the subject, for he himself was now suffering the embarrassment arising from investments made in just such a time of fictitious prosperity and unreal fortunes.

A year later he writes in reference to the disastrous results of this spirit of speculation in Western lands, which swept the country in 1836:

We are gradually getting through this "valley of the shadow of death," which the whole busy world has had for some few years past to traverse, and I am in hopes that the severe lessons received this time will be held in remembrance, and have a wholesome effect for the residue of our existence. The world at large is suffering the penalty of its own avarice;

for avarice for a time was as extensive and deleterious in its sway as the cholera. Every one was seized with the mania of becoming suddenly rich; and, in yielding to the frantic impulse, has impoverished himself. The only consolation to each individual sufferer is, that he is not worse off than most of his neighbors. It has been a mania, too, that has infected the most knowing as well as the most simple minded; indeed, some of the shrewdest calculators have been the most taken in.

November 25th, 1840, after having contributed to the *Knickerbocker* "Sketches in Paris in 1825, from the Travelling Note-book of Geoffrey Crayon," he writes to his sister, Mrs. Van Wart:

If times ever again come smooth and flush with me, so that I can command a decent income independent of the irksome fagging of my pen, I shall think nothing of an occasional trip across the Atlantic, now that steam has made the voyage short and commodious; but cares and claims multiply upon me as I advance in years.

Then follows this agreeable picture of the neighborhood in which he had fixed his residence, so much changed from the "old Tarrytown" of his correspondent's recollection:

I find, by your correspondence with sister Catherine, that she gives you many details of our country neighborhood and circle, and that you take great interest in everything relating to "old Tarrytown." You would scarcely recognize the place, however, it has undergone such changes. These have in a great degree taken place since I have pitched my tent in the neighborhood. My residence here has attracted others; cottages and country seats have sprung up along the banks of the Tappan Sea, and Tarrytown has become the metropolis of quite a fashionable vicinity. When you knew the village, it was little better than a mere hamlet, crouched down at the foot of a hill, with its dock for the accommodation of the weekly market sloop. Now it has mounted the hill; boasts of its hotels, and churches of various denominations; has its little Episcopalian church with an organ—the gates of which, on Sundays, are thronged with equipages belonging to families resident within ten or a dozen miles along the river banks. We have, in fact, one of the most agreeable neighborhoods I ever resided in. Some of our neighbors are here only for the summer, having their winter establishments in town; others remain in the country all the year. We have frequent gatherings at each other's houses, without parade or expense, and I do not know when I have seen more delightful little parties, or more elegant little groups of females. We have, occasionally, excellent music, for several of the neighborhood have been well taught, have good voices, and acquit themselves well both with harp and piano; and our parties always end with a dance. We have picnic parties also, sometimes in some inland valley or piece of wood, sometimes on the banks of the Hudson, where some repair by land, and others by water. You would be delighted with these picturesque assemblages, on some wild woodland point jutting into the Tappan Sea, with gay groups on the grass under the trees; carriages glistening through the woods; a yacht with flapping sails and fluttering streamers anchored about half a mile from shore, and rowboats plying to and from it, filled with lady passengers. Country life with us, at present, is very different from what it was in your youthful days. There is more of morning visiting, like in country life in England; still it differs essentially from English rural life. The nature of our climate influences our habits. We have so much sunshine and fine warm weather during the genial months of the year, that we live more out of doors, and in a more free and unceremonious style. Our very winters, though sometimes intensely cold, are brilliant and beautiful from the purity of the atmosphere and the prevalence of sunshine. For my part, I am almost a worshipper of the sun. I have lived so much of my life in climates where he was all-powerful, that I delight in his vivifying effect on the whole face of nature, and his gladdening influence on all animate creation. In no climate within the range of my experience is sunshine more beautiful in its effect on landscape than in this, owing to the transparency of the atmosphere, and, at the same time, the variety of clouds with which our skies are diversified. To my mind, neither Spanish nor Italian skies, so bright and cloudless, can compare with ours, forever shifting in their tints, and at times so gorgeous with their floating regions of "cloud-land."

To the same sister he gives the following picture of the holidays, under date of December 26th:

We have had a pleasant Christmas gathering at the cottage. The day was bright and sunny, but the weather changed in the night, and now a snowstorm is prevailing, which promises to be a severe one. This, however, is rather a welcome event in the country, as it produces fine sleighing, and sets all the country in movement. I know nothing more exhilarating than the first sleigh rides; skimming over the sparkling snow, the air so pure and bracing, the sunshine so splendid; the very horses seem to share your animation and delight, and dash forward merrily to the jingling of the sleigh bells.

Mr. Irving had recently written a biography of Goldsmith for Harper's Family Library, which was intended merely as a sketch to accompany a collection or selection of his writings. He afterward, as will be seen, prepared another, which is now known as his best and only biography of his favorite author.

The following letter to Mrs. Van Wart has some allusion to this sketch of Goldsmith, and touches also upon another interesting biography upon which he had been employed during his engagement with the *Knickerbocker*. It opens, as will be seen, with a notice of the prolonged absence from the cottage of Ebenezer, his only surviving brother, whose character is feelingly portrayed:

It is now nearly a month since brother Ebenezer has been at the cottage. I never have known him to be so long absent before, unless when on a journey. Business has detained him in town. * * * I think him one of the most perfect exemplifications of the Christian character that I have ever known. He has all father's devotion and zeal, without his strictness. Indeed, his piety is of the most genial and cheerful kind, interfering with no rational pleasure or elegant taste, and obtruding itself upon no one's habits, opinions, or pursuits. I wish to God I could feel like him. I envy him that indwelling source of consolation and enjoyment, which appears to have a happier effect than all the maxims of philosophy or the lessons of worldly wisdom.

I promised, in a late letter, to send you a copy of my biography of Goldsmith, recently published. I have not been to town since, but when I do go, I will procure a copy and forward it. In the spring I shall publish a biography of Miss Margaret Davidson, with her posthumous writings. She was a sister of Lucretia Davidson, whose biography * you may have read—a lovely American girl, of surprising precocity of poetical talent, who died at the age of seventeen or eighteen. The one whose biography I have just written died a year or two since, between sixteen and seventeen years old. I saw her when she was about eleven years old, and again when about fourteen. She was a beautiful little being, as bright and as fragile as a flower, and like a flower she has passed away. Her poetical effusions are surprising, and the spirit they breathe is heavenly. I think you will find her biography one of the most affecting things you have ever read. It is made up in a great degree from memorandums furnished by her mother, who is of almost as poetical a temperament as her children. The most affecting passages of the biography are quoted literally from her manuscript. You may recollect the family of Mrs. Davidson; she is one of a number of sisters—very beautiful girls—of the name of Miller, who, in your younger days, lived in Maiden lane.

Mr. Irving transferred to the mother the copyright of the biography of Margaret Davidson, reserving merely the right to publish it at any time in connec-

* Written by Miss Catherine Sedgwick.

tion with his other writings. The success which it met with he was not disposed to attribute to any merit of his, but to the extreme interest and pathos of the materials placed in his hands. It has not yet appeared in a collective edition of his works.

It was during his engagement with the *Knickerbocker*, now about to close, that its editor, Clark, made the visit to Mr. Irving of which he has given a published account. The little brook on the place had lately broken bounds, and he found him engaged in making, as his host expressed it, "a dam and some other profane improvements." In the afternoon they drove out together in an open one-horse carriage, to explore the wizard region of Sleepy Hollow. A sudden and violent shower coming up, accompanied with thunder and lightning, Mr. Irving stopped the horse, and took refuge under a large tree, leaning against the trunk, where, however, he soon became thoroughly drenched. All this while Clark was standing out in the pouring rain. "Why don't you come under a tree," asked Mr. Irving, facetiously, "and be dry and comfortable like me?" Clark excused himself on the ground that his father had once taken refuge from a sudden thunder shower under a spreading chestnut tree, which was struck, his father prostrated and rendered insensible for four hours; and that on his recovery he gave him an injunction never to stand under a tree, in an open field, in a thunder storm. "Oh!" replied Mr. Irving, with a look in which you could see the humorous thought before he gave expression to it, "that makes all the difference in the world. If it is hereditary, and lightning runs in your family, you are wise."

CHAPTER VIII.

LETTER TO MRS. STORROW, WITH TRANSCRIPTS OF LETTERS FROM VAN BIBBER, G. P. R. JAMES, AND DICKENS—ALBERT GALLATIN—VISITS IN THE HIGHLANDS—LETTER FROM HONESDALE—SEIZED WITH FEVER ON HIS RETURN—LETTER AFTER RECOVERY.

THE following letter is addressed to a niece, recently married, the only surviving daughter of his sister Catherine, who had embarked on the 1st of May for Europe, and was now to find a home for many years in the gay capital of France. Identified with the cottage and its concerns from its building, and forming one of the domestic circle of Sunnyside—as the rural retreat was now named—from the time the establishment was fairly set up, the separation across the wide Atlantic was felt by Mr. Irving as a bereavement. In adverting to it in one of his letters to Mrs. Van Wart, he writes:

Thus you see, though a bachelor, I am doomed to experience what parents feel, when their children are widely separated from them by marriage. But this is a world of changes; and we were all too happy in our delightful little nest, for our domestic quiet to remain uninterrupted.

The letter will be found to contain passages from

his correspondence with Van Bibber, an early literary pilgrim to Sunnyside, G. P. R. James, the novelist, with whom he became acquainted at Bordeaux in 1825, and Charles Dickens, whom he had never yet seen, but to whom he had expressed his delighted interest in the Story of Little Nell. I give mainly these portions of his letter, omitting much that could be of no interest to the general reader:

[*To Mrs. Storrow.*]

SUNNYSIDE, May 25, 1841.

MY DEAR SARAH.

* * * I am glad to fancy you on firm land, and at the end of your voyage, for it was painful to think of you every day and hour and minute urging your way across the broad Atlantic, and adding to the space that separated us from each other. * * *

I have received two or three letters recently, which I know would please you; and as I have not you at my elbow to hand them to, as I always did all my correspondence of an interesting nature, I will transcribe them. The first is from that eccentric but excellent fellow, Van Bibber; of this I will merely give a scrap, as the greater part relates to his private concerns, and to a drama, in two acts, which he has just finished, and is disposed to risk on the stage. His whole letter is charmingly written, and evidences a mind imbued with classical literature, and with the golden old literature of England. I give you merely his conclusion, which is quaint but picturesque, full of kindness, and not deficient in beauty:

"Avon Dale, sweet lady, has just donned her annual

garniture of buds and flowers; her head is crowned with a garland of lilac, beech and apple blossoms, her feet covered with slippers of woven cowslips and polyanthus. Every morning I catch her twining some new bud or wreathing some new floweret into her coronet. Come, sir, I must renew my invitation for a visit. Our means will not allow us to offer you those costly juices ripened beside the Rhine or Marne, to which you have doubtless been ever accustomed; but if you are fond of rich cream, fresh milk, and clear water (with ever and anon a sparkling glass of aromatic mint julep); if you love deep woodland solitude, and the voice of plaintive turtle doves (I never in any other place knew half so many or half such musical ones), then come, dear sir, to Avon Dale, and I will insure you a hearty welcome, a room (when you wish it) to yourself, a horse to ride on when you list, abundance of pure fresh air, and a glorious view of the distant mountains of Cotockton. But if you still turn a deaf ear to my invitations, and prefer to all this the company of your fair nieces, the manifold pleasures of Sunnyside cottage, and the delicious reveries inspired by Sleepy Hollow, then—my only wish is, that your own orchard may shower down its choicest blossoms on your head, and that, during all this merry springtime, you may have sweet thoughts, pleasant dreams, and frequent visits from the muses."

Is not that delightfully said? and does it not give a delightful idea of the man, and his wildwood retreat? I declare to you, that, if I could possibly tear myself from the cottage at this moment, when it is all in bloom and beauty, and fragrant with lilacs, I should be delighted to pay a visit to the poetic retreat of the Van Bibbers.

The next letter is from my friend James, the novelist, dated from Bruxelles, 7th January last:

"MY DEAR IRVING:

"I cannot let slip the opportunity of the return of my young acquaintance, Mr. Meline, to the United States, to write you a few lines, though it is now, alas! many a year since we met, and the broad Atlantic rolls between us, perhaps forever. The memory of our intercourse while you were resident in the Old World still remains fresh and pleasurable with me, and I trust that I am not forgotten either, but that when you see the name of one of my paper things, you think of him who wrote it. My productions in that way have been many—yours all too few; but those that you have written have given me intense delight, especially Astoria, every word of which I dwell upon with feelings of excitement and interest, and longings for adventure, which I thought were gone with my boyhood. I am even now writing something for the *Knickerbocker*, which I hear you take an interest in—as, indeed, you should in your godchild; and what I shall require as payment shall be a few lines from your hand, to tell me how you are, and that you have not forgotten your English friends. My address, for the present, must be at Messrs. Longmans, Paternoster Row, for I am now wandering, having lately met with a severe family affliction, which made change of scene and air advisable for me. I shall soon, however, settle again; and if ever you should be tempted once more to cross the broad stream, I trust that one of the first firesides at which you sit down will be that of Yours ever truly, &c."

Is not this a most kind and friendly letter? And how

little have I deserved it! I, who have let his former letter remain unanswered, and a book, which he sent me, unacknowledged and unthanked for. But I will reform!

And now comes the third letter—from that glorious fellow, Dickens (Boz), in reply to the one I wrote, expressing my heartfelt delight with his writings, and my yearnings toward himself. See how completely we sympathize in feeling:

"My dear Sir:

"There is no man in the world who could have given me the heartfelt pleasure you have, by your kind note of the 13th of last month. There is no living writer, and there are very few among the dead, whose approbation I should feel so proud to earn. And with everything you have written upon my shelves, and in my thoughts, and in my heart of hearts, I may honestly and truly say so. If you could know how earnestly I write this, you would be glad to read it—as I hope you will be, faintly guessing at the warmth of the hand I autobiographically hold out to you over the broad Atlantic.

"I wish I could find in your welcome letter some hint of an intention to visit England. I can't. I have held it at arm's length, and taken a bird's-eye view of it, after reading it a great many times, but there is no greater encouragement in it this way than on a microscopic inspection. I should love to go with you—as I have gone, God knows how often—into Little Britain, and Eastcheap, and Green Arbor Court, and Westminster Abbey. I should like to travel with you, outside the last of the coaches, down to Bracebridge Hall. It would *make my heart glad to compare notes* with you about that shabby gentleman in the oilcloth hat and red nose, who sat in the nine-cornered back parlor of the Masons' Arms; and about

Robert Preston, and the tallow chandler's widow, whose sitting room is second nature to me; and about all those delightful places and people that I used to walk about and dream of in the daytime, when a very small and not over-particularly-taken-care-of boy. I have a good deal to say, too, about that dashing Alonzo de Ojeda, that you can't help being fonder of than you ought to be; and much to hear concerning Moorish legend, and poor, unhappy Boabdil. Diedrich Knickerbocker I have worn to death in my pocket, and yet I should show you his mutilated carcass with a joy past all expression.

"I have been so accustomed to associate you with my pleasantest and happiest thoughts, and with my leisure hours, that I rush at once into full confidence with you, and fall, as it were naturally, and by the very laws of gravity, into your open arms. Questions come thronging to my pen as to the lips of people who meet after long hoping to do so. I don't know what to say first, or what to leave unsaid, and am constantly disposed to break off and tell you again how glad I am this moment has arrived.

"My dear Washington Irving, I cannot thank you enough for your cordial and generous praise, or tell you what deep and lasting gratification it has given me. I hope to have many letters from you, and to exchange a frequent correspondence. I send this to say so. After the first two or three, I shall settle down into a connected style, and become gradually rational.

"You know what the feeling is, after having written a letter, sealed it, and sent it off. I shall picture you reading this, and answering it before it has lain one night in the post office. Ten to one that before the fastest packet could reach New York I shall be writing again.

"Do you suppose the post-office clerks care to receive letters? I have my doubts. They get into a dreadful habit of indifference. A postman, I imagine, is quite callous. Conceive his delivering one to himself, without being startled by a preliminary double knock!

"Always your faithful friend,

"CHARLES DICKENS."

May 26th.—Since copying the foregoing letters, I have answered them all, so you see I am becoming quite a prompt correspondent. * * * I shall be anxious to know whether you have seen any of my literary friends in England, to whom I gave Mr. Storrow letters. Among the artists, I learn that Sir David Wilkie was absent on a visit to the Holy Land. I regret that you have missed him; the letter, however, will answer for another time.

I have commenced the barricade at the foot of the bank, and trust, before long, to be protected against all the surf and surges of the Tappan Sea, and the evil influence of the Erie railroad. Our neighborhood is filling up for the summer. The Hamiltons are at home; Mrs. C. I. and her family came up yesterday, and Mrs. Sheldon is to come up about the beginning of the month.

* * * And now, my dear Sarah, I must conclude this letter, which has been so much taken up with myself. I only ask, in return, that you will in your letters be equally egotistical. Tell me all about yourself—your movements, your occupations, your amusements; all that you see, think, and feel; let me have as much of yourself as possible, that I may not feel as if we are severed in spirit by the distance between us. I shall be eager to hear of your final establishment in your

own habitation at Paris, and in what quarter of the great city you are fixed, and how you acquit yourself in housekeeping. Mr. Storrow, however, is an able and experienced hand, who will arrange everything, I make no doubt, to your heart's content. Remember me to him most kindly and heartily, and believe me, my dear, dear Sarah,

Ever your affectionate uncle,

WASHINGTON IRVING.

In July I find him among the Highlands, on a visit to his friend, Gouverneur Kemble—a visit somewhat saddened by the recent death of that gentleman's sister, Gertrude, the wife of James K. Paulding, whose image was linked with the familiar scene. It is to her that the extract which follows, from a letter to Mrs. Storrow, makes the brief and touching allusion. West, his companion in the visit, was William E. West, the amiable American artist, whose likeness of Lord Byron had made him famous.

I arrived here the evening before last, in company with Mr. West. We had a splendid evening's voyage through the Highlands, which looked to me more magnificent than ever. I found Mr. Kemble's house a real "bachelor's hall," having no longer a lady to preside there. * * * The glorious being who used to grace and gladden this little mansion with her presence is gone forever! I cannot express to you how dreary I have occasionally felt since I have been here.

I give this further extract from the same letter, for

its interesting allusion to the venerable Albert Gallatin, then long withdrawn from public life:

The day before I left the cottage I dined at the Sheldons', to meet Mr. and Mrs. Gallatin (the old people), who were on a visit there. Mr. George Jones was the only guest besides myself from the neighborhood. We had a very cheerful dinner. Mr. Gallatin was in fine spirits, and full of conversation. He is upward of eighty, yet has all the activity and clearness of mind and gayety of spirits of a young man. How delightful it is to see such intellectual and joyous old age; to see life running out clear and sparkling to the last drop! With such a blessed temperament, one would be content to linger and spin out the last thread of existence.

From Kemble's, Mr. Irving proceeded to visit his friend, Henry Brevoort, who had taken the old Beverley House in the Highlands, which formerly belonged to the family of the Robinsons, and was associated with the history of the Arnold treason. It was distant about five miles from the residence of Gouverneur Kemble. It was while here that he was unexpectedly tempted into an excursion, of which he gives some description in the extract which follows:

[*To Mrs. Van Wart, Birmingham.*]

HONESDALE, Aug. 1, 1841.

MY DEAR SISTER:

I write from among the mountains in the upper part of Pennsylvania, from a pretty village which has recently sprung into existence as the deposit of a great coal region, and which is called after our friend Philip Hone, who was extremely efficient in directing enterprise into this quarter. I came here along the Delaware and Hudson Canal, which extends from the Hudson River near the Catskill Mountains, upward of a hundred miles into the interior, traversing some of the most beautiful parts (as to scenery) of the State of New York, and penetrating the State of Pennsylvania. I accompanied the directors of the Delaware and Hudson Canal in their annual visit of examination. Among the directors are Philip Hone and my friend Brevoort. I do not know when I have made a more gratifying excursion with respect to natural scenery, or more interesting from the stupendous works of art. The canal is laid a great part of the way along romantic valleys, watered by the Rondout, the Lackawaxen, &c. For many miles it is built up along the face of perpendicular precipices, rising into stupendous cliffs with overhanging forests, or strutting out into vast promontories; while on the other side you look down upon the Delaware, foaming and roaring below you at the foot of an immense wall or embankment which supports the canal. Altogether it is one of the most daring undertakings I have ever witnessed, to carry an artificial river over rocky mountains, and up the most savage and almost impracticable defiles; and all this, too, has been achieved by the funds of an association composed of a handful of individuals. For upward of ninety miles I went through a constant succession of scenery that would have been famous had it existed in any part of Europe; the Catskill Mountains to the north, the Shawangunk Mountains to the south, and between them lovely valleys, with the most luxuriant woodlands and picturesque streams. All this is a region about which I had heard nothing—a region entirely unknown to fame; but so it is in our country. We have some main routes for the fashionable traveller, along which he is hurried in steamboats and railroad cars; while on every side extend regions of beauty, about which he hears and knows nothing. Some of the most enchanting scenes I have beheld since my return to the United States, have been in out-of-the-way places, into which I have been accidentally led.

A letter to Mrs. Storrow, dated Sunnyside, Sept. 1st, more than three weeks after his return, shows that he did not gain in health by the exposures of this wild expedition into the mining regions:

SUNNYSIDE COTTAGE, Sept. 1, 1841.

MY DEAR SARAH:

Your mother, I believe, has given you, in her letter, a daily bulletin of my health during my recent malady; finding myself, however, fairly emerged out of the "dark valley," I hasten to give you, under my own hand, assurance of my returning health. I have indeed received a lesson which will cure me hereafter of that heedless confidence in my constitution, which made me think myself proof against heat or cold, wind or rain, and rendered me regardless of every exposure. I believe the last day of my tour to the coal region, where, for the sake of seeing the mountain scenery, I sat from morning till night beside the driver, exposed to the intense heat of the sun, after my system had been deranged by previous fatigues and exposures, gave the effectual blow to my health. I returned home completely out of order, and in the course of three or four days my indisposition terminated in a violent fever. I have never known before what a real fever was;

indeed, my health has been so uniformly good, that I have scarcely ever had a serious malady of any kind. Perhaps this may have made my actual illness appear the more severe to me. At times, when I lay panting with fever, my whole frame in a state of indescribable irritability, my mind at intervals wild with delirium, it seemed to me as if I could not exist under it—as if the fever must seize upon my brain, deprive me of my senses, and hurry me out of existence. But how can I express myself in sufficient terms of affectionate gratitude for the tenderness, the watchful, the devoted, the unwearied tenderness with which I have been treated! * * * It is almost worth being ill to experience such tenderness. I used to look forward with doubt and distrust to the time when, through age and infirmity, I might be unable to take care of myself, and, having no child of my own to cherish and bear with me, I might become an irksome burden upon others. I have no longer such apprehension. I feel that I have affectionate, tender-hearted beings about me, that would be to me like children, and love and cherish me the more for my very infirmities. Thank God, my malady has passed away, and I begin to be myself again. Yesterday, for the first time, I drove out in the carriage with your mother and Julia (Sanders' wife). We had a lovely drive past Mr. Constant's, through the new road to the Sawmill River, and up that delightful valley and by the Dobbs' Ferry road home. Oh! how beautiful everything looked; my heart was full of love and gratitude and enjoyment.

This morning opens bright and exhilarating; a pure, bracing northwest wind has made the air light and elastic, and seems to give new vigor to my frame. I feel in the happiest of moods, and my happy feelings are reflected from every affectionate countenance around me. It is the fifth anniversary of our taking up our residence at the dear little cottage, which has proved such a happy home to us all.

His brother Ebenezer had now become a member of the domestic circle of Sunnyside, which was henceforth to be his permanent home, his growing deafness and advancing years disqualifying him for further active occupation in the city.

CHAPTER IX.

EXTRACTS OF LETTERS TO MRS. STORROW—ANNIVERSARY OF THE ST. NICHOLAS SOCIETY—THE LIFE OF WASHINGTON BEGUN—APPOINTED MINISTER TO SPAIN —SECRETARIES OF LEGATION—JOSEPH G. COGSWELL—ALEXANDER HAMILTON—THE DICKENS DINNER—LETTER FROM BOZ—EMBARCATION AND FAREWELL.

IN a communication to Mrs. Storrow, of October 29th, Mr. Irving writes:

What do you think?—Dickens is actually *coming to America.* He has engaged passage for himself and his wife in the steam packet for Boston for the 4th of January next. He says: "I look forward to shaking hands with you with an interest I cannot (and I would not if I could) describe. You *can* imagine, I dare say, something of the feelings with which I look forward to being in America. I can hardly believe I am coming."

Three weeks later, November 19th, he thus apologizes for the somewhat desponding vein of a recent letter:

I have written you rather a gloomy letter lately, and am sorry for it; but for a time I was depressed in spirit by a concurrence of uncomfortable circumstances. I have always had a principle of reaction in my nature, however, which I am happy to find is not extinguished. I have taken pen in hand, and have been writing steadily for some weeks past. I do not know that what I have written will be of a nature to command much popularity or circulation, nor do I think I shall offer it soon to the press; but the manner in which I have executed it satisfies me that I have "good work in me yet," and I am determined to keep on until I have fairly worked it out. The effect, too, has been immediate on my spirits. * * * The moment I finish the work I am busied upon, I shall throw it aside and commence something else. If I continue in health and good spirits, I shall soon have a little capital lying by me in manuscript.

On the 1st of December he writes to his niece in Paris:

I have been about a week in town, and begin to long most heartily after the cottage, where, if nothing occurs imperatively to call me away, I shall remain through the winter, hard at work, that I may once more get a little ahead of the world, and cast dull care behind me.

On the 7th of the same month he writes:

I have stayed until to-day, to be present at the anniversary of the St. Nicholas Society, which went off yesterday in great style. The dinner was more numerously attended than on any former occasion. We had Lord Morpeth there, who of late has been the universal guest. He made a very neat speech on the occasion. My health was drunk in the course of the evening, and I was absolutely hurried upon my legs to make a speech, but, agitated and abashed as usual, and overcome by the prolonged and deafening testimonials of good will, I blundered through two or three indistinct sentences, and sat down amidst thundering applause. I never shall figure as an orator.

Toward the close of the same month he again expresses regret at the boding vein, so unusual in him, of some of his late letters:

I have written you two or three very uncomfortable letters lately, and am sorry for it; but I was discouraged by evils that seemed thickening around me, and felt doubtful whether I still retained mental force and buoyancy sufficient to cope with them. Thank God, the very pressure of affairs has produced reaction; a stout heart, not yet worn out, has rallied up to the emergency, and I am now in a complete state of literary activity. I shall keep on without flagging or flinching, as long as health and good spirits are continued to me. * * * Never did I feel the value of life and health more than at this moment, and never did I take a deeper interest in existence. I believe it is good for man to be thus roused to new exertion (even though by the stimulus of adverse circumstances), when the game of life would otherwise be growing tedious and uninteresting.

Tell Mr. Storrow I have received the books which he was so kind as to procure for me. * * * They are very rare works, not to be met with in this country, but indispensable to a work which I have in contemplation.

I am now so much engrossed by my literary avocations, that I shall not be able to write to you as often or as circumstantially as before; but you know the reason, and I am sure will not complain.

The work he had in contemplation was his Life of Washington, upon which he had actually commenced and got fairly under way, when he received the appointment of Minister to Spain—an honor totally unsought and unlooked-for by himself and his friends. It was on the 10th of February, in the city of New York, where he had been passing the winter, that he first heard of his nomination. "Washington Irving," said Daniel Webster, the distinguished Secretary of State, when he supposed a sufficient time had elapsed for him to have received the tidings of his nomination, "Washington Irving is now the most astonished man in the city of New York." I saw him at my office within an hour after he had received the news, and he had not yet got over the surprise and excitement of this unexpected event. Yet, as he paced up and down, revolving the prospect of a separation from home and home scenes, he appeared less impressed with the distinction conferred, than alive to the pain of such an exile. "It is hard—very hard," he half murmured to himself, half said to me; "yet," he added, whimsically enough, being struck with the seeming absurdity of such a view, "I must try to bear it. *God tempers the wind to the shorn lamb.*"

At a later period, and in a different mood, he spoke of this appointment to me as "the crowning honor of his life;" yet I am persuaded he would have declined it, but for a confident belief that a diplomatic residence at Madrid need work no interruption to his Life of

Washington, the literary task upon which he had now set his heart.

The following letter was written after he had been dubiously balancing the pros and cons for a time in my presence, and had concluded by a determination to accept. It is addressed to his brother Ebenezer at Sunnyside, now, as we have seen, his home:

NEW YORK, Feb. 10, 1842.

MY DEAR BROTHER:

I have been astounded, this morning, by the intelligence of my having been nominated to the Senate as Minister to Spain. The nomination, I presume, will be confirmed. Nothing was ever more unexpected. It was perfectly unsolicited.

I have determined to accept. Indeed, under all the circumstances of the case, I could not do otherwise. It will be a severe trial to absent myself for a time from dear little Sunnyside; but I shall return to it better enabled to carry it on comfortably.

In the following unofficial letter from Mr. Webster, we find that the appointment had taken place:

WASHINGTON, Feb. 14, 1842.

MY DEAR SIR:

You will have heard of your nomination and appointment as Envoy Extraordinary and Minister Plenipotentiary to the Court of Madrid. I assure you it gives me pleasure to have been instrumental in calling you to so distinguished a post in the public service. If a gentleman of more merit and higher qualifications had presented himself, great as is my personal regard for you, I should have yielded it to higher considerations.

The time of your departure from this country will be left to your own convenience. We have some confidential subjects, depending between the United States and Spain, in regard to which it would be well that you would confer with the Department, before you repair to your post.

I am, truly and cordially, yours,

DANIEL WEBSTER.

The suggestion of this appointment, however readily it may have been adopted by the President, John Tyler, originated with Mr. Webster, who, in the first month of his Secretaryship, had been agitating Mr. Irving's name for a diplomatic post. The sudden death of the President, General Harrison, very probably effected a change in his views at that time, but his purpose would seem, from this evidence, to have remained. Mr. Irving's old friend, William C. Preston, then a Senator of the United States from South Carolina, is also linked in this testimonial. "I have rarely performed," writes that gentleman in a letter to Gouverneur Kemble now before me, dated February 18th, "an official duty with more pleasure than that of reporting Irving from the Committee of Foreign Relations, and moving his confirmation. Such things make pleasant little green spots amid our wearisome pitching and tossing here. It was very gratifying, the cordial feeling manifested on both sides of the Senate. This was a very good thing on the part of Webster, and makes me sorry to see him so bedevilled by the Whigs, the Democrats, and the duns."

Nothing could be more gratifying [writes Washington to his brother, February 16th] than the manner in which this appointment has been made. It was suggested by Mr. Webster to the President, immediately adopted by him, heartily concurred in by all the Cabinet, and confirmed in the Senate almost by acclamation. When it was mentioned, Mr. Clay, who has opposed almost all the other nominations, exclaimed: "Ah, this is a nomination everybody will concur in! If the President would send us such names as this, we should never have any difficulty." What has still more enhanced the gratification of this signal honor, is the unanimous applause with which it is greeted by the public. The only drawback upon all this is the hard trial of tearing myself away from dear little Sunnyside. This has harassed me more than I can express; but I begin to reconcile myself to it, as it will be but a temporary absence.

To the same brother, now entered upon his sixty-sixth year, he writes the next day:

I now abandon the care of the place entirely to you. You will find, in my little library, books about gardening, farming, poultry, &c., by which to direct yourself. The management of the place will give you healthful and cheerful occupation, and will be as much occupation as you want. * * * So content yourself at Sunnyside, and never think of seeking any other "berth" for the rest of your days. Try if you cannot beat me at farming and gardening. I shall be able to bestow a little more money on the place now, to put it in good heart and good order.

Tell the girls they must not repine at my going away for a time, but must cheer me off with pleasant faces. The parting from Sunnyside will be hard for me, and must be rendered as cheerful as possible. * * * I shall apply myself steadily and vigorously to my pen, which I shall be able to do at Madrid, where there are few things to distract one's attention, and in a little while I shall amass a new literary capital. I shall therefore return to Sunnyside with money in both pockets, be able to "burn the candle at both ends," and to put up as many weathercocks as I please.

The following is his letter of acceptance:

NEW YORK, Feb. 18, 1842.

The Hon. DANIEL WEBSTER, *Secretary of State, Washington:*

SIR: I accept, with no common feelings of pride and gratitude, the honorable post offered me by the Government, of Envoy Extraordinary and Minister Plenipotentiary to Spain. It will take some little time for me to arrange my affairs preparatory to so sudden and unexpected a change of position and pursuits, but I trust to be ready to depart early in April, previous to which time I will visit Washington, to receive my instructions. I am, sir, very respectfully yours,

WASHINGTON IRVING.

Previous to the date of this formal acceptance, Mr. Irving had intimated a desire to have Mr. Joseph G. Cogswell appointed as Secretary of the Legation. "He is a gentleman," he wrote, "with whom I am on terms of confidential intimacy, and I know no one who, by his various acquirements, his prompt sagacity, his knowledge of the world, his habits of business, and his obliging disposition, is so calculated to give me that counsel, aid, and companionship so important in Madrid, where a stranger is more isolated than in any other capital of Europe."

It was an object of great solicitude to him to get the right person for this important and confidential relation; but just as he had succeeded in procuring the appointment for Cogswell, Mr. John Jacob Astor, finding that he was likely to lose the invaluable services of this gentleman in organizing the Astor Library, made him librarian of that embryo institution; and Mr. Irving, unwilling to stand in the way of a selection so admirable and of so much public importance, set about procuring the appointment of another in his place. His personal comfort and happiness were somewhat at stake in this matter, and it was a little doubtful whether he could get his inclinations consulted in another choice. He was most fortunate, however, in accomplishing the appointment of Alexander Hamilton, Jr., for the post; though not without some political scruples on the part of Mr. Tyler, which were finally yielded to a conviction of his fitness for the place, and a disposition to oblige the newly appointed Minister.

On the eve of his departure, President Tyler wrote him that he was most happy to say the difficulties in the way of Mr. Hamilton's nomination as his Secretary of Legation had been removed, and that his name would immediately be sent up to the Senate. "I am sorry," writes afterward the eloquent Hugh S. Legaré, "Cogswell does not go with you, but this appointment of his successor makes all possible amends, especially as the motive of his remaining is, with a view both to the public and to himself, of so much importance." His wishes, in fact, could not have been better accommodated than by this appointment of Hamilton, and his satisfaction was the greater that he was the son of a friend and near neighbor. "It will be like taking a bit of home with me," said Mr. Irving to the mother of the youthful Secretary.

Taking no lady with him to preside over his bachelor establishment at Madrid, his Secretary of Legation and two young gentlemen, Hector Ames, a son of Barrett Ames, of the city of New York, and J. Carson Brevoort, a son of his old friend, Henry Brevoort, would comprise his diplomatic family—the two last as attachés.

It was just when Mr. Irving had received the appointment of Minister to Spain, that Charles Dickens, the renowned author, made his first appearance in New York, having arrived shortly before at Boston.

The genial and lamented Felton, at this date Professor, afterward President of Harvard University, was visiting New York at the same time; and, after the death of Mr. Irving, in his remarks before the Massachusetts Historical Society, in paying his tribute to his memory, gives the following delightfully characteristic picture of their intercourse at that period:

> The time when I saw the most of Mr. Irving, was the winter of 1842, during the visit of Charles Dickens in New

York. I had known this already distinguished writer in Boston and Cambridge, and while passing some weeks with my dear and lamented friend, Albert Sumner. I renewed my acquaintance with Mr. Dickens, often meeting him in the brilliant society which then made New York a most agreeable resort. Halleck, Bryant, Washington Irving, Davis, and others scarcely less attractive by their genius, wit, and social graces, constituted a circle not to be surpassed anywhere in the world. I passed much of the time with Mr. Irving and Mr. Dickens; and it was delightful to witness the cordial intercourse of the young man, in the flush and glory of his fervent genius, and his elder compeer, then in the assured possession of immortal renown. Dickens said, in his frank, hearty manner, that from his childhood he had known the works of Irving; and that, before he thought of coming to this country, he had received a letter from him, expressing the delight he felt in reading the Story of Little Nell; and from that day they had shaken hands *autographically* across the Atlantic. Great and varied as was the genius of Mr. Irving, there was one thing he shrank with a comical terror from attempting, and that was *a dinner speech.* A great dinner, however, was to be given to Mr. Dickens in New York, as one had already been given in Boston; and it was evident to all that no man but Washington Irving could be thought of to preside. With all his dread of making a speech, he was obliged to obey the universal call, and to accept the painful preëminence. I saw him daily during the interval of preparation, either at the lodgings of Dickens, or at dinner or evening parties. I hope I showed no want of sympathy with his forebodings, but I could not help being amused with the tragi-comical distress which the thought of that approaching dinner had caused him. His pleasant humor mingled with the real dread, and played with the whimsical horrors of his own position with an irresistible drollery. Whenever it was alluded to, his invariable answer was, "I shall certainly break down!"—uttered in a half-melancholy tone, the ludicrous effect of which it is impossible to describe. He was haunted, as if by a nightmare; and I could only compare his dismay to that of Mr. Pickwick, who was so alarmed at the prospect of leading about that "dreadful horse" all day. At length the long-expected evening arrived; a company of the most eminent persons, from all the professions and every walk of life, were assembled, and Mr. Irving took the chair. I had gladly accepted an invitation, making it, however, a condition that I should not be called upon to speak—a thing I then dreaded quite as much as Mr. Irving himself. The direful compulsions of life have since helped me to overcome, in some measure, the post prandial fright. Under the circumstances—an invited guest, with no impending speech—I sat calmly, and watched with interest the imposing scene. I had the honor to be placed next but one to Mr. Irving, and the great pleasure of sharing in his conversation. He had brought the manuscript of his speech, and laid it under his plate. "I shall certainly break down," he repeated over and over again. At last the moment arrived. Mr. Irving rose, and was received with deafening and long-continued applause, which by no means lessened his apprehension. He began in his pleasant voice; got through two or three sentences pretty easily, but in the next hesitated; and, after one or two attempts to go on, gave it up, with a graceful allusion to the tournament, and the troops of knights all armed and eager for the fray; and ended with the toast, "Charles Dickens, the guest of the nation." "There!" said he, as he resumed his seat under a repetition of the applause which had saluted his rising; "there! I told you I should break down, and I've done it."

There certainly never was made a shorter after-dinner speech; I doubt if there ever was a more successful one. The manuscript seemed to be a dozen or twenty pages long, but the printed speech was not as many lines. I suppose that manuscript may be still in existence; and if so, I wish it might be published.* Mr. Irving often spoke with a good-humored envy of the felicity with which Dickens always acquitted himself on such occasions.

The following letter is addressed to his brother from Washington, where he and "Boz" had gone shortly after the Dickens dinner:

[*To Ebenezer Irving.*]

WASHINGTON, March 16, 1842.

MY DEAR BROTHER:

My reception in Washington, by all persons and parties, has been of the most gratifying kind. The Government seems disposed to grant me every indulgence as to the time and mode of my embarcation, my route, &c. I shall remain here until some time in the early part of next week, to read the correspondence and documents connected with my mission, and to make myself acquainted with the affairs of the legation, after which I shall return home to make my final preparations for departure.

I dined with Mr. Granger yesterday; Mr. Webster to-day; I dine to-morrow with Mr. Preston, of the Senate, the next

* The manuscript, which consisted, no doubt, only of notes or hints, was probably destroyed at the time.—ED.

day with the President, and on Saturday with Mr. Tayloe; so you see I am launched in a complete round of dissipation. Last evening I was at the President's *levee*—a prodigious crowd. I set out to walk, with Julia Sanders on my arm, but was penned up against the wall, and for an hour had to stand shaking hands with man, woman, and child from all parts of the Union, who took a notion to *lionize* me. I thought I had become so old a story as to be past all such bozzing, but they seem to think me brought out in a new edition at Washington. * * *

March 17th he resumes:

I have nearly finished my business here. I have read all the correspondence and documents of importance connected with my mission, and had private conversations with the Secretary of State. I have received my letter of credit on the Rothschilds, London, for my salary, which, I find, commences from the date of my commission—10th of February last. I shall receive a draft for my outfit on Tuesday next. I intend paying a visit to Mount Vernon on Monday, and hope to leave this for Baltimore on Tuesday afternoon. As I shall stop in Philadelphia to see my booksellers, I shall not reach New York until toward the end of the week. I still shall endeavor to make all my arrangements so as to sail in the Liverpool packet on the 7th April, as I am anxious to get out to Europe early enough to have a portion of the fine season for travelling.

Yesterday I dined at the President's, and had a very pleasant dinner. Mr. Tyler has all the air of a very good-hearted, fine-tempered man, and I have experienced the most cordial reception from him. I sat next to his daughter-in-law, a daughter of my early friend, Mary Fairlie, and we had much interesting conversation about her mother, among whose papers she had found many of my letters during the time that, in our young days, we kept up an amusing correspondence.

In the following, we have a further glimpse of Boz and Diedrich:

[*Charles Dickens to Washington Irving.*]

WASHINGTON, Monday afternoon, March 21, 1842.

MY DEAR IRVING:

We passed through—literally passed through—this place again to-day. I did not come to see you, for I really have not the heart to say "good-by" again, and felt more than I can tell you when we shook hands last Wednesday.

You will not be at Baltimore, I fear? I thought, at the time, that you only said you might be there, to make our parting the gayer.

Wherever you go, God bless you! What pleasure I have had in seeing and talking with you, I will not attempt to say. I shall never forget it as long as I live. What *would* I give, if we could have but a quiet week together! Spain is a lazy place, and its climate an indolent one. But if you have ever leisure under its sunny skies, to think of a man who loves you, and holds communion with your spirit oftener, perhaps, than any other person alive—leisure from listlessness, I mean—and will write to me in London, you will give me an inexpressible amount of pleasure.

Your affectionate friend,

CHARLES DICKENS.

The following letter from Henry Clay has reference to the nomination of Alexander Hamilton as Secretary of Legation, some difficulties, as before hinted, having been interposed in the way of his appointment, which were not removed until the 7th of April, when his name was sent into the Senate, and immediately confirmed. I introduce the brief epistle of this eloquent and illustrious man for the genial tone of its closing paragraph:

WASHINGTON, March 29, 1842.

MY DEAR SIR:

I received your favor, and, should I be in the Senate when the nomination to which it refers shall be acted upon, *your* wishes are sufficient to command my vote.

Take with you, my dear sir, the fervent wishes of one whose sentiments of regard have remained unabated during twenty-eight years, for your success in your public mission, and for increased fame in your literary pursuits.

I am, truly and faithfully, your friend and obedient servant,

H. CLAY.

Philip Hone, who presents Mr. Irving with the following invitation to a public dinner on the eve of his departure, was an old friend and his next-door neighbor in their boyhood, and had served the city, at one period, with great acceptance, as its Mayor:

Friday, April 1, 1842.

MY DEAR IRVING:

The pleasant duty is assigned to me of handing you the

enclosed; and I am directed to request you will communicate your answer (which it is hoped will be favorable) to,

Dear sir, your obedient servant and sincere friend,

PHILIP HONE.

The letter of invitation which follows, is signed by some of the most honored names in New York, without distinction of party, and is worth giving as a testimony that his appointment was regarded as gratuitous and national, and not in return for claims of a political nature. Among the signers are William Cullen Bryant, Charles King, Gulian C. Verplanck, William Kent, Daniel Lord, Samuel B. Ruggles, Thomas J. Oakley, Samuel Jones, Charles Augustus Davis.

NEW YORK, March 29, 1842.

DEAR SIR:

It is now nearly ten years since a number of the citizens of New York, prompted by personal affection, and an honest pride in the high literary character of their townsman, assembled at the festive board to welcome your return from Europe; to renew with you the recollection of former days of pleasant intercourse, and to participate in the rich stores of information, the fruits of your sojourn of seventeen years in foreign parts.

An occasion now occurs to repeat this "feast of reason," which dwells so pleasantly on the memory of many of us. You have been appointed, in a manner alike honorable to the Government and yourself, unassisted by intrigue, and unpledged to party, the nation's representative at the Court of Spain—a station which seems to be universally conceded as your peculiar right. You have studied the language of that interesting country, searched her archives, embellished her story, and made her literature familiar to your countrymen.

Understanding that your departure is nigh at hand, we are desirous to give you a "God speed" upon your honorable mission, to convince you that the hearts of your "brethren and friends" here in your native city beat warmly as ever toward you, and that their pride in your literary fame has suffered no abatement. With this view we offer ourselves, as the representatives of a large number of your fellow citizens, to invite you, most affectionately, to dine with them previous to your departure for Spain, on any day most convenient to yourself.

We are, dear sir, with respect and affection, your friends and townsmen,

PHILIP HONE, &c.

The reply was as follows:

[*To Mr. Philip Hone.*]

NEW YORK, April 4, 1842.

MY DEAR HONE:

I have just received your kind noto of the 1st inst., enclosing an invitation, signed by a number of my townsmen, to partake of a public dinner, as a farewell expression of their regard, prior to my departure for Spain.

I cannot but remember with deep sensibility a similar testimonial of their good will with which I was surprised and overpowered ten years since, on my return home from so long an absence that I had almost feared it had alienated me from their affection; and it is a proud gratification to me to find that, after ten years of familiar intercourse, the same good will still appears to be exhibited. Indeed, the manifestations of public regard have thickened upon me rather than declined with the lapse of years. And when I have made up my mind to find myself naturally waning in popular favor, and rightfully giving place to younger and fresher candidates, I am surprised by new marks of popular esteem and national confidence, surpassing all that have gone before. Thus have I continually been paid, and overpaid, and paid again for all the little good I may have effected in my somewhat negligent and fortuitous career, until, at times, I feel as if, in acquiescing in such over-measured rewards, I am tacitly pocketing what is not due to me.

In the present instance that shall not be the case. Indeed, the nature of my preparations, on the eve of departure for a post of important and untried responsibility, leaves me neither the leisure nor the frame of mind necessary to participate in such a festivity as is proposed; but I beg you to assure my townsmen that, while I excuse myself from accepting their proffered banquet, I will treasure up in my heart of hearts the cordial "farewell" intended by it, as one of the dearest of the many testimonials of regard received by me from my native place.

To you, my good friend, who have known me "from my childhood on," accept my thanks for the kind expressions with which you have accompanied this invitation, and my sincere wish that, should I live once more to return to my native land, I may find you in the full enjoyment of health and prosperity.

Yours very faithfully,

WASHINGTON IRVING.

Seven days later, when his departure was close at hand, he addresses the following letter to his niece, Sarah Irving, at his cottage:

NEW YORK, April 7, 1842.

MY DEAR SARAH:

I have given Pierre M. Irving a full power of attorney to act in my name, and have made arrangements with him for the conduct of my pecuniary affairs. * * *

And now, my dear, good little girl, God bless you! You have been like a daughter, and an affectionate one, to me, and so have all your sisters; and have, by your kind attentions, made the years I have lived among you one of the happiest portions of my life. In a little while we shall come together again, I trust, and then we will have merry times at sweet little Sunnyside.

With my love to all the flock, your affectionate uncle,

WASHINGTON IRVING.

On the 10th of April he embarked, with fine weather and a fair wind.

CHAPTER X.

MR. IRVING IN LONDON — LEVEE — RECEPTION AT COURT — QUEEN VICTORIA — PRINCE ALBERT—MEETING OF OLD ACQUAINTANCES—ROGERS—LESLIE—JAMES BANDINEL — MONASTIC SECLUSION IN WESTMINSTER ABBEY — ANNIVERSARY DINNER OF THE LITERARY FUND — HIS STRUGGLE ABOUT GOING — EXTRACT FROM MOORE'S DIARY ON THE SUBJECT—THE QUEEN'S GRAND FANCY BALL—AT PARIS—A GUEST OF MRS. STORROW—PASSAGES FROM LETTERS TO SARAH IRVING AND MRS. PARIS—MR. CASS—LETTER TO MRS. HENRY VAN WART—LETTER TO MRS. PARIS—PRESENTMENT TO LOUIS PHILIPPE AND OTHER MEMBERS OF THE ROYAL FAMILY AT NEUILLY—HIS RECEPTION—FETE AT COLONEL THORN'S—PASSAGES OF LETTERS TO PIERRE M. IRVING AND WIFE.

THE following letter to his sister, written at a scanty moment snatched from amidst the hurry of various occupations, gives the first tidings of his arrival in England, where the members of the family at Birmingham, from whom he had now been separated ten years, were looking forward with impatience to a meeting:

[*To Mrs. Paris, at Tarrytown.*]

LONDON, May 3, 1842.

MY DEAR SISTER:

I have arrived in England *before my ship*, and in London before visiting Birmingham; and these are the circumstances of the case: We had a fair wind and fine voyage until we made the Irish coast, when the wind came ahead. After beating for a day or two in the channel, with the prospect of passing several more days on shipboard, a steam packet hove in sight. A signal brought it within hail. It was bound from Cork for Bristol, where it would arrive on the following day. Several of my fellow passengers and myself, therefore, got on board, and were landed on the following day (April 30th) at Bristol. * * * We landed after dark, and the next morning I set off in the railroad cars for London. These railroads have altered the whole style and course of travelling in England. You fly through the country rather than ride. We were about four hours travelling a distance of one hundred miles; and such admirable vehicles. I sat as comfortably cushioned and accommodated as in my old Voltaire chair at the cottage. The railroads, too, are so well finished, that you experience none of the jarring and vibration that are felt in ours. In this way we were whirled through a succession of enchanting scenery, in all the freshness of spring; the weather was lovely, and the sunshine worthy of our own country.

I had intended merely to touch in London, and proceed by railroad to Birmingham, which is now but a five-hours' journey from the metropolis. I found, however, once here, it was impossible to get away as readily as I had supposed. I waited on our Minister, Mr. Edward Everett, and had some matters to arrange with him, and understood that it would be proper for me to appear at the levee, and be presented to the Queen on Wednesday morning (to-morrow). Then I had to order some addition to my diplomatic uniform for the occasion—to get clothes, &c., &c. It worries me extremely to be thus detained from seeing sister Sarah, and I fear she will be grieved at my delay. I shall endeavor to break away from town the day after to-morrow, and put off all further business and arrangements until my return. In fact, I am not in mood and trim to enter upon the bustle and agitation of public life. The hurried transitions of the latter part of my voyage, and of my arrival, have excited me too much. I arrived here flushed, and heated, and agitated, and since that have experienced something of depression. I have avoided making any calls that might involve me in engagements, and have felt a singular reluctance to commit myself once more to the current of society and the turmoil of the world. * * * However, all this will pass away. When I have made my visit to Birmingham, I will come back and plunge into the stream, and trust to the buoyancy and activity of my spirit to enable me once more to buffet with the waves. I find that, by getting on board the steamer, and landing at Bristol, I escaped the bother of a public dinner which they were prepared to offer me at Liverpool. This is a great comfort. * * * I question whether I shall get away from England until toward the end of the month; and then I shall hurry on to Paris, where I expect to be joined by Mr. Hamilton. * * *

[*To Mrs. Paris, at Tarrytown.*]

THE SHRUBBERY, May 7, 1842.

MY DEAR SISTER:

I wrote you a hasty scrawl, a few days since, from London. I was detained in town three or four days by business, and then set off for Birmingham, where I arrived in about five hours by railroad, travelling without the least fatigue. My meeting with our dear sister was, as you may suppose, most affecting.

* * * * * *

While I was in London I attended the levee, to be presented. I know the great interest you take in the young Queen, and that you will expect some account of her. She is certainly quite low in stature, but well formed and well rounded. Her countenance, though not decidedly handsome, is agreeable and intelligent. Her eyes light blue, with light eyelashes; and her mouth generally a little open, so that you can see her teeth. She acquits herself in her receptions with great grace, and even with dignity. Prince Albert stood beside her—a tall, elegantly formed young man, with a handsome, prepossessing countenance. He is said to be frank, manly, intelligent, and accomplished; to be fond of his little wife, who, in turn, is strongly attached to him. It is rare to see such a union of pure affection on a throne.

I experienced a very kind reception at court; was warmly welcomed by many members of the diplomatic corps, though most of them were strangers to me; but I met several of my old acquaintances among the ministers—Lord Aberdeen, Sir Robert Peel, &c.—who were very cordial in their recognitions, and seemed to be in high good-humor at having, themselves, got once more into office.

Among the most gratifying meetings with old friends during my brief sojourn in London, I must mention those with Mr. Rogers, and with Leslie. Mr. Rogers was quite affected on meeting with me (it was at a dinner party at our Minister's, Mr. Everett's). The old man took me in his arms quite in a paternal manner. He begins to show the marks of his advanced age, though he still goes out to parties, and is almost as much in company as ever. Leslie is occupied in painting a picture of the Royal Christening. His picture of the Coronation has been the making of him. He has more orders for paintings than he can execute.

LITTLE CLOISTERS, WESTMINSTER ABBEY, *May 9th.*—I returned to town on Saturday, after passing two days in Birmingham, intending to pay it another and a longer visit before I leave England. I am here ensconced in the very heart of this old monastic establishment, with an old friend who keeps bachelor's hall in one of the interior buildings connected with the Abbey. My host is Mr. James Bandinel, of the Foreign Office, with whom I became acquainted during my former diplomatic residence in London. He is a peculiar character; a capital scholar, a man variously and curiously informed, of great worth, kindness, and hospitality. His quarters in the old Abbey are a perfect "old curiosity shop," furnished with all kinds of antiquities and curiosities: quaint old furniture; the walls hung with ancient armor; weapons of all ages and countries; curious pictures, &c., &c.; cases and shelves of old books in every room. The entrance to this singular and monkish nest is through the vaulted passages and the long arcades of the cloisters, over the tombstones (inserted in the pavements) of the ancient abbots, which I have mentioned in the Sketch Book, and past that mural monument with a marble figure reclining on it, which frightened Sarah so much that evening when she was brought to the Abbey unexpectedly by Mr. Storrow. I have repeatedly passed through these cloisters and by that monument at midnight, on my way home from a party, and on one occasion the Abbey clock struck twelve just as I was passing. How strange it seems to me that I should thus be nestled quietly in the very heart of this old pile, that used to be so much the scene of my half-romantic, half-meditative haunts, during my scribbling days. It is like my sojourn in the halls of the Alhambra. Am I always to have my dreams turned into realities?

May 13*th*.—I have kept this letter by me several days, but have been unable to add a word, such is the hurry of engagements, visits, calls, notes, &c., &c., in this overwhelming metropolis. I have neither rest by day nor sleep by night, and am almost fagged out. I had hoped to enjoy some delightful quiet in this glorious seclusion in the heart of the cloisters, but the claims of the world follow me here, and keep me in continual agitation. Last Sunday, it is true, I had a delicious treat in hearing the cathedral service performed in a noble style, with the chaunts of the choir, and the accompaniment of the organ; but besides this, I have seen nothing of the Abbey excepting to pass to and fro, by night and day, through the cloisters, making the vaults and monuments echo with my footsteps at midnight.

I have not been able to call on many of my old friends, but have met some of them on public occasions. Many of the literary men I met at an anniversary dinner of the Literary Fund, at which Prince Albert presided. Here I sat beside my friend Moore, the poet, who came to town to attend the dinner. He looks thinner than when I last saw him, and has the cares and troubles of the world thickening upon him as he advances in years. He has two sons; both had commissions in the army. The youngest has recently returned home, broken in health, and in danger of a consumption. The elder, Tom, has been rather wild, and is on his return from India, having, for some unknown reason, sold his commission. The expenses of these two sons bear hard upon poor Moore, and he talks with some despondency of the likelihood of his having to come upon the Literary Fund for assistance. The Literary Fund dinner was very splendid, and there was much dull speaking from various distinguished characters. I had come to it with great reluctance, knowing that my health would be drunk; and, though I had determined not to make a speech in reply, yet the very idea of being singled out, and obliged to get on my legs and return thanks, made me nervous throughout the evening. The flattering speech of Sir Robert Inglis, by which the toast was preceded, and the very warm and prolonged cheering by which it was received, instead of relieving, contributed to agitate me, and I felt as if I would never attend a public dinner again, where I should have to undergo such a trial.

There is an amusing description, in the Diary of Thomas Moore, of his endeavors to persuade Mr. Irving to be present at this annual dinner of the Literary Fund Society, which I am tempted to extract in this place, though, in so doing, I break off from the letter, to return to it, however, again:

[*From the Diary of Thomas Moore.*]

May 10*th.*—Started for town, leaving our dear boy somewhat better. Found, with my usual good luck, a note from Murray, asking me to meet at dinner, *to-day*, the man of all others I wanted to shake hands with once more—Washington Irving. Called at Murray's, to say "Yes, yes," with all my heart.

11*th.*—Went to the Literary Fund Chambers to see what were the arrangements, and where I was to be seated, having, in a note to Blewitt, the Secretary, begged him to place me near some of my own personal friends. Found that I was to be seated between Hallam and Washington Irving. All right. By-the-by, Irving had yesterday come to Murray's, with the determination, as I found, not to go to the dinner, and all begged of me to use my influence with him to change this resolution. But he told me his mind was made up on the point; that the drinking his health, and the speech he would have to make in return, were more than he durst encounter; that he had broken down at the Dickens dinner (of which he was chairman) in America, and obliged to stop short in the middle of his oration, which made him resolve not to encounter another such accident. In vain did I represent to him that a few words would be quite sufficient in returning thanks. "That *Dickens* dinner," which he always pronounced with strong emphasis, hammering all the time with his right arm, *more suo*, "that *Dickens* dinner" still haunted his imagination, and I almost gave up all hope of persuading him. At last I said to him, "Well, now, listen to me a moment. If you really wish to distinguish yourself, it is by saying the fewest possible words that you will effect it. The great fault with all the speakers, *myself* among the number, will be our saying too much. But if you content yourself with merely saying that you feel most deeply the cordial reception you have met with, and have great pleasure in drinking their healths in return, the very simplicity of the address will be more effective, from such a man, than all the stammered-out rigmaroles that the rest of the speechifiers will vent." This suggestion seemed to touch him; and so there I left him, feeling pretty sure that I had carried my point. It is very odd, that while some of the shallowest fellows go on so glib and ready with the tongue, men whose minds are abounding with matter should find such difficulty in bringing it out. I found that Lockhart also had de clined attending this dinner under a similar apprehension, and only consented on condition that his health should not be given.

Whether Moore's suggestion was adopted or not, certain it is that Mr. Irving did little more than bow his thanks to the toast of Sir Robert Inglis. Happily, the brilliant Everett, never at a loss, was there to speak for the honor of American literature.

I now resume with some further passages from the letter to his sister:

I believe I told you, in a previous letter, of the public dinner that had been intended me at Liverpool. I have since received an invitation to accept a public dinner at Glasgow, which, of course, I declined; indeed, the manifestations of public regard which I have continually experienced since my arrival have been quite overpowering.

Last evening I was at the Queen's grand fancy ball, which surpassed, in splendor and picturesque effect, any courtly assemblage that I ever witnessed or could imagine. The newspapers are full of details of this magnificent pageant, and I must refer you to them for particulars, for the whole is a scene of bewilderment in my recollection. There were at least two thousand persons present, all arrayed in historical, poetical, or fanciful costumes, or in rich military or court uniforms. A kind of scheme was given to the whole, by making it the representation of the visit of Anne of Brittany (the character sustained by the Duchess of Cambridge) to the Court of Edward III (Prince Albert) and his Queen Philippa (Queen Victoria). The respective sovereigns had all their courtiers and attendants in the costumes of the times, faithfully executed after old historical paintings and engravings. There was a reality mingled with the fiction of the scene. Here royalty represented royalty, and nobility represented nobility. Many of the personages present played the parts of their own ancestors, their dresses being faithfully copied from old family paintings by Vandyke and other celebrated persons. There was no tinsel nor stage trumpery in the dresses and jewels; all was of the richest materials, such as the characters represented would have worn; and there was on all sides a blaze of diamonds beyond anything I had ever seen. The saloons of the palace were of great size, so that there was ample room for display; and nothing could surpass the effect of the various groups, processions, &c., or the splendor of the assemblage in the Throne Room, where Albert and Victoria, as Edward and Philippa, were seated in state, receiving the homage of the brilliant throng.

I had a very favorable situation in one part of the evening, near the royal party, when the different quadrilles, each in uniform costumes, danced before them. The personage who appeared least to enjoy the scene seemed to me to be the little Queen herself. She was flushed and heated, and evidently fatigued and oppressed with the state she had to keep up, and the regal robes in which she was arrayed, and especially by a crown of gold, which weighed heavy on her brow, and to which she was continually raising her hand to move it slightly when it pressed. I hope and trust her real crown sits easier. Prince Albert looked uncommonly well in his costume. He would have realized the idea you have no doubt formed of a prince, from all that you have read in fairy tales. He came up to where I was standing, and held some little conversation with me. He speaks English very well, and his manner is extremely bland and prepossessing.

THE SHRUBBERY, *May* 16*th*.—I was interrupted in my letter, and had to abandon it. Yesterday I made my escape from London, in spite of a host of tempting invitations, and came off here, glad to get a little repose. I arrived wearied, exhausted, rheumatic (which I have been ever since my arrival on the coast of England); and yesterday afternoon, and all last evening, could do little else than sleep, to make up for nights of broken rest. * * *

The Shrubbery, from which he dates on the 16th of May, was the residence of his sister, Mrs. Van Wart.

A few days afterward he embarked at Southampton for France, in company with Hector Ames, of New York, who was to be attached to the Legation at Madrid, and form one of his household.

To his sister, at Birmingham, he writes, June 8th:

I arrived at Havre at an early hour on the Sunday morning after I left you, having had a very smooth voyage across the channel. I passed the day at the delightful little half-rural retreat of my friend Beasley, which is situated in a garden on the descent of the hill overlooking Havre and the surrounding extent of land and sea. I stayed there until Monday morning, Hector being quartered there with me. We then ascended the Seine in a steamboat to Rouen; passed a night there, and the next day proceeded by steamboat and railroad to Paris, where we arrived on Tuesday evening. My visit to my excellent friend Beasley, and my voyage up the Seine, however gratifying in other respects, were full of melancholy associations; for at every step I was reminded of my dear, dear brother Peter, who had so often been my companion in these scenes. In fact, he is continually present to my mind since my return to Europe, where we passed so many years together, and I think this circumstance contributes greatly to the mixture of melancholy with which, of late, I regard all those scenes and objects which once occasioned such joyous excitement. There is one little, quiet, conventual garden, with shady walks, and shrubberies, and seats, behind the old Gothic church of St. Ouen, at Rouen, which used to be his favorite resort during his solitary residence in that city, and where he used to pass his mornings with his book, amusing himself with the groups of loungers and of nursery maids and children. I felt my heart completely give way when I found myself in that garden. I was for a time a complete child. My dear, dear brother! As I write, the tears are gushing from my eyes.

The following characteristic extract is taken from a letter to his niece, Sarah Irving, an inmate of Sunnyside, in reply to some welcome intelligence from home. It is dated five days after his arrival in Paris, and is addressed to her from beneath the roof of Mrs. Storrow, with whom he was residing, and who, it may be remembered, had not long before been domesticated with him at the "Roost."

May 29th, 1842.— * * * My visit to Europe has by no means the charm of former visits. Scenes and objects have no longer the effect of novelty with me. I am no longer curious to see great sights or great people, and have been so long accustomed to a life of quiet, that I find the turmoil of the world becomes irksome to me. Then I have a house of my own, a little domestic world, created in a manner by my own hand, which I have left behind, and which is continually haunting my thoughts, and coming in contrast with the noisy, tumultuous, heartless world in which I am called to mingle. However, I am somewhat of a philosopher, and can accommodate myself to changes, so I shall endeavor to resign myself to the splendor of courts and the conversation of courtiers, comforting myself with the thought that the time will arrive when I shall once more return to sweet little Sunnyside, and be able to sit on a stone fence, and talk about politics and rural affairs with neighbor Forkel and Uncle Brom.

In a similar vein he writes to his sister, Mrs. Paris, the same day:

* * * Hitherto, since my arrival in Paris, I have been living very quietly, avoiding all engagements, that I might pass my time as much as possible with Sarah; but now I shall have to launch in some degree into society. I have to make diplomatic calls in company with our Minister, General Cass, and these will lead, more or less, to various engagements. Fortunately, the fashionable season is over; the royal family are absent, and there is less call for visits of ceremony and crowded entertainments. Still I feel a mortal repugnance to launching into the stream of public life, and I cling as long as possible to the quiet shore I am about to leave. I endeavor to conform to our old family motto, *Sub sole sub umbra virens* (flourishing in the sun and in the shade); but I think, upon the whole, I am more calculated for the shade.

My predecessor, Mr. Vail, expects me early in July, and is

anxious to leave Madrid with his family before the intense heats of summer. I have made a kind of half arrangement, by letter, with Mr. Vail, by which I shall take up my quarters with him when I arrive, and pretty much take his establishment, carriage, furniture, and servants off his hands. * * * I shall thus have a home at once on my arrival, without being subjected to the loss of time and trouble, the bother, and perplexity, and cheatery which I would otherwise incur in forming an establishment. I mention this to you because I know you are anxious on this point.

* * * * * *

Not long after, he entertains the same correspondent with the following:

PARIS, June 10, 1842.

MY DEAR SISTER:

A few days since, I drove out, in the evening, with our Minister, General Cass, to Neuilly, one of the royal country residences near Paris, to be presented to the King. Neuilly is situated in the midst of an English park, through which we had a pleasant drive. I observed sentinels stationed here and there about the park—a precaution taken in consequence of the repeated attempts upon the life of the King. Louis Philippe, I am told, is extremely annoyed, in his rides on horseback about the park, at finding himself thus under perpetual surveillance. He says he is almost as badly off as Napoleon at Longwood, who could never find himself out of sight of a sentinel.

A suite of saloons on the ground floor of the palace were lighted up. Very little formality is observed in these country receptions. Passing through a number of domestics in the entrance hall, we found our way from one chamber to another, until we came to where the company were assembled in a central saloon. The Queen and Madame Adelaide (sister to the King) were seated, with several ladies, at a round table, at work. The King was conversing by turns with gentlemen who were standing in groups round the room, some few of whom (General Cass and myself among the number), who were there on ceremony, were in court uniforms. The King was simply dressed in black, with pantaloons and shoes. I am thus particular in noting his dress, knowing your curiosity with respect to royalty, and lest you should suppose that kings and queens are always in long velvet robes, with golden crowns on their heads. I experienced a very kind reception from the King and Queen and Madame Adelaide, each of whom took occasion to say something complimentary about my writings. The King has altered much since I last saw him (which was in 1830, when he took the oaths of office). Age may begin to weigh upon him, but care, no doubt, still more. He is less erect than he used to be, and at times stoops considerably. How different from what he was when I first saw him, nearly twenty years since—as the Duke of Orleans, in hussar uniform, mounted on a superb horse, in a public procession, the admiration of every eye. Still he is a fine-looking man for his years, and appeared to be in good health and good spirits, laughing heartily with some of those with whom he was conversing. In his conversation with General Cass and myself, he spoke of American affairs, and showed himself to be minutely observant of all that was passing in our country, and of the state of its relations with its neighbors in Canada, Texas, and Mexico. I am told he keeps a vigilant eye upon the newspapers, and thus informs himself of what is going on in all parts of the world.

I am sure this will recommend him to the good opinion of our worthy brother, the present Laird of Sunnyside [whose devotion to the newspapers nearly excluded all other reading].

The Queen, who is a most excellent, amiable person, is pale and thin, with blue eyes, and hair quite white. Nothing can be kinder than her manners. Her life is an anxious one. The repeated attempts upon the life of her husband, and even of her sons, have filled her with alarm, and I am told she is in a state of nervous agitation whenever they are absent on some public occasion of ceremony. She is a devoted wife and mother, a perfect pattern in the domestic relations of life. The King's sister, Madame Adelaide, is a woman of more force of character; resembles the King in features, possesses vigorous good sense and great ambition. She is said to take great interest in public affairs, and in the stability of her brother's throne.

* * * * * *

June 14th.—I had intended to write something in this letter every day, but I have been so much taken up by the usual demands of society, and so oppressed by the heat of the weather, that I have found it impossible to do so. Two or three days since, Mr. Storrow, Sarah, and myself dined at the country seat of Mrs. Welles, and passed the evening delightfully in strolling about the grounds. The day after to-morrow we intend going to Versailles, to pass two or three days there. * * *

I shall be glad to get out of Paris into the country. The weather is uncommonly warm, and, in spite of all my holding back, I have got launched into society, and find myself obliged to dine out almost every day. Yesterday I dined at the British ambassador's (Lord Cowley, brother to the Duke of Wellington). The dinner, however, was very pleasant. Lady Cowley I knew some years since, in England. I was treated most cordially. General Cass dined there also, and Mr. Rumpf, son-in-law to Mr. Astor, besides other persons of my acquaintance. In the evening I was at a magnificent fête given by our countryman, Colonel Thorn, on the occasion of one of his daughters' marriage with a French baron. You know the history of Colonel Thorn, and the stand he has taken among the old French noblesse by dint of his wealth. His fête was really magnificent. His hotel was brilliantly lighted up, the extensive gardens fancifully illuminated, and singers and musicians stationed among the distant groves, who occasionally regaled the company with concerted pieces of instrumental music, or romantic choruses and glees. The whole was one of those fairy scenes that would have enchanted me in my greener years of inexperience and romance; but I have grown too wise to be duped by such delusions, so I sagely came away just as the thoughtless throng were beginning to dance. It is wonderful how much more difficult it is to astonish or amuse me than when I was last in Europe. It is possible I may have gathered wisdom under the philosophic shades of Sleepy Hollow, or may have been rendered fastidious by the gay life of the cottage; it is certain that, amidst all the splendors of London and Paris, I find my imagination refuses to take fire, and my heart still yearns after dear little Sunnyside. This letter, I trust, will find you up there, and must answer for the household, for I have not time to write any more. Give my love to all the girls. I will not name any one in particular, lest it might appear like giving a preference; and God knows I love them all with all my heart. Oh! what would I not give to be once more among them.

The following is in reply to a letter from myself, informing him how I had invested some funds left in my hands, and giving some personal details:

[*To Pierre M. Irving.*]

PARIS, June 26, 1842.

MY DEAR PIERRE:

I have just received your most welcome letter of May 31st, and have read it with great interest. I thank you heartily for your kind attention to my pecuniary affairs, and am well pleased with the investment you have made.

* * * I am delighted with the account you give of your nest at the bank. * * * I presume the iron safe which you extol as such a "convenient fixture," must have become necessary to hoard up the bags of money you are now accumulating. * * *

* * * Since I begun this letter, Alexander Hamilton and Carson Brevoort have reached Paris, and have brought me a thousand interesting details about home. Being now joined by my household, I shall set forward for Spain as soon as possible, though I suppose they will want a little time at Paris to fit themselves out. I am anxious to be at my post, to have my establishment formed, my books and papers about me, and to get settled. The restless life I have led for some months past has grown extremely irksome, and the continual shifting of the scene, and of the *dramatis personæ*, distracts my mind without interesting me. I am too old a frequenter of the theatre of life to be much struck with novelty, pageant, or stage effect, and could willingly have remained in my little private *loge* at Sunnyside, and dozed out the rest of the performance.

Do write often, and let me know all about your own concerns, and the concerns of those around you. My heart dwells among you all at home, and my thoughts are continually reverting thither. Your affectionate uncle,

WASHINGTON IRVING.

To a postscript added to my letter by my wife, he replied as follows:

MY DEAR HELEN:

If you knew with what avidity and relish I devoured your *half* letter, you would immediately sit down and write me a whole one. * * * The merest gossip about home and its everyday concerns would be more prized by me than the finest turned periods. The accidental mention you make in your letter about the green sodded bank before the cottage, and about Julia and Mary in their new bonnets and dresses, has presented home pictures that speak at once to my heart.

* * * I have been living as quietly as I could for some time past, in Sarah's pretty little establishment, trying to keep out of the turmoil of the great world; for my desire has been not to *mount the Minister*, if possible, until my arrival in Spain, having no great relish for the pageantry of courts, or the thronged saloons of fashionable life; but I am drawn into the vortex occasionally in spite of myself, so am kept in a half-drowned state, neither one thing nor t'other; neither enjoying repose nor dissipation; like a poor drenched Yankee fisherman whom I once met with, shivering, and drying himself before a fire in a little seashore inn at Martha's Vineyard, and who, tired of being neither fish nor flesh, wished he was "clever-*ly* dead." The fact is, I am spoiled by the life I have led at

Sunnyside, and have not, during the whole time that I have been in Europe, had one of those right-down frolicksome moods that I have enjoyed at the cottage; but, indeed, they would not be becoming in diplomatic life. I shall therefore put by all my merriment until my return home, and will endeavor, in the mean time, to be dignified and dull.

* * * I am, my dear Helen, your affectionate uncle,

WASHINGTON IRVING.

CHAPTER XI.

PASSAGES OF A LETTER TO HENRY BREVOORT—LETTER TO MRS. PARIS FROM BAYONNE—BORDEAUX REMINISCENCES—ARRIVAL AT MADRID, AND OCCUPATION OF HIS NEW HOME—DOMESTIC DETAILS—DUKE DE GOR—AUDIENCE OF THE MINISTER OF FOREIGN AFFAIRS—INTERVIEW WITH THE REGENT AT HIS PALACE OF BUENA VISTA—AUDIENCE OF THE QUEEN AT THE ROYAL PALACE—LETTER TO MRS. ROMEYN—PASSAGES FROM LETTERS TO EBENEZER IRVING.

THE following lines were addressed to Henry Brevoort from the office of the Legation at Paris, in reply to a letter from that gentleman brought by his son, J. Carson Brevoort, whom he was to have with him as an attaché at Madrid. "I am delighted to have him with me," he writes. "My heart warms toward him, not merely on his own account, but also on your own. He seems like a new link in our old friendship, which commenced when we were both about his age, or even younger, and which I have always felt as something almost fraternal." Then, after giving a reason for his being detained eight or ten days longer in Paris, he adds:

I am anxious to get to my post and relieve my predecessor, Mr. Vail, who wishes to get to the mountains with his family for the health of his children. I am desirous, also, of forming my establishment, and feeling myself once more settled. The unsettled life I have led for some months past begins to be extremely irksome. I have enough to do to bother me, yet no settled occupation to interest me. My mind is perplexed by arrangements for my domestic establishment and solicitude about my new career, and, with all this, I am harassed by the claims of society, which, with all my exertions, I cannot fight off Paris and London are terrible places for these kind of claims, which cut up one's time, disturb one's quiet, and render life a continual round of empty toils. I am amused with the solicitude of our friend ——— on my account, who thinks I am turning my back upon fortune, and ruining my prospects in life by neglecting to follow up the friendships proffered me in saloons. He could restrain his feelings no longer, a few evenings since, at an evening party, where the Duchess of ——— had sought an acquaintance with me, and held me for some time in very amiable conversation. On leaving her, ——— took me aside, and implored me to leave a card the next day for the duchess, and at the same time read me a most affectionate lecture on my neglect of this piece of etiquette with respect to various other persons of rank. He attributes all this to my excessive modesty, not dreaming that the empty intercourse of saloons with people of rank and fashion could be a bore to one who has run the rounds of society for the greater part of half a century, and who likes to consult his own humor and pursuits.

In the following letter, written when he was accomplishing his journey from Paris to Madrid, in company with the future members of his diplomatic family, we have a touching allusion to his former sojourn at Bordeaux, where he and his brother Peter spent four months, prior to their entrance into Spain in 1826:

[*To Mrs. Paris, New York.*]

BAYONNE, July 20, 1842.

MY DEAR SISTER.

Here I am, in the frontier town of France, with the Pyrénées in view, which I shall be traversing in the course of the day. My journey from Paris hither has been very pleasant. * * * We stopped at several fine old historical places, such as Orleans, Tours, Poitiers, and Angoulême. My fellow travellers are excellent companions, young and fresh and buoyant, and we get on joyously together. I have picked up a most valuable servant at Paris, a mulatto named Benjamin Gowien, native of South Carolina, who came out with Mr. Middleton when he went Minister to Russia, remained with him ten or twelve years, and has been travelling about Europe in various capacities for twenty-four years past. He speaks most of the European languages fluently, is a capital travelling servant, and, indeed, a valuable servant at all points, steady, quiet, respectful, and trustworthy. He has already been three times at Madrid, and made himself well acquainted with the language and with the customs of the country. I write particularly on this point, as I know you will feel some solicitude about my personal comforts. I passed between four and five days at Bordeaux, among my excellent friends the Guestiers, Johnsons, and Bartons. I was received by them as if I were one of their family connection. That good old lady, Mrs. Johnson, the great friend of our dear brother Peter, I found still in good health, though complaining of advanced age. My heart was full on meeting with her, for I thought of the many happy hours I had passed in her company and under her hospitable roof, with our dear brother. The good old lady received me with the warmest affection, and talked in the kindest and most touching manner about past times. My sojourn at Bordeaux was indeed full of heartfelt recollections, for here my dear brother was constantly by my side, enjoying the cordial intercourse with these excellent people, who all cherish the kindest remembrances of him. Indeed, who ever knew him without loving him? For my own part, never have I felt his loss more deeply than since my return to Europe, where every step I take recalls him to my mind, and recalls something he has done or said; some happy observation, some tasteful remark, some delightful pleasantry, from him whose whole life was an exemplification of every excellence.

At the close of his journey, after reaching Madrid on the morning of July 25th, and reconnoitring his establishment, he writes to his sister, Mrs. Paris:

I found the house in good order, and commodious. Juana (late head maid to Mrs. Vail, now my housekeeper) showed me through the rooms. Benjamin, my valet, who had travelled with me from Paris, brought my trunks to the house, and I at once found myself at home. The young gentlemen have since been here, chosen their rooms, and are to bring their luggage in the course of the day. Until my china ware, linen, &c., &c., arrive from France, we have to make shift by hiring bedding, table furniture, &c.; but we shall all feel delighted to be under our own roof, and settled. I like the appearance of my new servants, especially Lorenzo and Juana; their countenances, deportment, and mode of dressing themselves are highly in their favor, and I make no doubt I shall find them to answer to the high recommendations of Mr. Vail, with whom they have resided ever since he has been here. My cook, Antonio, who is a Greek, is said to be excellent in his art. He is not very brilliant in appearance, but, as he will be among pots and kettles, it is not of much moment.

It seems strange to me to find myself, all at once, the master of a new home, walking from room to room, all having the look of a long-established abode; strange servants running at my call, and bowing to me with profound respect. My own chamber, which is a very spacious one, is already all in order, my trunks all emptied, and their contents neatly arranged by Benjamin in the various drawers and presses, and everything has an air as if I had been master here for a long time past.

To the same, he writes, five days later (July 30th), giving a glimpse into the composition of his household, and a sketch of his meeting with his Granada friend, the Duke de Gor:

I am completely installed in the late residence of Mr. Vail, and shall probably continue to reside there for some time to come, as it is not easy to find a suitable habitation in that part of the city which I should prefer. I am in one wing, or half, of the hotel of the Duke of San Lorenzo; the opposite wing is occupied by Mr. Albuquerque, Brazilian resident Minister, who married one of the Miss Oakeys, of New York, so that we have a very pleasant and intelligent countrywoman for near neighbor. We are not far from the royal library and the royal palace.

I have made Benjamin my butler, or upper servant, as I

found he best understood the business, and had the most judgment. He appears to manage the house extremely well. Lorenzo is footman, or valet. Juana is housemaid, and has charge of the linen, &c., &c. Antonio is cook. The young gentlemen have made a page, or tiger, of a nephew of Lorenzo, a boy, whom they keep to loiter in the antechamber, run their errands, &c. Such is my household. As I have no horses yet, I have not engaged a coachman, though I have bespoken a trusty one, who is well recommended.

The other morning, as I was seated in the saloon, conversing with a gentleman, the servant announced the Duke de Gor; in a moment I was in his arms. You may remember that this was the nobleman with whom I was so intimate at Granada, at whose house I was so often a guest, and who, with his children, made me frequent visits in the Alhambra. He is now resident with his family in Madrid. I cannot express to you how rejoiced I was to see him. He is a most estimable character in every respect. One of the *Moderados*, and therefore not exactly in favor with the party in power. He is a leading man, however, in all public institutions, and the Duchess is at the head of many of the charitable institutions. The Duke gave me anecdotes of my friends in Granada. Mateo, on the strength of my writings, is quite the cicerone of Granadá and the Alhambra. Dolores and her husband reside elsewhere. The lovely little Nina, the daughter of the old Count, she who was quite my admiration and delight, is dead. * * * The Duke was accompanied by a young gentleman, whom he recalled to my recollection as little Nicholas, *alias*, *el rey chico*, who, a very small boy, had chased bats about the vaulted halls of the Alhambra. * * *

An evening or two since, I had my audience of the Minister of Foreign Affairs, the Count Almodovar, who received me in the most courteous manner, expressing his satisfaction at my being sent to this court. I delivered him an official copy of the President's letter to the Queen, and requested that a day might be assigned for me to present the original to the Regent. The day after to-morrow (Monday), at one o'clock, is appointed for the ceremonial. Mr. Albuquerque (hitherto *chargé d'affaires*) will present his letters of credence as resident Minister at the same time. This ceremony over, I shall be a regularly accredited Minister, and will then make my visits of ceremony to the heads of departments and the gentlemen of the diplomatic corps. I am curious to have this presentation, that I may have an interview with Espartero, the Regent, who certainly is one of the most remarkable men of the age. I have as yet only seen him one day in public, on the Prado, when I was pleased with his soldier-like air and manly deportment.

The following letter relates his audience with the Regent and the Queen, and reads, in some of its particulars, like a chapter in the romance of history. In sending it unsealed to Mrs. Storrow, at Paris, to be read and forwarded, he writes: "You are curious about the little Queen and her sister. The enclosed letter to your mother will give you some particulars about them. I feel a great interest in them, isolated as they are at such a tender age, surrounded by dreary magnificence, and by the political and military precautions incident to the present position of the Government."

[*To Mrs. Paris, New York.*]

MADRID, Aug. 3, 1842.

MY DEAR SISTER:

The day before yesterday I had my audience of the Regent, Espartero, Duke of Victoria, to present to him my original letter of credence from the President to the Queen. I was accompanied by Mr. Vail, who went to take leave, and by Alexander Hamilton as Secretary of Legation. We were in diplomatic uniform. The Regent resides in a very spacious palace called Buena Vista, formerly belonging to the Prince of the Peace. It has an elevated site, with terraces in front, so that it might resist an attack and maintain a respectable defence—an important consideration in the residence of the present military head of the Government, who is surrounded by dangers, and the object of incessant machinations.

We passed by sentinels posted at the entrance and in various parts of the palace, and were introduced into an anteroom of spacious dimensions, with busts of Espartero in two of the corners, and a picture of him in one of his most celebrated battles. Some of his officers and aides-de-camp were in this room, as well as Mr. Cavalcanti de Albuquerque, *chargé d'affaires* of Brazil, who came to deliver letters of credence as resident Minister. After a little while, we (Mr. Vail, Hamilton, and myself) were ushered into an inner saloon, at one end of which Espartero stationed himself, with Count Almodovar, Minister of State, on his right hand. I advanced, and read in Spanish a short address, stating that I had the honor of delivering the letter of the President to the Queen into his hands, as Regent of the kingdom, and expressing the sentiments of respect and good will entertained by my Government for the sovereign of this country, for its institutions, and its people; its desire to draw still closer the bonds of comity which exist between the two nations, and its ardent wish for the prosperity and glory of Spain under its present constitutional form of government. I concluded by expressing my own feelings of gratification in being appointed to a mission, the only object of which, I trusted, would be to cultivate the relations of good will between my own country and a country which I had ever held in the highest consideration. My address was well received, and the Regent replied in a manly, frank, cordial, and courteous manner, responding to the expressions of national good will, and ending with some complimentary expressions to myself. I then introduced Mr. Hamilton as Secretary of Legation; after which Mr. Vail, having taken leave of the Regent, with mutual expressions of respect and good will, we retired to the anteroom, to make way for the Brazilian Minister.

It being signified to us that the Queen would receive us at the royal palace, we drove thither, but had to wait some time in the apartment of Count Almodovar. After a while, we had notice that the Queen was prepared to receive us. We accordingly passed through the spacious court, up the noble staircase, and through the long suites of apartments of this splendid edifice, most of them silent and vacant, the casements closed to keep out the heat, so that a twilight reigned throughout the mighty pile, not a little emblematical of the dubious fortunes of its inmates. It seemed more like traversing a convent than a palace. I ought to have mentioned, that on ascending the grand staircase, we found the portal at the head of it, opening into the royal suite of apartments, still bearing the marks of the midnight attack upon the palace in October last, when an attempt was made to get possession of the persons of the little Queen and her sister, to carry them off, that their presence might give strength and authority to the party of the Queen Mother (Queen Maria Christina, now at Paris), in any contemplated insurrection or invasion of the country to regain the authority which she had abdicated. The marble casements of the doors had been shattered in several places, and the double doors themselves pierced all over with bullet holes, from the musketry that played upon them from the staircase during that eventful night. What must have been the feelings of those poor children, on listening, from their apartment, to the horrid tumult, the outcries of a furious multitude, and the reports of firearms, echoing and reverberating through the vaulted halls and spacious courts of this immense edifice, and dubious whether their own lives were not the object of the assault!

After passing through various chambers of the palace, now silent and sombre, but which I had traversed in former days, on grand court occasions in the time of Ferdinand VII, when they were glittering with all the splendor of a court, we paused in a great saloon, with high vaulted ceiling incrusted with florid devices in porcelain, and hung with silken tapestry, but all in dim twilight like the rest of the palace. At one end of the saloon a door opened to an almost interminable range of other chambers, through which, at a distance, we had a glimpse of some indistinct figures in black. They glided into the saloon slowly, and with noiseless steps. It was the little Queen, with her governess, Madame Mina, widow of the general of that name, and her guardian, the excellent Arguelles, all in deep mourning for the Duke of Orleans. The little Queen advanced some steps within the saloon, and then paused; Madame Mina took her station a little distance behind her. The Count Almodovar then introduced me to the Queen in my official capacity, and she received me with a grave and quiet welcome, expressed in a very low voice. She is nearly twelve years of age, and is sufficiently well grown for her years. She has a somewhat fair complexion, quite pale, with bluish or light gray eyes; a grave demeanor, but a graceful deportment. I could not but regard her with deep interest, knowing what important concerns depended upon the life of this fragile little being, and to what a stormy and precarious career she might be destined. Her solitary position, also, separated from all her kindred except her little sister, a mere effigy of royalty in the hands of statesmen, and surrounded by the formalities and ceremonials of state, which spread sterility around the occupant of a throne. I must observe, however, that the little Queen and her sister are treated with great deference and protecting kindness; that in Madame Mina, and in the upright, intelligent, and kind-hearted Arguelles, they have the best of guardians. * * *

As I was retiring from the presence chamber, I was overtaken by Arguelles, who accosted me in the most cordial manner, reminding me of our having met in London, at the time of my return from Spain, when he was in a state of exile. I had not recollected the circumstance, though I well remembered having heard him often spoken of during my former residence in Spain, as one of the best spirits of the nation. He promised to call upon me, and I look forward with interest to cultivating an intimacy with a man who holds in his hands a sacred trust, so important to the future destinies of Spain. He and Espartero are men I felt extreme interest in seeing. Espartero is a fine, manly, soldier-like fellow, with a frank deportment, a face full of resolution and intelligence, and a bright, beaming, black eye. He was dressed in full uniform, with various orders. He has before him a grand career, if he follows it out as he has begun, and is permitted to carry it to a successful termination. I am inclined to think his ambition of the right kind, and that he has the good of his country at heart. If he can conduct the affairs of Spain through the storms and quicksands that beset his regency; if he can establish the present constitutional form of government on a firm basis, and, when the Queen arrives at the age to mount the throne, resign the power into her hands, and give up Spain to her, reviving in its industry and its resources, peaceful at home and respected abroad, he will leave a name in history to be enrolled among the most illustrious of patriots.

I cannot but feel a deep interest in the fortunes of this harassed, impoverished, depressed, yet proud-spirited and noble country, and a most earnest desire to see it relieved from its troubles and embarrassments, and reëstablished in a prosperous and independent stand among the nations.

* * * * *

I am looking for the arrival of my books and papers, which were forwarded from New York to Cadiz. As soon as I receive them, I shall set to work at my Life of Washington, and foresee that I shall have abundant leisure here for literary occupation.

These expectations of leisure for literary occupation were doomed to be sadly frustrated by a long indisposition, and other interruptions consequent upon his diplomatic position.

The following is addressed to a niece, a daughter of his deceased sister, then residing temporarily at Sunnyside, and gives an interesting picture of a day's life at Madrid:

[*To Mrs. Eliza Romeyn.*]

MADRID, Aug. 16, 1842.

MY DEAR ELIZA:

* * * * * *

Having no news to tell you that is not in the other letters to the family, I shall give you a picture of the routine of one day, which will serve pretty much for a specimen of every day in the week. I rise about five o'clock, that I may have a good start of the sun, which rules like a tyrant throughout the day. Throwing open the doors and windows of my chamber, to dmit a free current of the morning air, I occupy myself reading and writing until about eight o'clock. At this time the distant sound of military music gives notice of the troops on their way to relieve guard at the royal palace. In a little while the horse guards pass under my window, with a band of music on horseback, performing some favorite march or military air. I watch and listen as they prance down the street, between spacious dwellings of the nobility, and turn into the passage leading to the palace; by this time another band of music comes swelling from a distance, and the foot guards approach in quick step to some glorious march or waltz; by the time these have disappeared, I am summoned to breakfast, which is always a lively meal with us. While we are seated at breakfast, we again hear the strains of military music, and the troops come back from relieving guard, reversing the order of their march—the foot guards coming first, and the horse guards afterward. This pageant, which invariably takes place at the same hour every morning, is a regale of which we never get tired. On our breakfast table are laid the Madrid gazettes, which seldom contain anything of peculiar interest. Shortly after breakfast arrives the mail, with Paris and London papers, which occupy us some time in reading and discussing news. Should the mail bring, as it sometimes does, a packet of letters for the different members of the household, giving us the news and gossip of home, there is a complete scene of excitement, each hurrying on his letters, and calling out, every moment, some piece of intelligence, or some amusing anecdote. This over, we separate to our different rooms and pursuits, exchanging visits occasionally, as circumstances may require or humors dictate. The front windows of my apartments look into one of the main streets, traversing the city from the Prado, or public walk, to the royal palace, so that every movement of consequence is sure to pass through it. Immediately opposite some of my windows is a small square, with the *ayuntamiento*, or town hall, on one side, and a huge mansion on the other, in a tower of which Francis I is said to have been confined when a prisoner in Madrid. In the centre of this square is a public fountain, thronged all day, and until a late hour of the night, by water carriers, male and female servants, and the populace of the neighborhood, all waiting for their turns to replenish their kegs, pitchers, and other water vessels. An officer of police attends to regulate their turns; but such is the demand for water in this thirsty climate at this thirsty season, that the fountain is a continual scene of strife and clamor. The groups that form around it, however, in their different costumes, are extremely picturesque. My day, during the hot weather, is chiefly passed in my bedroom, which I likewise make my study. It is lofty and spacious, about thirty feet by twenty-two. The heat of day is shut out, as in the rest of the house, and just sufficient light admitted to permit me to read and write. Indeed, a kind of twilight reigns throughout a Spanish house during the summer heats. At five o'clock we dine, after which some take a siesta, or lounge about until the evening is sufficiently advanced to take a promenade either on the Prado, or on the esplanade in front of the royal palace. Such is the dull heat, however, that occasionally lingers in the streets, that I frequently remain at home all the evening, taking my seat in the balcony of my room, where I can catch any night breeze that is stirring, and can overlook the street. Between nine and ten a running footman gives notice, by the sound of a bugle, of the approach of the Queen, on her return from her evening's drive in the Retiro and in the Prado. Next come three or four horsemen in advance; then the royal carriage, drawn by six horses, in which are the little Queen and her sister, and their *aya*, or governess, Madame Mina. As the carriage is an open barouche, and passes immediately under my balcony, I have a full view of these poor, innocent little beings, in whose isolated situation I take a great interest. Mounted attendants ride beside the carriage, and it is followed by a troop of horse, after which comes another carriage and six, with those whose duties bring them in immediate attendance upon the persons of the Queen and Princess. After this cortege has passed by, I continue in my balcony until a late hour, enjoying the gradually cooling night air, which grows more and more temperate until toward midnight, when I go to bed.

Such is the routine of most of my days during this hot weather, occasionally varied by a sultry visit of ceremony in the course of the day, or a stroll late in the evening to the Prado, or the esplanade about the palace.

* * * * * *

I have as yet been but once to the royal museum of paintings, but it was like a peep into a gold mine. The collection was one of the very best in Europe when I was here before, but such treasures have been added to it of late years, that, to my mind, it surpasses all others that I have seen. This of itself will be an inexhaustible resource to me.

* * * * * *

Write to me as often as you feel disposed. Your letters just such as I delight to receive.

Your affectionate uncle,

WASHINGTON IRVING.

will be seen, by the following extracts from his letters to his brother Ebenezer, still his agent in negotiating with the booksellers, that he could make no further arrangements with Lea & Blanchard, of Philadelphia, for the right of publishing his works. He had not expected a renewal of the arrangement such as the last, which was about to expire, at a positive yearly stipend, but it had occurred to him that an arrangement might be made by which they might continue to sell his works already printed, they allowing him a stipulated sum on each copy sold. This would enable them to trade off the stock on hand, and him to participate in the profits.

MADRID, *Sept. 8th*, 1842.— * * * I observe that Lea & Blanchard decline the arrangement I proposed. I presume, therefore, the source of income from that quarter is effectually dried up for the present. * * *

To the same brother he replies, somewhat later:

* * * You give me a sad account of my literary harvest; everything behind me seems to have turned to chaff and stubble, and if I desire any further profits from literature, it must be by the further exercise of my pen. * * * If I can have one good course of literary occupation, I may produce another profitable crop, though I cease to be very sanguine of profit.

* * * I have all my books and papers now around me, and am about to set to work. I find I have no copies of the Crayon Miscellany, containing the Tour on the Prairies, the Legends of the Conquest of Spain, and Abbotsford and Newstead Abbey. I wish you would send me a set of each. * * * You may send them by the captain of any ship bound to Cadiz, and direct them to the care of Alexander Barton, Esq., Consul of the United States at that port.

He was now meditating to use what leisure he could spare from more important literary occupations, in preparing revised and improved editions of all his works, to be put forth at some future period, when business had revived, and the world was once more prosperous. Hence his request for the copies of the Crayon Miscellany.

I close this chapter with the following extract of a letter to his brother Ebenezer, upon which I venture no comment, further than to state that the remains of his brother Peter were now deposited in a churchyard about three miles south of Sunnyside, and were afterward transferred to the spot where he himself hopes "some day or other to sleep" his "last sleep."

I mentioned, in a former letter, my wish that you would have an iron railing put around the grave of our dear brother Peter, and a gravestone within, with a simple inscription of his name, age, date of his birth, &c. Have honeysuckles and shrubs planted inside of the inclosure, that they may, in time, overrun it. I had intended to have his remains transported to a family vault or burying ground which I contemplated establishing at the old Dutch Sleepy Hollow church. * * * Even now, perhaps, it might be as well to buy of the widow Beekman a few yards square of the woody height, adjacent to the north end of the burying ground, and have it enclosed with a paling for the family place of sepulture. * * * I think a family burying place, with a gate opening into the main burying ground, would be preferable to a vault. If this should be determined upon, it would not be necessary to put up the iron railing above mentioned, as our dear brother's remains might be conveyed to the above-mentioned place. Think of all this, and carry it into effect. It is a thing that lies near my heart. I hope, some day or other, to sleep my last sleep in that favorite resort of my boyhood.

P. S.—You do not mention, in any of your letters, whether neighbor Forkel has still the superintendence of Mrs. Jones' property. I like to hear occasionally how all my country neighbors are coming on—the Manns, the Forkels, the Ackers, &c. Give a kind word to them occasionally in my name. They have always proved good neighbors to me.

CHAPTER XII.

LETTER TO MRS. PARIS—SKETCH OF SPANISH POLITICS, AND SPANISH CHARACTERS — THE INSURRECTION IN OCTOBER, 1841 — ATTEMPT TO GET POSSESSION OF THE PERSON OF THE QUEEN—THE ROYAL PALACE—ITS SITUATION—DETAILS OF HIS FIRST AUDIENCE WITH THE QUEEN — HIS SYMPATHY IN HER POSITION—DIPLOMATIC THEMES—CURIOSITY ABOUT THE DELIVERY OF HIS CREDENTIALS—LOUIS PHILIPPE.

THE long domestic letter which I now offer, gives a peep into the affairs of the Court, and abounds in details which will account to us for the deep interest Mr. Irving took in his first audience with the little Queen. "I must confess," he writes to Mrs. Pierre M. Irving, "the more I get acquainted with the present state of Spanish politics and the position of the Government, the more does the whole assume a powerful dramatic interest, and I shall watch with great attention every shifting of the scene. The future career of this gallant soldier, Espartero, whose merits and services have placed him at the head of the Government, and the future fortunes of these isolated little princesses, the Queen and her sister, have an uncertainty hanging about them worthy of the fifth act of a melodrama."

[*To Mrs. Paris, Tarrytown.*]

MADRID, Sept. 2, 1842.

MY DEAR SISTER.

In the letter last received from you, dated July 19th, you give me, as usual, a world of news from the *cottage*. I will, in return, give you a little history of the *palace*. I know you like to hear, now and then, what is going on in the grand world, and, from your little sheltered country nook, to "take a peep at royalty." So I will perform the promise I made you in a former letter, to give you an inkling of Spanish politics, that you may understand the present state of this harassed country.

Spain, having long experienced the evils of an absolute monarchy, where the will of the monarch was supreme law, has made repeated struggles to establish a constitutional form of government, such as is enjoyed in England and France, where the power of the king is limited and controlled by the constitution, and where the people have a voice in affairs through elective chambers of legislation. It succeeded in forming such a constitution in 1812, with the approbation of its sovereign, Ferdinand VII, who was at that time detained by Napoleon in France. The constitution was overthrown by Napoleon, who placed his brother Joseph on the throne. At the downfall of Napoleon, Ferdinand regained his throne; but, false to the nation, he refused to restore the constitution, persecuted those who had supported it, and reigned absolute monarch. A revolution, in 1820, was the consequence; the constitution was again proclaimed, and Ferdinand again swore to support it, declaring that, in opposing it, he had acted under the influence of bad advisers. A French army, sent by Charles X, again trampled down the constitution, and replaced the faithless Ferdinand in absolute power, which he exercised for the remainder of his worthless life. At the time of my former visit to Spain, he was on the throne, and the French troops which had placed him there still lingered in the country. The liberties of Spain seemed completely prostrate, and many of her most enlightened, virtuous, and patriotic men were in exile.

In 1829, Ferdinand married, for his fourth wife, Maria Christina, sister of the King of Naples, and niece of the present Queen of France. By her he had two daughters, his only children. In 1833, being low in health, without prospect of recovery, he became anxious to secure the succession to the throne to his own progeny; but here arose a difficulty. By long usage, the *Salique* law of France, which excludes females from the exercise of regal authority, had become naturalized in Spain. According to this, the King's eldest brother, Don Carlos, being next male heir, would inherit the crown. Ferdinand, however, supported by the opinions of men learned in the law, revived the old Spanish law of succession, which made females equally entitled to inherit with males, and quoted the reign of the illustrious Isabella of glorious memory as a case in point. The question agitated the country even before the death of Ferdinand. Don Carlos insisted on his rights, and had a strong party in his favor, composed of many of the aristocracy, who knew him to be an absolute monarchist; and by the monks and a great part of the clergy, who knew him to be a bigot. The Queen, Maria Christina, of course, stood up for the rights of her infant daughter, and her cause was the popular one, having all the *Liberals*, or those who were anxious for a constitutional government, in its favor.

Ferdinand died in 1833, and, in conformity to his will and

testament, his eldest daughter, then but three years of age, was proclaimed Queen, by the name of Isabella II, and her mother, Maria Christina, Queen Regent, to exercise the royal authority in the name of her daughter, until the latter should be fourteen years of age; when, according to Spanish law, she is of age to ascend the throne. Maria Christina was likewise constituted guardian to the Queen during her minority.

Don Carlos immediately raised the standard of rebellion, and here commenced the modern "war of succession" which desolated Spain for seven years. The Liberals rallied round the standard of the Queen Regent, and for a time she was exceedingly popular. Indeed, never had a woman a better opportunity of playing a noble part as a mother and a sovereign; but she proved herself unworthy of both characters. What first impaired her popularity with the Liberals was the opposition which she manifested to all their plans of salutary reform; to this, it was suspected, she was secretly instigated by her uncle, Louis Philippe, King of France, who, though his own power originated in constitutional reform, has constantly been hostile to constitutional reform in Spain.

Another deadly blow to the popularity, and, indeed, respectability of the Queen Regent, was an unworthy connection which she formed, not very long after the death of her husband, with one of the royal body guards, named Muñoz, whom she subsequently advanced in rank and fortune. This scandalous connection, it is said, was ultimately reconciled to ideas of decency by a private marriage; though such a marriage was not valid in point of Spanish law, and, if promulgated, would have incapacitated her from acting as Regent, or as guardian to the Queen. The effect of this connection, in fact, was to render Maria Christina remiss in the exercise of her high office as Regent, and, what was still worse, neglectful of her sacred duties to her legitimate children; and the little Queen and her sister were left to the interested and venial services of the attendants about a court, to supply the want of the vigilant tenderness of a mother.

At length, in 1836, a popular movement wrung from the fears of Maria Christina what it was impossible to obtain from her gratitude or her sense of justice, and she was compelled to restore the constitution of 1812. From this time, it is thought, she contemplated the probability of a retirement from Spain. She had already amassed great property from her yearly allowance of two millions of dollars. This was sent out of the kingdom, as were large sums arising from the sale of every object under her control that she could convert into money. Muñoz, her minion, who formerly appeared everywhere with her in public, had for some time ceased to make himself conspicuous; but it was known that she had lavished much of her wealth on him and his family, and that her children by this degrading union had alienated her thoughts from her regal offspring.

At length, in 1839, the civil war was brought to a close, and Don Carlos driven from the kingdom. A patriot general, Espartero, had risen to great popularity and influence by his successful campaigns, and was now commander-in-chief of the army, which idolized him, and virtually controller of the politics of the kingdom. By this time Maria Christina had made herself an object of *popular* distrust, and she gave a finishing blow to her ascendency, by signing an act vesting the appointment of all municipal officers in the Crown; thereby violating one of the grand principles of the constitution, and restoring, in a great measure, the absolute power of the throne. This rash measure she was secretly prompted to by the French Minister resident at this Court; but, before signing the act, she repaired to Barcelona, under pretence of taking the royal children there for sea bathing, but, in fact, to get the support of General Espartero and his victorious army, who were quartered in that city. Maria Christina miscalculated on her own reputed powers of persuasion, and on the *persuasibility*, if I may use the term, of Espartero. That general remained true to the popular cause, and warned her against the consequences of the act she contemplated. She disregarded his advice and his remonstrances, and signed the act. The consequence was, a burst of indignation from all parts of Spain, under the appalling effects of which, and the public obloquy of her connection with Muñoz, she abdicated the regency and retired from Spain, leaving her royal children to their fortunes. The little Queen and her sister, then of the respective ages of ten and eight years, were reconducted in state by Espartero to Madrid, where they were received with acclamation, replaced in their usual residence in the royal palace, and surrounded with the usual state and ceremony accorded to their rank and station. The office of regent being vacant by the abdication of Maria Christina, Espartero was elected, and has hitherto discharged the sovereign duties with great integrity. Maria Christina having also forfeited her claims to the guardianship of the Queen and her sister, that important trust was confided to Don Augustin Arguelles, one of the most intelligent, upright, and patriotic men of Spain, who, for his lofty principles, suffered exile under the perfidious Ferdinand. A kind of maternal care has likewise been exerted over the children by the Countess Mina, widow of a patriot general. She fills the station of *aya*, or governess, and is a woman of amiable character and unblemished virtue. Their education is superintended by Quintana, one of the most learned men of the kingdom; the royal children, therefore, are more likely to be well educated and trained up in pure principles under the persons of worth who now have charge of them, than they were under the former misrule of a corrupt and licentious court. They are treated, too, with mingled respect and tenderness; still they cannot but feel their isolated situation, without a mother's care, and separated from all their kindred. * * *

Maria Christina, on leaving Spain, repaired to the Court of France, where she was received with great distinction, and where she has since resided, countenanced and favored by Louis Philippe and his Queen; the latter of whom, as I have before observed, is her aunt. Her residence at Paris and in its vicinity has become the focus of all kinds of machinations against the constitutional government of Spain. Her immense wealth gave her the means of fomenting insurrections, and the relics of the rebel armies, and the rebel generals and nobles ejected from the kingdom, have lent themselves to her plans. Louis Philippe is accused, and with apparent justice, of having countenanced her, and secretly promoted her plans, in the hope of increasing the power of his family by effecting a match between one of his sons and the little Queen. The consequence of all these plots beyond the Pyrénees, was an insurrection in the north of Spain, in the month of October last, when General O'Donnell (a Spaniard in spite of his name) seized upon the citadel of Pamplona, and proclaimed Maria Christina Queen Regent. The most nefarious part of this plot was an attempt to get possession of the persons of the little Queen and her sister, and bear them off to the rebel army, so as to give it the sanction of the royal presence. To promote this plan, immense sums had been spent in Madrid, to corrupt the soldiery and the people about the palace, and the evening of the 7th of October was the time appointed for the attempt. The royal palace stands on the confines of the city, on the brow of a steep descent sweeping down into the valley of the Manzanares; it overlooks the open country toward the Guadarrama mountains, which is so lonely, in the very vicinity of Madrid, that ten minutes' gallop from its walls takes you into scenes as savage and deserted as any of Salvator Rosa's. The palace is guarded every night by a body of troops, and is capable of a powerful defence; but the troops who were to mount guard that night were mostly under the influence of Generals Concha and Leon, who had been gained over to the conspiracy. Concha was an artful man, related by marriage to Espartero, so that, in this affair, he was guilty of a double treason. Leon was a brave, warm-hearted, weak-headed fellow, who, from his popularity with the soldiery, was made use of as a tool. It was a dark, tempestuous evening when the attempt was made. A part of the armed force was left to guard the avenues of the palace, and Concha and Leon, with a number of their followers, entered the main portal, rushed up the grand staircase, and expected to gain immediate entrance through the door leading into the Queen's suite of apartments, being guarded merely by a band of eighteen veteran halberdiers. To their astonishment, they met with a vigorous repulse from these gallant fellows, and several of the assailants were shot down. Repeated attempts were made to force an entrance, but were uniformly repelled with loss. The halberdiers ensconced themselves within the apartment, and fired through the woodwork of the door the moment they heard footsteps at the head of the staircase. In this way the door became completely riddled with bullet holes, which remain to this day, and many of the assailants were slain and wounded. In the mean time, the situation of the poor little Queen and her sister may be more easily imagined than described. The repeated discharges of firearms, which reverberated through the courts and halls of the palace; the mingled shouts and curses and groans and menaces which accompanied the attack, joined to the darkness of the night and the howling of the storm, filled their hearts with terror. They had no one with them but their *aya*, or governess, Madame Mina, and some of their female attendants, excepting their poor singing-master, who was as much frightened as any of the women. Ignorant of the object of this attack, and fearful that their own lives were menaced, the poor children gave themselves up to tears and outcries. The Queen threw herself into the arms of her governess, crying, "*Aya mia* (my dear *aya*), who are they? Are they rebels? What do they want of me?" The Princess was in convulsions in the arms of an attendant, making the most piteous exclamations. It was with the greatest difficulty that the governess was able to soothe them into some degree of calmness. The noise of firearms continued; attempts were heard to force a door leading through a private passage; two or three musket balls broke the windows of the apartment, but were stopped by the inside shutters. In the midst of these horrors, the poor little princess, trembling and sobbing, called to one of the ladies in attendance, "Inez, I wish to say something to you; Inez, I want to pray!" The wish of the innocent child was gratified; they all knelt down at the couch of the Queen, and prayed: "And I felt relieved," says Madame Mina, in her narrative of this eventful night, "I felt relieved by the tears which I shed on contemplating the situation of those two innocent beings, who, full of fervor, directed their supplications to Heaven to protect and deliver them from a peril, the extent of which no one knew so well as I." The clamor of the attack subsided, the firing became less frequent. The attendants now spread mattresses for the Queen and her sister in a corner of the apartment where they would be safe from any random shot; and the poor little beings, exhausted by the agitation and fatigue they had suffered, at length fell asleep.

The gallant defence of the handful of halberdiers effectually defeated this atrocious attempt. They kept the assailants at bay until assistance arrived. The alarm spread through Madrid. The regular troops and national guards assembled from all quarters; Espartero hastened to the scene of action, and the palace was completely surrounded. Concha and Leon, seeing the case was desperate, left their followers in the lurch, and consulted their own safety in flight. They spurred their horses to the open country, but Concha, being in ordinary dress, returned unobserved, concealed himself in Madrid, and ultimately escaped out of the kingdom. The heedless Leon, being in full general's uniform, was a marked object. He was discovered and arrested at some distance from Madrid, and, though great interest was made in his favor, was ultimately shot.

* * * * * *

The result of this brutal attempt has been to throw complete odium on the course of Maria Christina, to confound the enemies of the constitution, and to strengthen the hands of Government. The insurrection in the provinces was speedily put down. Maria Christina hastened to disavow all share in the conspiracy; but proofs are too strong against her, and the French Government stands chargeable with at least connivance. The stand which England has taken, of late, in the matter, and the declaration of ministers in Parliament that they would not quietly permit the hostile interference of any foreign power in the affairs of Spain, has had a happy effect in checking the machinations of France. Spain now enjoys a breathing spell, and, I hope, may be enabled to regulate her internal affairs, and recover from the exhausting effects of her civil wars. The little Queen is now nearly twelve years of age; in about two years more her minority will terminate, and, with it, the regency of Espartero. I hope, while the power still remains in his hands, he may be enabled to carry out his proposed plans of reform, and to confirm the constitutional government, so that it may not easily be shaken.

* * * * * *

The foregoing sketch will, I trust, enable you to form an idea of the position of Spanish affairs, and to take an interest in any particulars about this Court which I may hereafter have to relate. You will understand that Spain is now a constitutional monarchy, having its *Cortes*, or representative bodies of legislature, consisting of a senate and chamber of deputies; and that, until the Queen is fourteen years of age, Espartero (Duke of Victoria) holds the reins of government as Regent, in her name. He is a soldier of fortune, who has risen by his merits and his services, and been placed in his present elevated situation by the votes of the *Cortes*.

* * * * * *

You will now understand something of the jealousy and ill will that exists between this country and France, and of the failure of the embassy of Mr. Salvandy, which made so much noise last winter. However, as the last affair may have escaped your notice, and as you and I are now embarked in diplomacy, I will call your attention to it.

After the abdication and departure of Maria Christina from Spain, the French Government, by way of slight, suffered itself for a time to remain unrepresented at the Spanish Court, excepting by a temporary *chargé d'affaires*, whereas it has usually maintained a full embassy at Madrid. At length Louis Philippe, finding that he was exciting the indignation of the Spanish people against himself, and increasing their antipathy to his nation, determined to send an ambassador. Mr. Salvandy, a man of conspicuous talents, accordingly appeared at Madrid with a brilliant train; but here a difficulty arose: his letter of credence was addressed to the Queen, and he was instructed to deliver it *into her hands.* He demanded an audience of her for that purpose. It was objected, on the part of the Spanish Government, that the Queen, being yet a minor, was disqualified by the constitution from the performance of any public act; that a regent had been appointed, to whom, under that constitution, the regal power had been delegated, and who, in the name and stead of her Majesty, and at his own palace, would receive Mr. Salvandy, and from his hands the credentials of which he was the bearer. The ambassador refused to deliver his letters at any other place than at the royal palace, or into any other hands than those of the Queen herself; though, he observed, the Regent, if he thought proper, might be present at the ceremonial. The Spanish Government repeated its objections, and the ambassador wrote to Paris for new instructions. The Court of France approved of what he had done, and instructed him to persist; Louis Philippe doubtless being disposed to pass a slight upon the constitutional government, and to pass by the Regent as not being the actual head. The ambassador again demanded an audience of the Queen, adding, that if he were refused, he should require his passports, take down the French arms from the front of the embassy, and withdraw with the whole embassy from the country. The Spanish Government stood firm; the matter was discussed and argued on both sides, but the Spaniards were not to be argued into the admission of any slight or indignity to the constitutional Regent of their own election. Mr. Salvandy, after several days of fruitless discussion, at length demanded passports for the embassy, which were immediately granted, and he left Madrid with his retinue the same night. He moderated so much of his diplomatic threat, however, as to leave the escutcheon of the French arms standing over the gate of the embassy, and his second secretary, as *chargé d'affaires*, to take temporary care of the affairs of the mission; otherwise a complete departure would have been tantamount to a rupture between the two nations.

You will now understand why some little importance was given to my arrival as Minister at this court. There was a curiosity to know how I would act with respect to the delivery of my credentials. My written instructions were to present the President's letter of credence *to the Queen;* but, from conversations with the Government at Washington before my departure, I understood that I might regulate my conduct by circumstances. As it is a principle with us, therefore, to deal always in our diplomacy with the actual government of a country, I made no hesitation in delivering my letter into the hands of Espartero, at an audience given at his palace, specifying in my address that it was from the President to the Queen, and delivered into his hands as Regent of the kingdom. You have no doubt seen the bad translation of my address, as the

Government was careful to obtain from me a copy of it for publication, as it was the first time a foreign Minister had presented his credentials since the regency of Espartero. It was considered also as a precedent; and, indeed, the resident Minister of Brazil, who presented his credentials at the same time, but after me, and who is rather opposed to the present form of government, told me he should not have presented his letter of credence to Espartero, unless I had broken the way and set the example. Whether France will get over her pique, and make a step toward reconciliation with Spain, by sending a full mission, and authorizing her representative to acknowledge Espartero as the legitimate head of the Government, by delivering the letter of credentials into his hand, is yet to be seen. The conduct of France toward Spain, of late years, has been anything but fair and magnanimous; and Louis Philippe, in manifesting such hostility to the constitutional forms of the Government, and such a disposition to discountenance Espartero, the constitutional depositary of the regal power, seems singularly to have forgotten the history of his own elevation.

And now, having discussed these royal and diplomatic themes, I find it impossible, my dear sister, to descend to subjects of ordinary import, so shall conclude, for the present, with a promise of giving you some further anecdotes of courts, kings, and queens, in my future letters, finding these matters are so much to your taste. I would observe, however, that as this letter is really meant merely for your private amusement, I do not wish it to be shown about; a Minister ought not to be gossiping about diplomatic affairs. Keep it, therefore, *strictly among yourselves in the family.*

And so God bless you. Your affectionate brother,

WASHINGTON IRVING.

To myself, who had been left in charge of his pecuniary affairs, he writes, three days after the date of the preceding epistle:

MY DEAR PIERRE:

I have written so many family letters, of late, relative to myself and my Madrid concerns, of all of which you will probably learn the contents, that I have little to say to you on that head, not being able, like Paganini, to play a thousand variations on one string of my fiddle.

I find my home resources are drying up in various quarters, by the cessation of my arrangement with booksellers, the non-payment of dividend on stocks, &c. I trust, however, you have the ways and means to keep my home establishment on the usual footing. * * * Get all my funds, as soon as you can judiciously, out of these fluctuating stocks, and invest them safely, even though at less interest. I cannot afford to risk more losses for the chance of extra profits. * * *

I shall soon be comfortably settled in new quarters, with my books and papers about me, and shall then open a literary campaign, which I shall have ample leisure to prosecute, and which, I trust, will furnish me with the ways and means to abridge my absence from home, for I am anxious to pass as much as possible of the evening of my days among my relatives and friends at sweet little Sunnyside.

Of that "dear home," he had written to Mrs. Irving, the day before:

It seems to me as if I did not half enough appreciate that home when I was there, and yet I certainly delighted in it; but the longer I am away, the more the charm of distance gathers round it, until it begins to be all romance. I sometimes catch myself calculating the dwindling space of life that's left to me, and almost repining that so much of the best of it must be passed far away from all that I hold most dear and delightful; but I check such thoughts, and recollect how much there is around me to interest and exercise my mind. * * *

In the following letter to a juvenile niece, the youngest daughter of his brother Ebenezer, and one of the inmates of Sunnyside, he announces his change of habitation at Madrid, and gives a picture of his new abode. The letter opens, it will be perceived, in quite a sportive vein:

[*To Miss Charlotte Irving.*]

MADRID, Sept. 16, 1842.

MY DEAR CHARLOTTE:

Your letter of July 28th reached me three or four days since, and brought me a world of intelligence. First of all, your first appearance at the Tarrytown and Dobbs' Ferry *soirées*, held that evening at Mrs. Sheldon's, at which, I trust, you produced a proper sensation. Then the invasion of Sunnyside, by sea, by a roving *piragua*, fitted out at the port of Yonkers, and manned by Edgar and a desperate crew of ladies and gentlemen. Then the invasion by land, by Mrs. ——— and Mrs. ———'s mother, and Mrs. ———'s sister and Mr. ———'s mother—no, Mr ———'s aunt, and a Miss P., who was staying with Mrs. ———. And then the influx of all the ———s and of all the Dr. ———s. And then a second invasion by sea, of all the Hamiltons in the Dream, and the carrying off of half the garrison of Sunnyside to Rockland Lake and the mountains; and then the great party at Mr. ———'s, given to Mr. and Mrs. ———, to which Mrs. ——— did *not* think herself invited, but to which she afterward found she *was* invited, and which turned out a most delightful party. Guide us and keep us! what an eventful period of history we live in! Why, my dear Charlie, if matters go on at this rate, I shall find Sleepy Hollow wide awake by the time I come back.

And now, my exceeding good and very dear little woman, I will try to give you, in return for your very agreeable letter, some little inkling of my Spanish home and its affairs. I have just changed my residence, and have taken the principal apartment in a great Spanish house belonging to a bachelor nobleman named the Marquis de Mos, who has a bachelor's nest in one wing of it. I have such a range of *salons*, that it gives me quite an appetite to walk from my study to the dining room. Then the windows of the *salons* all face the south, and look into a little dilapidated garden, in the centre of which is an old, half-ruined marble fountain, with gold fish swimming about in it, and a superannuated triton in the middle, blowing a conchshell, out of which, in his younger days, there no doubt rose a jet of water. My own private apartment, consisting of a bedroom and study, is in one end of the building. My bedroom formerly served as an oratory or chapel to the mansion. It is a small octagon room, rising to a little cupola or dome, with little windows in the top, about fifteen feet from the floor, by which the chamber is lighted. These windows catch the first rays of the rising sun, and, as the oratory is prettily painted of a delicate pink, yellow, and pale green, and as the centre of the dome is gilded, the whole becomes beautifully lighted up. You have no idea what a splendid waking up I have sometimes in the morning. I don't think "glorious Apollo," with his bedchamber of sun-gilt clouds, has much the advantage of me. * * * My study is immediately adjacent to the oratory; one window overlooks the garden of an old convent, and has a fine view of the Regent's palace, and the distant groves of the Retiro.

* * * * * *

I have experienced a kind of home feeling of enjoyment since I have got into this house, that I have not felt before since my arrival in Madrid. My other residence was excessively noisy, and abounded with inconveniences, so that I could never feel at home in it; indeed, the very idea that I should remove as soon as I could find a house more to my mind, kept me unsettled and comfortless. Now, I trust, I am fixed for the whole of my sojourn in Madrid, and I consider myself singularly fortunate in finding in this uncomfortable metropolis so pleasant an abode.

The subjoined letter was written soon after the happy adjustment of the long-standing dispute between Great Britain and the United States respecting the Northeastern boundary, the amicable settlement of which the shipowning husband of his correspondent was about to commemorate by a design, to which he suggests, with humorous significance, a ludicrous heightening. The lady to whom it is addressed was a daughter of his deceased brother William, and was occupying the former homestead of Abijah Hammond, at Throgg's Neck, on the East River, a country retreat about fourteen miles from the city of New York, of which Washington remarks: "I recollect the place well, having visited it occasionally in my frolicking and dancing days, when it was the seat of great hospitality. One of the pleasantest balls I ever attended was in that mansion, at which divers respectable old ladies of the present day sparkled as belles."

[*To Mrs. Moses H. Grinnell.*]

MADRID, Sept. 30, 1842.

MY DEAR JULIA:

I have just received your delightful letter of August 25th, which was, indeed most welcome. I wrote to you not long since, in hopes of drawing from you a letter in return, but you have kindly anticipated me. I can easily imagine your satisfaction with your country residence; I know the old mansion well, and the delightful country in which it is situated, with its splendid advantages of water. I should think it would just hit Mr. Grinnell's fancy, and hope he may find loose spending money enough in his pocket to buy it. * * * Tell him not to cast all his bread upon the water in the shape of ships, however shipshaped they may be, but to anchor a little upon land in fast property. I like your idea of Lord Ashburton and Mr. Webster shaking hands, as an ornament for the stern of the new ship to be called after the former: perhaps the effect might be heightened, if you could bring in the boundary line, running across his lordship's toes.

I am delighted with the treaty; it has been negotiated in a fine spirit on both sides, and is a great achievement for Mr. Webster. He has remained in the Cabinet to some purpose, and now, if he thinks proper, may retire with flying colors; yet I should be loth to see such a statesman retire from the management of our affairs. What successor will give us such state papers? Who would have managed our Mexican correspondence in such style? Would to God he could remain in with satisfaction to himself, and have a good majority in Congress to back him.

I have just got myself settled in a pleasant habitation, which, I think, will be my home during my residence in Madrid. It is spacious, as all Spanish houses are, but quiet and clean, which are rare qualities in Madrid mansions. I have just given my first dinner; not such feasts as you give in New York, one of which would exhaust a Madrid market, but in a pretty French style, and to a small party; never, if I can help it, intending to exceed the limits of a social round table. I have, indeed, to play the Ambassador on a cautious scale. * * * Fortunately, there is no rivalry in expense in the diplomatic corps at Madrid, the British Minister being the only one that entertains, and his immense fortune putting competition out of the question. I find him very frank and cordial, and we are already on the most social terms.

I have had some brooding spells of homesickness since my arrival in Europe, but they are gradually wearing away, and I am now about to enter upon a career of literary occupation that will effectually dispel them.

* * * * * *

Mr. Grinnell, in his appendix to your letter, says that Mr. Webster inquired particularly after me, and expressed much interest in my mission. As yet my mission has called for but little exertion of diplomatic skill, there being no question of moment between the Governments, and I not being disposed to make much smoke where there is but little fuel. * * * I have been very quiet ever since my arrival in Madrid, getting my domestic affairs in order, and making myself acquainted with the complicated and entangled state of Spanish politics, but I shall now gradually take my stand in the diplomatic circle, and endeavor that it shall be an unobtrusive, but a firm one. * * *

It was not long after the date of this letter, that Mr. Irving addressed his fifth diplomatic despatch to the Honorable Secretary of State, presenting a sketch of the political affairs of Spain, which were just then rising to fever heat, as the time for the opening of the *Cortes* was approaching, and powerful preparations were making to displace the existing Cabinet. Mr. Webster used to speak in high terms of the interest of these papers, and once remarked to a friend, that he always laid aside every other correspondence to read a diplomatic despatch from Mr. Irving.

The following half-melancholy letter to his old companion at Madrid, Prince Demetri Ivanovitch Dolgorouki, now Russian Minister at Naples, was written when his young housemates, Hamilton, Brevoort, and Ames, were absent on a tour in Andalusia, to be gone four or five weeks, and he was living "in solitary dignity, pacing (his) great empty saloons to the echoes of his own footsteps."

Madrid, Oct. 18, 1842.

My dear Dolgorouki:

You certainly are one of the most faithful, long-suffering, and indulgent of friends, still to write to me, notwithstanding my neglect to answer your previous letters. But I am reforming as a correspondent, and henceforth, I trust, you will find me more punctual in my replies. In fact, I had grown quite indolent and self-indulgent in my happy little retreat on the banks of the Hudson, and needed something to rouse me into action. This most unlooked-for appointment to the Legation at Madrid has completely drawn me out of the oblivious influence of Sleepy Hollow, and thrown me once more into the midst of the busy world and its concerns.

And here I am, on our old campaigning ground, where we first became acquainted; but either I am or the place is greatly changed, for we seem to be quite strange to each other. I miss all my former intimates. Navarrete, grown old and infirm, has been absent from Madrid ever since my arrival. I look with an eye of wistful recollection at the house once inhabited by the D'Oubrils, which was my familiar and favorite resort. It is undergoing great repairs and alterations, to become the residence of some millionaire who has made a fortune by speculation. How often I recall the happy, happy hours I have passed there, and summon up the recollections of that most amiable and interesting family. Years have passed without my learning anything concerning them. Can you give me any information? I understand Mr. D'Oubril is Minister at Frankfort; the children, of course, are all grown up, some, perhaps, married. When I was recently in Paris, I heard from an American gentleman that he had been acquainted with Mademoiselle Bolvilliers, who, with her mother, was at Florence. Have you seen her lately?—and how is she?

My return to Europe, after such a long absence, is full of half-melancholy recollections and associations. I am continually retracing the scenes of past pleasures and friendships, and finding them vacant and desolate. I seem to come upon the very footprints of those with whom I have associated so pleasantly and kindly, but they only serve to remind me that those who made those footprints have passed away.

What would I not give to have that house of the D'Oubrils once more inhabited by its former tenants, just as they were when I was here in 1826. I long for such a resort; I long for such beings in whom I can take interest and feel delight. Madrid is barren, barren, barren to me of social intimacies. The civil wars, the political feuds and jealousies, seem to have cut up society, and rendered the Spaniards unsocial except in their own peculiar tertullias and cliques. Besides, I am not one to forage at large in general society; my intimacies are generally few and cherished.

I can give you but little intelligence of the gay world that used to assemble at the *soirées* of Madame D'Oubril. If you may remember, I mingled generally as a mere spectator, and seldom took sufficient interest in individuals to bear them in distinct recollection. When I have done so, I do not find the recollection productive of present satisfaction. Time dispels charms and illusions. You remember how much I was struck with a beautiful young woman (I will not mention names) who appeared in a tableau as Murillo's Virgin of the Assumption? She was young, recently married, fresh and unhackneyed in society, and my imagination decked her out with everything that was pure, lovely, innocent, and angelic in womanhood. She was pointed out to me at the theatre, shortly after my recent arrival in Madrid. I turned with eagerness to the original of the picture that had ever remained hung up in *sanctity* in my mind. I found her still handsome, though somewhat matronly in appearance, seated, *with her daughters*, in the box of a fashionable nobleman, younger than herself, rich in purse but poor in intellect, and who was openly and notoriously her *cavalier servente.* The charm was broken, the picture fell from the wall. She may have the customs of a depraved country and licentious state of society to excuse her; but I can never think of her again in the halo of feminine purity and loveliness that surrounded the Virgin of Murillo.

And so you have got my fellow traveller of the American wilds, and buffalo hunter of the prairies, Count Pourtales, in your neighborhood. When next you see him, remember me to him most cordially. Many, many pleasant scenes have we had together. He was full of talent, and had wonderful aptness at anything he turned to, but he seemed careless of turning his talent to account.

And now, my dear Dolgorouki, let me hear from you again, and before long. I envy you your beautiful residence at Naples, which is one of the lovely spots of earth that must unquestionably have dropped from the sky. Would that I could exchange for it the sterile vicinity of Madrid.

Believe me, ever yours most truly,

WASHINGTON IRVING.

CHAPTER XIII.

LETTER TO MISS CATHERINE IRVING—PASSAGES FROM LETTERS TO MRS. PARIS—THE QUEEN GIVING AUDIENCE—DIPLOMATIC CONVERSATION WITH ROYALTY—INSURRECTION IN BARCELONA—DEPARTURE OF THE REGENT—THE SOLITARY RAVEN—ATTACKS OF THE SOUTHERN LITERARY MESSENGER AND GRAHAM'S MAGAZINE—LETTERS ON THE SUBJECT—LITERARY OCCUPATION.

THERE is a vein of drollery in a portion of the following, to one of the youthful members of his home establishment, quite in character:

[*To Miss Catherine Irving.*]

MADRID, Nov. 15, 1842.

MY DEAR KATE:

Your letter of October 1st reached me a few days since, and gave me a very sunshiny account of affairs at pleasant little Sunnyside. I thus enjoy, by reflection, the bright days which pass at that brightest of little homes. My present home is enlivened by the return of the young travellers from their tour in Andalusia, which has been a very satisfactory one, excepting that they have not been robbed, at which they appear rather disappointed, an adventure with robbers being looked upon as essential to the interest and romance of a tour in Spain. They have a world of travelling anecdotes to relate about Granada and Malaga and Gibraltar and Seville, which make our repasts quite instructive as well as convivial. They are all in fine health and spirits, and, from their good tempers, good sense, good breeding, and perfect harmony, make a very pleasant household.

You seem to pity the poor little Queen, shut up, with her sister, like two princesses in fairy tale, in a great, grand, dreary palace, and "wonder whether she would not like to change her situation for a nice little cottage on the Hudson." Perhaps she would, Kate, if she knew anything of the gayeties of cottage life; if she had ever been with us at a picnic, or driven out in the Shandry-dran, with the two roans, and James, in his slip-shod hat, for a coachman, or *yotted* in the Dream, or sang in the Tarrytown choir, or shopped at Tommy Dean's; but, poor thing! she would not know how to set about enjoying herself. She would never think of appearing at church without a whole train of the Miss ———s and the Miss ———s and the Miss ———s, as maids of honor, nor drive through Sleepy Hollow except in a coach and six, with a cloud of dust and a troop of horsemen in glittering armor. So I think, Kate, we must be content with pitying her, and leaving her in ignorance of the comparative desolateness of her situation.

The last time I saw the little Queen was about ten days since, at the opera, with her sister. Espartero, the Regent, sat on her right hand. She is fond of theatricals, and appeared to take great interest in the performance. She is growing fast, and will soon be quite womanly in her appearance. I cannot say that she is strictly handsome, for which I am sorry, on account of your aunt; but you may console the latter, by assuring her that the Queen's sister is decidedly pretty enough to answer her notions of a princess. I shall give your aunt another diplomatic chapter on royalty and its concerns as soon as I can find leisure from my diplomatic communications to Government; but she must not let it get to Mr. Webster's ears how communicative I am to her on these subjects; he may not be disposed to admit her into our secrets.

* * * * * *

God bless you, my excellent, noble-hearted little girl! I can never enough express how deeply I feel the affection I have experienced and daily experience from you all. It constitutes the great happiness of my life.

After relating a second interview with the Queen, on her saint's day—the day of St. Isabella—in which she received congratulatory deputations from the Senate and the Chamber of Deputies at two o'clock, and from the *Corps Diplomatique* at three, and giving an account of her setting forth, followed by her sister, "on her awful journey along the diplomatic line," to receive and reply to a speech from each, "with the terrors of a schoolgirl," a letter to his sister remarks:

I believe, at first, I felt almost as much fluttered as herself, I entered so much into the novelty and peculiarity of her task —a mere child having to give audience to the official representatives of nations. Mr. Asten first addressed her. She had been accustomed to see him on other occasions, and that served to put her more at her ease. It was the same case with Count Lima; and, by the time she had finished with him, she began to smile. You will want to know what discourse I held with her, as my turn came next. I do not know whether I ought to impart these diplomatic conversations with royalty, as these are the verbal links that connect the destinies of nations. However, for once, I'll venture confiding in your secrecy. I had been so interested in contemplating the little sovereign, that I had absolutely forgotten to arrange anything to say; and when she stood before me, I was, as usual with me on public occasions, at a loss. However, something must be said, so I expressed my regret that my want of fluency in the Spanish language rendered it so difficult for me to address her as I could wish. "But you speak it very well," said she, with a smile, and a little flirt of her fan. I shook my head negatively. "Do you like Spain?" said she. "Very much," replied I, and I spoke sincerely. She smiled again, gave another little clack of her fan, bowed, and passed on. Her sister followed. She had not the womanly carriage of the Queen, being still more the child. I told her I hoped she had been pleased at the opera, where I had had the honor of seeing her a few nights before. She said, "Yes; she liked the theatre," and then glided on after her sister. When they had passed down the line, they returned to their places, and again, on being prompted, bowed to us; upon which we made respectful reverences, and retired, taking care, as we withdrew, not to turn our backs upon royalty.

I have thus, my dear sister, given you another peep into court scenes, and shown you the petty machinery of the great world. I can imagine you smiling in the serene wisdom of your elbow chair, at this picture of a row of dignified diplomatic personages, some of them well stricken in years, and all of them sage representatives of Governments, bowing with profound reverence, and conjuring up nothings to say to a couple of little girls. However, this is all the whipt syllabub of diplomacy. If I were to take you into one of our conferences with Cabinet Ministers, then you would know the solid wisdom required by our station; but this department of our official functions is a sealed book!

It was not long after this audience, that a popular paroxysm occurred, of which Mr. Irving gives this account, under date of November 25th:

An insurrection has taken place in Barcelona. This is the next city in importance to Madrid. It is the capital of the province of Catalonia, the most active and industrious province in Spain. The Catalans are to Spain what the New England people are to the United States. Wherever money is to be made, there is a Catalan. They are pushing, scheming, enterprising, hardy, and litigious. Catalonia is one of the most restless and insubordinate of the Spanish provinces, and frequently the seat of political disturbances. It borders on France, and is infested by half-robber, half-rebel bands, the remnants of the factions of the civil wars which lurk about the French frontiers. There is a small but busy party of republicans, also, at Barcelona, who would gladly pull down the present form of government, and establish a republic. Catalonia also has a strong manufacturing interest, having many cotton manufactories. This has taken the alarm at the rumor of a proposed commercial treaty with England for the introduction of her cotton goods at a lower rate of duties, so that there is a mixture of various motives in the present convulsion; and the whole has been thrown in a ferment by the intrigues of foreign agents, who seek the confusion of Spain and the downfall of its constitutional government. The present insurrection seems to have broken out suddenly and accidentally, some trifling affray with custom house officers having been the spark which has set the combustible community in a flame. There has been fighting in the streets, as in the famous "three days of Paris," and the troops have been obliged to evacuate the city, but hold it closely invested. The Regent set off from Madrid some days since for the scene of action, and troops are concentrating upon Catalonia from every direction; in the mean time, Madrid is full of rumors and reports that insurrections are breaking out in other provinces, but I believe, as yet, the insurrection is confined to Barcelona, and I think it probable it will be suppressed without much difficulty.

The departure of the Regent was a striking scene. All the uniform companies, or national guard of Madrid, consisting of several thousand men, well armed, equipped, and disciplined, paraded in the grand esplanade of the Prado in the neighborhood of the Regent's palace of Buena Vista. They really made a splendid appearance, and the air resounded with military music, several of the regiments having complete bands. It was a bright, sunshiny day. About two o'clock, the Regent sallied forth from Buena Vista, at the head of his staff. He is a fine martial figure, and was arrayed in full uniform, with towering feathers, and mounted on a noble gray charger with a flowing mane, and a long silken tail that almost swept the ground. He rode along the heads of the columns, saluting them with his gauntleted hand, and receiving cheers wherever he went. He stopped to speak particularly with some of the troops of horsemen; then, returning to the centre of the esplanade, he drew his sword, made a signal as if about to speak, and in an instant a profound silence prevailed over that vast body of troops, and the thousands of surrounding spectators. I do not know that ever I was more struck by anything, than by this sudden quiet of an immense multitude. The Regent then moved slowly backward and forward with his horse, about a space of thirty yards, waving his sword, and addressing the troops in a voice so loud and clear, that every word could be distinctly heard to a great distance. The purport of his speech was to proclaim his determination to protect the present constitution, and the liberties of Spain, against despotism on the one hand and anarchy on the other; and that, as on a former occasion, when summoned away by distant insurrection, he confided to the loyalty of the national guards the protection of the peace of the capital, and the safeguard of their young and innocent Queen. His speech was responded to by enthusiastic acclamations from the troops and the multitude, and he sallied forth in martial style from the great gate of Alcala.

I must note, to complete the scene, that just as Espartero issued forth from Buena Vista, and rode slowly down the Prado between the columns of the troops, a solitary raven came sailing down the course of the public promenade, passed immediately above him, and over the whole line of troops, and so flitted heavily out of sight. This has been cited, even in the public papers, as a bad omen; and some of the superstitious say Espartero will never return to Madrid. I should not be surprised, however, if the omen had been prepared by some of the petty politicians with which this capital abounds, and that the raven had been let loose just at this opportune moment. However, with this portentous circumstance I will close my letter, especially as I have just received despatches from Government, which, with the stirring events of the day, will cut out plenty of occupation for me.

With love to all, your affectionate brother,

WASHINGTON IRVING.

A fortnight later, he writes to the same correspondent:

My last letter ended, I think, with the departure of the Regent to quell the insurrection in Barcelona. He travelled in his own fearless style, pushing on in a post chaise ahead of his troops, and without escort, accompanied merely by an officer or two of his staff, and threw himself frankly among the people in the towns and villages, who showed the sense of this confidence in their loyalty, receiving him everywhere with acclamations. After his departure, Madrid was full of rumors; insurrections were said to be breaking out everywhere. The downfall of Espartero and of the existing Government was confidently predicted, and there were not wanting factious people and factious prints to endeavor to blow this hidden flame into a general conflagration. Thus far, however, they have been disappointed. Madrid has remained quiet under the guardianship of the national guards, and the insurrection did not extend beyond Barcelona. That factious city has once more been brought into submission to the Government, but not until it had suffered a bombardment of several hours. As yet, we have no particulars of the damage done, but it must have been considerable, and I fear we shall hear of some punishments inflicted upon those who have been most active in exciting this rebellion. Barcelona has sinned so often in this way, that it is deemed necessary to treat it, in the present instance, with rigor. The bombardment, though repeatedly threatened, and the day and hour assigned, was put off from day to day and hour to hour, in the hope that the insurgent city would surrender; but a band of desperadoes had got the upper hand, who refused to submit excepting on such terms as it would have been degrading to the Government to grant.

The year of Mr. Irving's departure on his interesting mission was memorable for two attacks on him, to which it is necessary to allude, to clear the way for the letters from him which I am about to quote. A writer in the *Southern Literary Messenger*, in March, 1841, had been at great pains to show that Mr. Irving's expressions of obligation to Navarrete, in the preface to his Life of Columbus, were not sufficiently explicit, while conceding that he had performed his historical task with "accuracy, judgment, and infinite beauty." In the writer's estimation, his statements implied, though perhaps unintentionally, he admits, a more extensive search into original documents than he could have made, while the history was mainly digested from documents already collected by Navarrete.

The article was sent to Mr. Irving, and, without a perusal, handed over by him to a candid and discriminating friend, with a request that he would read it, and tell him if there was anything in it which required an answer at his hands. If so, he would notice it; otherwise he did not care to be discomposed by reading it. He claimed no immunity from critical animadversion, but it was his practice to shun the perusal of all strictures that did not involve a point of character, and demand reply.

His friend read it, and, satisfied of the unsoundness of the strictures, and that his acknowledgments to Navarrete were ample, advised him to give himself no concern about it. He dismissed it, accordingly, from his thoughts.

In the May number of 1842 of the same magazine, after Mr. Irving had left the country, the writer returns to the attack, and, as more than a year had elapsed without any notice or refutation by the author, or his friends, of his "grave charges," he comes to the conclusion that he had preferred "the quiet disparagement of a judgment by default to the notoriety of a verdict after a fruitless contest." To this article there was a reply in the *Knickerbocker*, to which Mr. Irving was in no ways privy, and a rejoinder in the *Messenger*, in which the writer, with compliments to the purity and richness of his general style, still adhered to his original position that Mr. Irving had not sufficiently acknowledged his indebtedness to Navarrete.

The other attack was in *Graham's Lady's and Gentleman's Magazine*, then under the editorial management of the Rev. Rufus W. Griswold, a Baptist clergyman of some six-and-twenty years, who had recently given to the world a valuable compilation, styled "The Poets and Poetry of America." The *Magazine* was published in Philadelphia, had a circulation, it was said, of fifty thousand subscribers, and numbered, among its regular contributors, Cooper, Bryant, Dana, and other distinguished names. In a notice of the Critical and Miscellaneous Writings of Sir Walter Scott, contained in the October number of that periodical, was a statement which, after charging Scott with numerous "puffs of himself from his own pen," proceeded in this language: "Washington Irving has done the same thing, in writing laudatory notices of his own works for the Reviews, and, like Scott, received pay for whitewashing himself."

As Mr. Irving was not in the country to meet this coarse aspersion with instant denial, should he see fit to notice it, before communicating with him on the subject, I addressed a letter to Mr. Griswold, asking his authority for the statement, and requesting him to name the Reviews containing the laudatory notices in question. His reply gave a Mr. E . . . . . ., an English gentleman, with whom his acquaintance was limited to a single interview, as the person who informed him that "Mr. Irving wrote the articles in the *Quarterly Review*, on the Life of Columbus, and the Chronicles of Granada." I replied, that the *London Quarterly* contained no review of the Life of Columbus, "laudatory" or otherwise, and that the review it did contain of the Chronicles of Granada had not a commendatory expression of the work or its author, or a single sentence that might not have come from the pen of Mr. Irving without the slightest impeachment of his delicacy. If a self-review—and I did not then know whether it was or not—it was not, at any rate, a self-eulogy.

Pointing out these facts to Mr. Griswold, and referring him to the files of the *Quarterly* for proof, I appealed to his sense of equity whether it were not due to Mr. Irving that he should review the grounds upon which, thus publicly and uncalled for, he had sought to bring the delicacy of his character into suspicion.

In his reply, dated October 13th, he expressed great regret for the whole matter, and said he would do Mr. Irving justice in the December number of the *Magazine*, the November number being already printed. He was as good as his word, and in that number retracted, though rather ungraciously, the pitiful charge he had been too eager to catch up and circulate. The imputation upon Scott, I presume, had as little foundation.

On the sixth of October—before, of course, the receipt of Mr. Griswold's promise of recantation of the 13th—I wrote to Mr. Irving, enclosing the leaf of *Graham's Magazine* which contained the offensive imputation, and a copy of Mr. Griswold's answer to my first letter. In this answer, which named his authority for the assumed self-laudation, he took oocasion to add that he had strong ground for supposing Mr. Irving to have been a *frequent* contributor to the *London Quarterly*, while that periodical, more than any other in Europe, was distinguished for its unprincipled hostility to the United States.

With this preface, I submit the letters of Mr. Irving on the subject of these separate charges:

[*To Pierre M. Irving.*]

MADRID, Nov. 12, 1842.

MY DEAR PIERRE:

I have just received your letter of October 6th, enclosing an article from *Graham's Magazine*, charging me with writing laudatory notices of my own works for the Reviews, and alluding especially to the *Quarterly*. The only notice I ever took of any of my works, was an article which I wrote for the *Quarterly Review* on my Chronicle of the Conquest of Granada. It was done a long time after the publication of the work, in compliance with the wishes of Mr. Murray, who thought the nature of the work was not sufficiently understood, and that it was considered rather as a work of fiction than one substantially of historic fact. Any person who will take the trouble to read that review, will perceive that it is merely *illustrative*, not *laudatory* of the work, explanatory of its historical foundation. I never made a secret of my having written that review; I wrote it under the presumption that the authorship of it would become known to any person who should think it worth his while to make the inquiry. I never wrote any other article for the *Quarterly Review* excepting a review to call favorable attention to the work of my friend and *countryman*, Captain McKenzie (then Slidell), entitled "A Year in Spain, by a Young American," and another review, for the same purpose, of a work of my friend and *countryman*, Mr. Wheaton, at present Minister at the Court of Prussia. This last article, though written for the *Quarterly Review*, did not appear in that publication, but was published in the *North American Review*. The work of Mr. Wheaton which it reviews, was, I think, the History of the Northmen. These are the only articles that I am conscious of having ever written for the *Quarterly*, or any other European Review. I have never inserted in any publication in Europe or America a puff of any of my works, nor permitted any to be inserted by my publishers when I could prevent it; nor sought to procure favorable reviews from others, nor to prevent unfavorable ones where I thought they were to be apprehended. I have on all occasions, and in every respect, left my works to take their chance, and I leave them still to do the same. My present reply to your inquiry is only drawn forth by a charge that would affect my private character; though I hope *that* is sufficiently known to take care of itself on the point in question.

I understand a kind friend has recently been vindicating me against attacks made on me in the *Southern Literary Messenger*, on the subject of my Life of Columbus. I have never read those attacks, having been assured there was nothing in them that called for reply, and not being disposed to have my feelings ruffled unnecessarily. I understood they mainly charged me with making use of Mr. Navarrete's work without giving him due credit. Those who will look into my Life of Columbus, will find that in the preface I have cited the publication of Mr. Navarrete as the foundation of my work, and that I have referred to him incessantly at the foot of the pages. If I have not done so sufficiently, I was not aware of my "shortcomings." His work was chiefly documentary, and, as such, invaluable for the purpose of history. As my work was not a work of invention, I was glad to find such a store of facts in the volumes of Mr. Navarrete; and as I knew his scrupulous exactness, wherever I found a document published by him, I was sure of its correctness, and did not trouble myself to examine the original. My work, however, was made up from various sources, some in print, some in manuscript, all of which, I thought at the time, I had faithfully cited. Those who wish to know Mr. Navarrete's opinion of the work, will find it expressed in the third volume of his collections of documents, published after the appearance of Columbus, in which his expressions are anything but those of a man who felt himself wronged. I can only say, that I have never willingly, in any of my writings, sought to take advantage of a contemporary, but have endeavored to be fair in my literary dealings with all men; and if ever you hear again of my having practised any disingenuous artifice in literature, to advance myself or to injure others, you may boldly give the charge a flat contradiction. What I am as an author, the world at large must judge. You know what I am as a man, and know, when I give you my word, it is to be depended upon.

* * * * * *

Your affectionate uncle,

WASHINGTON IRVING.

P. S.—This letter is written in great haste on the spur of the moment, to go by the courier that sets off for Paris to-day. I have not yet read Helen's long letter, from which I promise myself a perfect treat. The foregoing letter is, of course, not intended for publication, but you may use it as "authority," quoting from it what you think proper. I must expect attacks of this and other kinds now. I have been so long before the public, that the only way to make anything now out of me is to *cut me up*. However, I shall follow the example of Sam Williams, whilome American banker at London, who, when his ship was sinking at sea, sprang on board of another one that had run foul of it, and was saved. As literature is sinking under me, I shall cling to diplomacy.

The following letter, written on the same day, has a more playful allusion to the same topic:

[*To Mrs. P. M. Irving.*]

MADRID, Nov. 12, 1842.

MY DEAR HELEN:

I did not intend to write to you by this opportunity, for I am fairly fagged out with letter writing by this courier, having, besides scribbling to friends, to send long despatches to Government; but I cannot suffer your long, delightful letter to remain unacknowledged, though, at present, I scrawl but a line of thanks. My dear Helen, you cannot imagine what a rich treat such a letter from home is to me. It fills my heart to the very brim, and with the very best of good feelings; and then, your details about sweet little Sunnyside—God bless my dear little cottage!—what a treasure of comfort and enjoyment it is to me! Every letter from it or about it gives me such a picture of true, innocent, home-dwelling happiness, and of such joyous meetings and gatherings together of those I love, that I feel for a time as if I had just heard a strain of delightful music, which is one of my purest of earthly pleasures. I had just been reading and answering one of Pierre's, wherein he had given a most indignant account of a charge made upon me, in a *Lady's Magazine*, of having puffed my own works. Don't tell Pierre, but absolutely he had put himself in such a passion on the subject, that I found all the indignation appurtenant to the matter was done to my hand, so I retained the smoothness of my temper without a wrinkle. As authorhood seems to be getting down in the world, and I have taken to the company of kings and queens and regents, and others of "the quality," I begin to think I'll give out that I am not the Washington Irving that wrote that farrago of literature they are occasionally cutting up, and that I have never followed any line of life but diplomacy, nor written anything but despatches. I certainly began life at the wrong end; it is only recently I have discovered what I was cut out for. However, don't mention it; people might think me vain. * * *

* * * And now, my dear Helen, as this letter was a perfect impromptu, totally unpremeditated, I must close it, to attend to other correspondents. I will take some other occasion to answer your long letter more at length; in the mean time, I beg you forthwith to sit down and write me such another one. And do, I again charge you, tell me everything that is pleasant and prosperous about yourself and Pierre; and tell Pierre not to take it so much to heart, if they make any further attacks upon that poor-devil author who has scribbled under my name.

Your affectionate uncle,

WASHINGTON IRVING.

Five days later, he returns to the subject of these attacks with the following supplementary letter, which relates, in his own words, particulars in his literary history heretofore hinted at by myself, and disposes of Mr. Griswold's epistolary intimation about the *frequency* of his contributions to the *London Quarterly*. I have already briefly refuted this charge, by which it was intended to prejudice his popularity at home, but the reader may be willing to see in what spirit it is met by Mr. Irving. Mr. Griswold, it will be understood, makes no such charge himself, but only reports it as a supposition which he was disposed to entertain.

[*To Pierre M. Irving.*]

MADRID, NOV. 17, 1842.

MY DEAR PIERRE:

I wrote to you, a few days since, in reply to your letter concerning the attack upon me in *Graham's Magazine.* As that reply was written hastily, I may not have been precise in one or two particulars. The review of the Conquest of Granada was written nearly, if not quite two years after the publication of the work, and after it had been very favorably noticed in several periodical publications. As I before observed, it was written in compliance with the wishes of Mr. Murray, to state the historical nature of the work; my use of the soubriquet of Fray Antonio Agapida, and the occasional romantic coloring, having led many to suppose it was a mere fabrication. I did not ask or expect any remuneration from Mr. Murray, but he sent me the sum he was accustomed to pay for similar contributions to his Review, and I did not hesitate to accept it, the article, in fact, being written for his benefit. Perhaps it would be as well to have the review republished in the *Knickerbocker*, and then the public will be able to judge whether or no it is "laudatory."

While I am upon these literary matters, I will furnish you with a fact or two in my literary life in Europe, which may enable you to reply to any similar charges that may be brought against me. In the early struggle of my literary career in London, before I had published the Sketch Book in England, I received a letter from Sir Walter Scott, inviting me to Edinburgh to take charge of a periodical publication, holding out the certainty of a liberal sum per annum, with other incidental advantages. Though low in purse and uncertain in my prospects at the time, I declined accepting the invitation, fearing it might implicate me in foreign politics.

When I was in Spain, I was offered, by Mr. Murray, £1,000 per annum to conduct a magazine which he had in contemplation, I to be paid, *in addition*, for any articles I might contribute. This I declined, because it would detain me in Europe, my desire being to return to the United States. Mr. Murray likewise offered me a hundred guineas an article for any article I might write about Spain for the *Quarterly Review*. I refrained from accepting his very liberal offer. As I mentioned in my former letter, I contributed but two articles to his *Review*—one explanatory of the historical grounds of my Chronicles of Granada, and the other a review of my friend McKenzie's "Year in Spain, by a Young American."

I do not recollect having written for any other reviews or magazines in Europe; and I again repeat, I never in any way sought to "puff" my works, or to have them puffed. I always suffered them to take their chance, and always felt that I was favored beyond my deserts.

At the close of the letter to me from which I have been quoting, dated November 17th, Mr. Irving gives this glance at his literary and diplomatic matters:

* * * I have, of late, been so much occupied in diplomatic business, that I have not had time to attend to the Life of Washington. Indeed, I have not done much at it since I have been here, but I shall soon take it earnestly in hand. I found it necessary to give up literary matters for a time, and turn my thoughts entirely into the subjects connected with my station. The statistics of trade about which I have had to

occupy myself, are new to me, and require close attention for a time to master them.

Five weeks later, December 21st, in a letter to his brother Ebenezer, he alludes in this way to his progress on the Life of Washington:

I have been much interrupted in my literary occupations for the last two or three months, by the necessity of applying my mind to the examination of some subjects connected with my diplomatic duties, and of preparing rather voluminous papers. Within this week or two past, however, I have been able to add a few chapters to my history.

CHAPTER XIV.

LETTER TO MISS SARAH IRVING—INDISPOSITION OF THE AUTHOR—LETTER TO MRS. PARIS—ALARMING ASPECT OF POLITICAL EVENTS—GLOOMY SOIREE OF THE REGENT, PREPARATORY TO HIS DEPARTURE—LETTERS TO MRS. STORROW—IN THE MIDST OF CONSPIRACIES AND INSURRECTIONS—A CITY IN A STATE OF SIEGE—SALLIES FORTH—STRIKING SCENES—NOTE OF THE DIPLOMATIC CORPS IN BEHALF OF THE QUEEN.*

THERE is a sly vein of humor in the following extract from a letter to a juvenile inmate of Sunnyside, who had been keeping him in the current of family affairs, and giving him a budget of New York gossip:

[*To Miss Sarah Irving.*]

January 13*th*, 1843.— * * * Your information that Mr. ——— had given Mrs. ——— a two-story house in Broadway, gave me great satisfaction; but when you added that the mantelpieces were of wood, it went to my heart. However, let us hope for the best. If the young couple really love each other, they may manage to have a happy fireside in spite of the mantelpiece; and who knows but the old gentleman's heart may soften toward them before his death, and he may leave them a marble mantelpiece in his will. Miss ———, on the contrary, who married according to his wishes, has been rewarded, I am told, with a three-story (I am not certain that it is not a *four*-story) house.

These two instances of the matrimonial fortunes of two sisters, my dear girl, should be held up as warnings to young ladies disposed to enter the connubial state, not to give away their soft and tender hearts without first consulting the harder hearts of all the old gentlemen they may happen to be related to. For my own part, I should take it in great dudgeon, if any of you girls at the cottage should throw yourselves away upon any agreeable young gentleman, without his first gaining the affections of your father and myself; though I trust I should not go to the length of condemning you to a wooden mantelpiece.

I thought of you all at dear little Sunnyside on Christmas day, and heartily wished myself there to eat my Christmas dinner among you. I hope you kept up Christmas in the usual style, and that the cottage was decked with evergreens. You must not let my absence cause any relaxations in the old rules and customs of the cottage; everything must go on the same as it did when I was there.

His own Christmas dinner he had eaten at the British embassy, where, he remarks, "we had the good old Christmas luxuries of plum pudding and minced pies, and our repast was a very pleasant one."

In the beginning of this year, Mr. Irving was confined to the house by an indisposition, the consequence of a cold, which was soon followed by an inflammatory disease of the skin, similar to that which he had experienced about twenty years before, but much more virulent. It was the result, as in the former instance, of having overworked himself, and fagging too incessantly at his literary, diplomatic, and epistolary tasks, while taking too little exercise. The malady, though annoying and obstinate, was not dangerous, but it required him to renounce the pen for awhile, as the least mental excitement aggravated his symptoms. From this tedious and harassing complaint, which in a measure unfitted him for everything, he was doomed to suffer more or less for two years, the remedies sometimes proving almost as irksome as the disease. At the time it first set in, he had been engaging with all his powers upon his Life of Washington, to which he had added some chapters, when he was compelled to throw by the pen, not, I think, to exercise it again on this task until his return to his own country. This interruption to his literary occupations, always cheering to him, brought additional discomfort in the midst of his malady. But, though incapable of working, he could direct others, and manage to carry on the business of the legation. He was a less attentive correspondent, however, than heretofore, though not incapable of letter writing, as the following will show:

[*To Mrs. Paris.*]

MADRID, June 21, 1843.

MY DEAR SISTER:

I have again to thank you for kind and cheering letters, full of precious home details. I am sorry I can make but such poor returns; but, though my malady has ceased in its virulence, I find writing still irksome to me, and, indeed, am prohibited by my physician from indulging in it. It is a great privation, and reduces me to a state of idleness foreign to my habits and inclinations. The doctor would also, if he could, put a stop to my almost incessant reading, as he thinks that any fixed attention for a length of time wearies the brain, and in some degree produces those effects on the system which originated my complaint; but I cannot give up reading, in my otherwise listless state. He has been very urgent for me to travel, not merely for a change of air, but because the succession of scenes and incidents amuses without fatiguing the mind, and thus operates healthfully upon the system. I have been recovering so much of late, however, that I hope to be able to dispense with this part of his advice, and to continue at my post. I should be loth to leave it in the present critical state of the country, when insurrections are breaking out in various parts of the kingdom, and Spain is once more threatened with civil war.

My illness has prevented me from giving you a detail of the political events of the country, which have of late assumed an alarming aspect. A coalition of various factions (opposite in their views and doctrines, and no one of them of sufficient magnitude to form a majority) has united in a vehement attempt to pull down the Regent, and put an end to the existing government. For this purpose, insurrections have been stirred up in various parts of the country, and, latterly, in Barcelona, that old seat of rebellion. To-day, the Regent sallies forth from the capital, to put himself once more at the head of his troops and endeavor to quell these insurrections. I heartily pray for his success; for, should he fail, and should he be ejected from power, a fearful state of anarchy would ensue The very coalition now combined against him would break into warring factions, each striving for the ascendency, and we might have civil war of the worst kind.

I have just returned from attending a levee held by the Regent, at twelve o'clock, preparatory to his departure. He made a frank, manly address to the diplomatic corps, declaring his disposition to cultivate cordial relations with all countries, but particularly with those who had representatives at this Court, and who recognized the constitution of Spain, the throne of Isabella II, and his regency; his loyal devotion to the constitution and the throne, and his sole and uniform ambition to place the reins of government in the hands of the youthful Queen on the 10th of October, 1844, when she should have completed her minority, and to place under her command a peaceful, prosperous, and happy country; but he expressed, at the same time, his determination to resist every attempt to throw the country into a state of anarchy, and to defend the throne of Isabella and the constitution of 1837 like a good soldier.

At four o'clock a general review of the national militia takes place in the Prado, as on a former occasion, when the Regent, as before, will no doubt make them a speech, confiding the safety of the city, and of the youthful Queen and her sister, to their patriotism and loyalty. At five o'clock he takes his departure. I cannot but feel that he sallies forth, this time, with much more doubtful prospects than in his former expedition against Barcelona. The spirit of rebellion is more widely diffused, and is breaking forth at various points. A few days, or a very few weeks at farthest, will decide his fate, and determine whether he is to maintain his post, and keep up some form of government for the remainder of the minority of the Queen (about fifteen months and a half), or whether his power, if not himself, is to be annihilated, and everything for a time thrown into chaos.

On Sunday evening last, I attended the *soirée* held weekly at the Regent's. It was the only one I have been able to attend for upward of four months; but I was anxious to go to it, as it would be the last before the departure of the Regent. It was thinly attended, and I remarked a general gloom on the faces of those attached to the Regent, or whose interests were connected with his fortunes. The Regent himself did not appear, being engaged in a Cabinet council. The Duchess was pale, and had a dejected air, complaining of headache. I rather fear it was heartache, for she feels their hazardous position, and the pitfalls which surround them. She is an amiable and a lovely woman, and her dejected air rather heightened her beauty in my eyes. I had not seen her since my illness, and I had to thank her for many kind inquiries she had made after my health, sending one of the Duke's aides-de-camp for the purpose. It will be a joyful hour for her, I am convinced, when the Duke lays down his regency, and returns to the quiet and security of private life. * * *

I have scrawled a longer letter than I had any idea of accomplishing, and must conclude. Tell Eliza R., Sarah Irving, &c., &c., that I have received their letters, giving me most acceptable cottage news, and beg them to write on without waiting for replies. I cannot write letters at present; indeed, I *must* not. Everything concerning dear little Sunnyside is interesting to me. My heart dwells in that blessed little spot, and I really believe that, when I die, I shall haunt it; but it will be as a *good spirit*, that no one need be afraid of. Though I cannot enjoy its delights in person, at present, I enjoy them at second hand, by the accounts given by others.

When I think of America, my thoughts all centre there; and I believe that, even though exiled from it, a great portion of my actual enjoyment in life is hearing and thinking about it, picturing it in my thoughts, dreaming about it, and flattering myself with the hope that I shall return and end my days there. In the mean time, thank God! it is a happy home for my dear brother and his family.

Ever, my dear sister, most affectionately your brother,

WASHINGTON IRVING.

At the date of the following letter, Mr. Hamilton, his Secretary of Legation, was setting off on an excursion to the Pyrenees. Brevoort had left the legation in April, to make the tour of Europe, and Ames had left in June, to return to France and embark for the United States in July. His man Benjamin, with whom he was so much pleased at first, had also gone, having lost favor in his eyes by "playing the old soldier" during his long malady, and leaving all the extra work and the care of him to the faithful Lorenzo, whom he had now put at the head of his establishment. The letter gives some further insight into the critical state of Spanish affairs, the observation of which still took up much of his time and thoughts. It is addressed to Mrs. Storrow, at Paris, and bears date June 27th:

* * * We are in the midst of plots, conspiracies, and insurrections, and know not what a day may bring forth. The Regent is on his way to one part of the kingdom which is in a state of insurrection; in the mean time, insurrections are

breaking forth in other quarters. Many predict that he will never return to Madrid; but so they predicted last year, when he sallied forth to put down the insurrection at Barcelona. For my part, I never expect to see Spain enjoy tranquillity and a settled form of government during the time I may sojourn in it, and fear I may have to witness some sanguinary scenes of popular commotion. I have looked upon Espartero as the only man likely to maintain the country in a tolerable state of tranquillity during the minority of the little Queen; but I now doubt if he will be able to keep up against the combination of factions bent upon his destruction. A few days will determine his fortunes.

* * * * * *

I am getting on very well, though it takes always a tedious time to get rid of maladies of the kind I have to struggle with. The weather has as much effect upon me as upon a barometer, and this season has been uncommonly capricious. It favors me in one respect, that we have none of the usual fervid heats of summer, which might debilitate me; but the cloudy, windy, and occasionally chilly weather irritates my system. However, I trust, in another month, to be superior to these influences.

Give my affectionate regards to Mr. Storrow, and kiss dear little good-for-nothing Kate for me.

Your affectionate uncle,

WASHINGTON IRVING.

[*To Mrs. Storrow, Paris.*]

MADRID, July 14, 1843.

MY DEAR SARAH:

I have just received your letter of the 8th, by which I find that the valiant Hector has arrived safely at Paris, after his adventurous journey. I have no news recently of Mr. Hamilton, who must be enjoying himself in the Pyrenees. The letters I have written to him I have reason to believe have been intercepted on the road by the insurgents.

We are here in the midst of confusion and alarm. I speak of the city and the people, for, as to myself, my mind is as tranquil and almost as stagnant as a millpond. A singular kind of rebellion is going forward. Armies marching and countermarching about the country; city after city declaring itself in a state of insurrection, but as yet no fighting. An insurgent army, under General Espiroz, has been hovering about Madrid for several days; another (under General Narvaez) is marching from a different direction to coöperate with it; and Government troops, under Generals Soane and Zurbano, are pushing in from a distance, to aid in the defence of the place. In the mean time, the city is declared in a state of siege, and placed under martial law; the gates are closed and guarded, and we are thus shut up within the walls. The day before yesterday I was sitting in my room writing, when I was attracted to the window by an uncommon bustle and confusion of voices in the street. I looked out, and saw men, women, and children scampering in every direction; as far as the eye could reach, there was the same hurry-scurry movement hither and thither. I summoned Lorenzo, and asked the reason. He told me there was "a revolution!" It appears the "General," or alarm, had been sounded, which is only done at moments of imminent peril, summoning every one to his post. The word was circulated that the enemy (an advanced guard of the army of General Espiroz) were at the Puerta de Hierro, or Iron Gate, which crosses the main road about half a league from the city gate. In a little while the national guards, or militia, were issuing from every side and corner, hastily equipped, and hurrying to their posts; women were gathering their children home, like hens gathering their chickens under their wings on the sight of a hawk. Before long, there were eighteen thousand men under arms within the city; all the gates were strongly guarded; the main squares were full of troops, with cannon planted at the entrances of the streets opening into them. The shops were all shut up, and the streets, in general, deserted and silent, all those not on duty keeping as much as possible within doors. At night the whole city was illuminated, as is generally the case when any popular movement is apprehended, so that an enemy may not have darkness to favor his designs.

I was advised not to stir out, as one may get involved in tumults at such times. I kept at home all day, but in the evening I could not resist the desire to see something of a city in a state of siege, and under an alarm. I accordingly sallied forth in my carriage, and drove to the Prado. Instead of being crowded by the fashionable world, it was full of troops, there having been a review of the national guards. I alighted, and walked among them. They seemed all to be in high spirits. There were but two carriages besides my own on the drive, usually so crowded. I drove from gate to gate of this end of the city, all closed and guarded. As the night advanced, I drove through most of the principal streets. The houses were illuminated from top to bottom. Few people were walking in the streets; but groups were gathered about every door. Troops were patrolling in every direction, and in the main squares, which formed military posts, both officers and men were bivouacking on the pavements. The appearance of a solitary carriage rumbling through the streets attracted universal attention, but no one offered to molest me. I drove to Madame Albuquerque's, took tea there, and returned home about eleven o'clock. I never saw Madrid under more striking and picturesque circumstances.

Yesterday was comparatively tranquil, but this morning the "General," or alarm, has been given at six o'clock. The enemy has approached a different gate of the city, and there is news that General Narvaez and his troops are at Guadalajara, a few leagues distant. The city is again under arms. I presume the shops are shut up, but I have not as yet been out of the house. The greatest evil I have as yet experienced, is the cutting off the supply of butter and cow's milk for my breakfast, both coming from the royal dairy beyond the Puerto de Hierro, or Iron Gate.

As the Government has prohibited the circulation of the opposition papers by the mail, they have all ceased to publish; the Government papers themselves are very scanty of intelligence, so that we are left in a state of ignorance of passing events, and are at the mercy of rumor, which fabricates all kinds of stories of plots, conspiracies to carry off the Queen, to blow up the powder magazines, &c., &c., &c.

Contradictory reports prevail also with respect to the Regent, who, by last accounts, was in La Mancha. Some say he is on his march back to Madrid, others that he is going to Cordova, others to Granada, to quell the insurrection in Andalusia. Some say his troops are in a high state of enthusiasm, others that they are deserting him. Every report has its counter report, so that one is reduced to mere conjecture.

I had looked forward to such a state of things, and I look forward to one still worse, when the hostile parties come to blows. There may also be perplexing questions for diplomatists, should the invading armies get possession of the capital, and of the person of the young Queen. The question may then arise, "Where is the actual Government?" and which party is to be considered legitimate? You will now understand why, at such a crisis, a diplomatic agent should not be absent from his post.

We have no regular troops in the city, but a large force of national guards, and of the national militia from the neighboring villages. Some feel great confidence in their maintaining the safety of the city; others doubt their being willing to fight, seeing that the invaders are their countrymen. My idea is, that if Soane and Zurbano arrive in the neighborhood with the force they are said to have, the invaders will have to retreat, or to make battle. Should no such succor arrive, I should not be surprised if, after a few days, the city should make terms, acknowledge the insurgent authority, and that a temporary government should suddenly be organized here—how long to last, it would be useless even to conjecture.

I am scrawling this hastily, to be sent off by the French courier. I doubt letters going safely at present by the mail, as the insurgent cities through which it passes are eager to get at news from the capital. As I have no time to write to your mother, send her this letter, when you have done with it. It will help to keep up the thread of Spanish affairs I have given her.

I miss much the delightful companionship of Hamilton, whom I have learned to prize more and more, the more I have known him. But I trust he will be here again before long, with renovated health and happy spirits. I am much cheered by the society of Mr. George Sumner, who dines with me almost every day, and is very intelligent and conversable.

My health is daily improving, and I am gradually getting freed from the malady which has so long clung to me. The weather continues generally cool for the season, and I find my large saloons very pleasant and airy for summer.

Let me hear of your plans and your whereabouts; I can make none for myself at present, as you must perceive. Give my kind regards to Miss Ledyard, and the young Ledyards.

With affectionate remembrances to your husband, and kisses to Kate,

Your affectionate uncle,

WASHINGTON IRVING

[*To Mrs. Storrow, Paris.*]

MADRID, July 13, 1843.

MY DEAR SARAH:

I have just learned that a French courier is about to set off from the French embassy, and I hasten to scrawl you a line by it, as letters by the mail are apt, at the present moment, to be intercepted, and you may be anxious to hear from me during these warlike times. I wrote to you about four days since, giving you some account of the critical state of affairs in this city. Since that time, we have been in a state of siege: the enemy at the gates; the whole body of national guards, &c., under arms; the main streets barricaded; every house illuminated at night; the streets swarming with military men; the shops shut; the publication of the newspapers suspended, and the public ear abused with all kinds of lying rumors. There has been brisk firing of musketry about some of the gates, and an occasional report of a cannon; but the besiegers calculated upon disaffection and treachery within the walls; upon a pronunciamento in favor of the insurrectional government, and upon the gates being thrown open to them. They therefore came without artillery. Thus far they have been disappointed. The national guards have remained firm and true, and have kept up a brisk fire whenever the enemy made any demonstrations. One of my windows commands a view of one of the city gates and its vicinity, and I could hear every discharge, and, at night, could see the flash of the guns. It has been extremely interesting to me, and, fortunately, I have so far recovered from the lingering of my malady, that I could go all about on foot, and witness some of the striking scenes presented by a city in a state of siege, and hourly in apprehension of being taken by assault. Troops were stationed in the houses along the main streets, to fire upon the enemy from the windows and balconies, should they effect an entrance; and it was resolved to dispute the ground street by street, and to make the last stand in the royal palace, where were the Queen and her sister, and where the Duchess of Victoria, wife of the Regent, had taken refuge, her own palace being in one of the most exposed parts of the city.

Apprehending that the lives of the Queen and her sister might be exposed to extreme hazard, as much in the defence as in the attack, the diplomatic corps addressed a note to the Government, urging the most scrupulous attention to the safety of these helpless little beings, and offering to repair in a body to the palace, and remain there during the time of peril. Our offer has been declined, the ministry thinking the safety of the Queen and her sister sufficiently secured by the devotion of the inhabitants of Madrid, &c.

Last evening it was confidently reported that there would be a grand attack at various points in the course of the night, and many were in a great state of alarm. I had returned home at a late hour, and had just got into bed, when I found a note lying on the table beside my bed, which proved to be from Mrs. Weismuller, the young and beautiful bride of Mr. Weismuller, a connection and representative of the Rothschilds, who arrived here recently from England, and whose residence was in the main street leading from the gate that would be attacked. She requested permission to take refuge in my house. It was already twelve o'clock, but I hastily dressed myself again, and repaired to the residence of Mr. Weismuller, escorted by Lorenzo. Groups of soldiers, with sentinels, were stationed at every corner. I found Mr. and Mrs. Weismuller in much anxiety, he having received what he considered certain intelligence that the attack would take place about four o'clock in the morning. I offered every accommodation my house would afford, and, after much deliberation, it was determined that, on the first alarm of the attack, they should repair to my residence. This being settled, I returned home, but did not get asleep until between one and two o'clock. This morning I awoke about four. There was the sound of a drum in the street, and the report of two or three distant shots. I thought the attack was about to commence, and prepared to rise; but all remained quiet, and there was no further alarm. It appeared that, instead of attacking, the enemy had drawn off in the night. They had heard of the approach of the forces under Generals Soane and Zurbano in one direction, and of a smaller force (about three thousand men) under Generals Iriarte and Enna in another direction. General Narvaez, therefore, has marched to encounter Soane and Zurbano, and General Espiroz to encounter Iriarte and Enna. Should they vanquish them, they will return upon

Madrid, which, in such case, will probably capitulate. Should Soane and the others be successful, the Regent's government will be strengthened in Madrid; should they fail, his government will be overthrown. However this present contest may end, I look upon it as but the commencement of another series of conflicts and struggles for rule that will desolate unhappy Spain. Espartero has been the only man that has presented, for many years, calculated to be a kind of keystone to the arch; but his popularity has been undermined, and, whether he be displaced or not, I fear he will no longer have power and influence sufficient to prevent the whole edifice falling to ruin and confusion.

I scrawl this in great haste, and have no time to write to any of the family; you must forward it, therefore, to your mother, that it may let all at home know that I am *safe*, and mean to continue so, whatever storms may prevail around me. I have just received a letter from Hamilton, dated from the Pyrenees. He will be much grieved at being absent from Madrid in these stirring and eventful times.

My health is continually improving, and I think the excitement of the last two or three days has been of great service to me. Yesterday I was on my feet from ten o'clock in the morning until twelve or one at night, and, though much fatigued, feel all the better for it.

CHAPTER XV.

LETTER TO MRS. PARIS—INCORRECT ACCOUNTS OF THE INTERPOSITION OF THE CORPS DIPLOMATIQUE—HIS VERSION—ESPARTERO DRIVEN OUT—IMPATIENCE TO DECLARE THE QUEEN OF AGE—SCENES AND CEREMONIALS IN THE ROYAL PALACE—VISITS THE DUCHESS OF VICTORIA (THE REGENT'S WIFE) IN HER REVERSE OF FORTUNE.

SOME of the letters of the foregoing chapter gave a glimpse or two of the scenes of warfare and confusion of which Mr. Irving was a witness, while alone in the legation, with the city in a state of siege, and in hourly expectation of a general assault. He had, as we have seen, recovered sufficiently from his tantalizing malady to be able to go about on foot, and felt so extremely interested and excited during the crisis, that he could not keep in the house day or night. "I sallied out with as much eagerness," he writes, "as, when a boy, I used to break bounds, and sally forth at midnight to see a fire." What added, no doubt, to his excitement, was that his residence was not far from the gate of Alcala, about which most of the skirmishing took place. He states that he could see the flash of firearms from his window, and was often roused from sleep by the report of them in the night. The consequence of this exposure and fatigue to one who had hardly yet regained the use of his legs, was a relapse.

We have seen, in a former letter, that when preparations were made for a last stand at the palace, in case the city should be carried by assault, he had joined with the rest of the diplomatic corps in an offer to repair thither, and be near the Queen in the hour of danger. In the following letter, written after the event of the siege and the catastrophe of Espartero's regency, who had been driven from the country by a successful insurrection, he enters into some particulars of his agency in proposing the diplomatic intervention, and the motives which prompted the offer. The letter is to Mrs. Paris, is dated August 10th, and, besides the theme to which I have referred, contains other interesting and striking details of the royal drama of which he was a spectator.

* * * I see the French and English papers have published incorrect accounts of an interposition of the *corps diplomatique* in relation to the safety of the little Queen and her sister, in case of the city being carried by storm. I am represented, by some, as having prepared a note under the direction of the French *chargé d'affaires*, by others as having prepared it in concert with the British Minister. The fact is, I prepared one according to my own conception of what would be likely to meet with the concurrence of both parties, whose disagreement was likely to defeat the whole measure. The intervention was in consequence of preparations being made to convert the royal palace into a citadel, where, in case the city were carried by

assault, the last desperate stand was to be made; and in consequence of a declaration of that fanfaron Mendizabal, who had the control of affairs, that, if pushed to the utmost, he would sally forth with the Queen and her sister in each hand, put himself in the midst of the troops, and fight his way out of the city. I looked upon this as empty swaggering, but I knew not how far the defence might be pushed, or to what dangers the poor little Queen and her sister might be exposed by those who might seek to screen themselves behind the fancied sanctity of their persons.

I entered, therefore, into the remonstrance of the diplomatic corps solely on account of the royal children. I was for protesting against any EXTREME, either of *attack or defence*, which might put their persons in imminent jeopardy, knowing that the protest of the diplomatic corps would be promulgated, and would reach the besieging army, with the leaders of which the objections of a part of the diplomatic corps would have influence; while that of another part would have an effect upon the leaders of the defence. I had, however, as I before observed, to modify the whole note, as the British Minister would only protest against the *attack*, while the rest of the diplomatic corps objected to omitting the word *defence*. I suggested the idea of offering to repair to the palace, and be near the Queen in any moment of danger; which was adopted, and incorporated in the note. Our offer was declined. Fortunately, events obviated the necessity of the measure. My only view in joining in the measure, as I before observed, was, as far as our interference could have effect, to prevent the poor little Queen and her sister from being personally exposed to the dangers of any ruffian contest between warring and desperate factions. I am happy to say, the storm has passed away, and they are at present safe.

The day before yesterday we had one of those transitions of scene and circumstance to which the melodramatic politics of this country are subject. Poor Espartero, as you will learn from the public papers, has been completely cast down, and driven out of the country. Notwithstanding all the obloquy heaped upon his name by those who have effected his downfall, I still believe him to have been loyal in his intentions toward the crown and the constitution; but of this, no more for the present. Those who were lately insurgents, now possess the power; have formed themselves into a provisional government, occupy the capital, and carry on the affairs of the country in the accustomed manner, at the public offices. Their great object now is to declare the Queen of age as soon as possible, so that there will be no need of a regency, and that they will be able to act immediately in her name and by her authority. Some were of opinion that the Government (or cabinet of Ministers) ought to declare her so instantly, as, authorized by the wish of the nation, expressed in the various *juntas* and *pronunciamentos;* but others objected that this would be unconstitutional; the *Cortes* only could, by its vote, abbreviate the minority of the Queen, and declare her of age to govern, and before the *Cortes* only could she take the necessary oaths on assuming the reins of government. It was determined, therefore, to defer the measure until the meeting of the *Cortes*, in October next, but, in the mean time, to have a grand ceremonial in presence of all the dignitaries of the kingdom and the diplomatic corps, whenever the measure should be recommended in an address to the Queen, and concurred in by her, and thus a solemn pledge given to the nation, that, *the*

Cortes concurring, the minority would cease, and the Queen begin to reign in her own person in October. Accordingly, the day before yesterday, at five o'clock in the afternoon, I was present at another imposing scene at that theatre of political events, the royal palace. I have given you two or three rather gloomy scenes there already, connected with the story of the little Queen. I will now give you one of a different character. As the recent change of affairs has been one in which the *moderados*, or aristocracy, have taken great part, a complete change has taken place in the affairs of the palace. Arguelles, Madame Mina, and all the official characters elevated into place about the royal person by former revolutions, are now superseded, and the old nobility, who stood aloof and refused to mingle at court with people who had risen from the ranks, now surround the throne, and throng the saloons of the palace. As my carriage drew up at the foot of the vast and magnificent staircase, I observed hosts of old aristocratic courtiers, in their court dresses, thronging the marble steps, like the angels on Jacob's ladder—excepting that they were all ascending, none descending. I followed them up to this higher heaven of royalty. I paused for a moment at the great portal opening into the royal apartments. The marble casings still bear marks of the shattering musket balls, and the folding doors are still riddled like a sieve—mementos of that fearful night when this sacred abode of royalty and innocence was made the scene of desperate violence. Now, all was changed; the doors, thrown open, gave access to an immense and lofty antisala, where we passed through lines of halberdiers and court servants, all in new and bright array. All the anterooms were swarming with courtiers, military and civic officers and clergy, in their different costumes. The magnificent hall of the ambassadors, which, at our last audience of the little Queen, was almost empty and silent, was now absolutely crowded. I have already mentioned this hall to you. It is of great size, very lofty, the ceilings painted with representations of the various climes and realms of Spain in her palmy days, when the sun never set on her dominions. The walls are hung with crimson velvet, relieved with rich gilding. The chandeliers are of crystal. All the furniture is sumptuous. On one side of the saloon, just opposite the centre windows, is the throne, on a raised dais, and under a superb canopy of velvet. In this saloon, as I observed, were congregated an immense throng: old and new courtiers, many of the ancient nobility, who had kept out of sight during the domination of Espartero, but who now crept forth to hail the dawn of what they consider better days. Here, too, were many of the generals and officers who had figured in the recent insurrection, or who had hastened back from exile to come in for a share of power. Here was Narvaez, who lately held Madrid in siege; here was Espiroz, his confederate in arms; here was O'Donnell, the hero of the insurrection of 1840, connected with the night attack on the palace. In short, it was a complete resurrection and reunion of courtiers and military partisans, suddenly brought together by a political *coup de theatre.* For a while, all was buzz and hum, like a beehive in swarming time, when, suddenly, a voice from the lower end of the saloon proclaimed, *La reina! la reina!* (the Queen! the Queen!) In an instant all was hushed. A lane was opened through the crowd, and the little Queen advanced, led by the venerable General Castaños, Duke de Bailen, who had succeeded Arguelles as tutor and guardian. Her train was borne by the Marchioness of Valverde, a splendid-looking woman, one of the highest nobility; next followed her little sister, her train borne by the Duchess of Medina Celi, likewise one of the grandees; several other ladies of the highest rank were in attendance. The Queen was handed up to the throne by the Duke of Bailen, who took his stand beside her; the Duchess of Valverde arranged the royal train over the back of the chair of state which forms the throne, so that it spread behind the little Queen something like the tail of a peacock. The little Princess took her seat in a chair of state on the floor, a little to the left of the throne; the Duchess of Medina Celi behind her, and the other noble ladies-in-waiting ranged along to her left, all glittering in jewels and diamonds. A little further off, likewise in a chair of state, was Don Francisco, the Queen's uncle, and beside him stood his son, the Duke of Cadiz, who is one of the candidates for the hand of her little Majesty. I had now a good opportunity of seeing this youth. He was in a hussar's uniform, and a much better-looking stripling than I had been led to suppose him. As I know I am now on a diplomatic theme that will be peculiarly interesting to you—good republican as you are—I wish I could detail to you, learnedly, the dresses of the little Queen and her sister, which, as usual, were alike. I know the body and skirt were of beautiful brocade, richly fringed with gold; there was abundance of superb lace; the trains were of deep-green velvet; the Queen wore a kind of light crown of diamonds, in which alone she differed from the Princess. They both had diamond pendants and necklaces, and diamond ornaments in their side locks.

The little Queen looked well. She is quite plump, and has grown much. She acquitted herself with wonderful self-possession, considering that she was thus elevated individually in the midst of such an immense and gorgeous assemblage, and the object of every eye. Her manner was dignified and graceful. Her little sister, however, is far her superior, both in looks and carriage. She has beautiful eyes, an intelligent countenance, a sweet smile, and promises to be absolutely fascinating. Her looks and her winning manners she is said to inherit from her mother. She seemed to be in fine spirits; indeed, both of the sisters appeared to enjoy the scene. It was the first time that the little Queen had been surrounded by the aristocratical splendors of a court.

When the Queen had taken her seat, the cabinet Ministers took their stand before the throne, and one of them read an address to her, stating the circumstances that made it expedient she should be declared of age by the next *Cortes*, and should then take the oaths of office. As the little Queen held her reply, ready cut and dry, in a paper in her hand, she paid but little attention to the speech, but kept glancing her eyes here and there about the hall, and now and then toward her little sister, when a faint smile would appear stealing over her lips, but instantly repressed. The speech ended, she opened the paper in her hand, and read the brief reply which had been prepared for her. A shout then burst forth from the assemblage, of *Viva la reina!* (Long live the Queen!). The venerable Duke of Bailen, taking the lead as tutor to the Queen, then bent on one knee, and kissed her hand. The Infanta Don Francisco and his son gave the same token of allegiance. The same was done by every person present, excepting the diplomatic corps. They also knelt and kissed the hand of the Princess, and some kissed the hand of Don Francisco, but those were his partisans. As the crowd was great, this ceremonial took up some time. I observed that the Queen and her sister discriminated greatly as to the crowd of persons who paid this homage, distinguishing with smiles, and sometimes with pleasant words, those with whom they were acquainted. It was curious to see generals kneeling and kissing the hand of the sovereign, who but three weeks since were in rebellion against her government, besieging her capital, and menacing the royal abode, where they were now doing her homage.

This ceremony over, the Queen and her sister took their stand in a balcony in front of the great hall of ambassadors, under a rich and lofty silken awning. The high dignitaries of her court attended on her. The ladies of the court were in a balcony on one side, and the diplomatic corps in one on the other; and every window of the royal suite of apartments was thronged by persons in court dresses or uniforms. The whole effect, in that magnificent palace, was remarkably brilliant. A vast throng was collected in the great square before the palace. In a little while, martial music was heard, and General Narvaez, with his staff, escorted by a troop of horse, came advancing under an archway on the opposite side of the square. In fact, the whole army that had lately besieged the city now came marching in review before the palace, shouting *vivas* as they passed beneath the royal balcony. It was really a splendid sight—one of those golden, cloudless evenings of this brilliant climate, when the sun was pouring his richest effulgence into the vast square, around which the troops paraded. Here were troops from various parts of Spain, many of them wayworn and travel stained, and all burnt by the ardent sun under which they had marched. The most curious part of this military spectacle was the Catalan legion—men who looked like banditti rather than soldiers—arrayed in half-Arab dress, with *mantas*, like horsecloths, thrown over one shoulder, red woollen caps, and hempen socks instead of shoes. They are, in fact, little better than banditti—a fierce, turbulent race, as are all the Catalans. I remained for a great part of an hour witnessing the passing of these insurgent legions, which were recently overrunning the country and menacing the capital, but which, by the sudden hocus pocus of political affairs, are transformed into loyal soldiers, parading peacefully before the royal palace, and shouting *vivas* for the Queen. This is the last act I have witnessed of the royal drama, and here I will let fall the curtain.

After writing the foregoing to his sister, he drove out to pay visits of ceremony to some of the persons who had suddenly been brought into official station by the recent change of government. The visit detailed below, however, was not one of form, and had a higher prompting than diplomatic etiquette. I have heard him say it provoked a courtier's scoff. When about to bring his long letter to an end, he writes to his sister, August 11th:

Before I conclude, let me say a word or two about that most amiable and excellent woman, the Duchess of Victoria. I have always esteemed and admired her, but never so much as since her great reverse of fortune. During the siege, as the palace of Buena Vista was near the point of attack, she took refuge in the royal palace. Since the capitulation of the city, the occupation of it by the insurgent armies, and the formation of the provisional government, she retired to the house of an aunt in the centre of Madrid. Here I visited her, and found her still attended by some faithful friends. I found her calm, self-possessed, and free from all useless repining or weak lamentation. In fact, she was in a far better state of mind than when I saw her at her *soirées* at Buena Vista, surrounded by something like a court, but harassed by doubts and forebodings. She said her conscience was clear; she had never been excited by her elevation as the wife of the Regent, and trusted her conduct had always been the same as when wife of a simple general. She felt no humiliation in her downfall. She spoke of the charges made against her husband of grasping ambition, artifice, love of power—he, said she, whose habits were so simple, whose desires so limited; who cared not for state, and less for money; whose great pleasure was to be in his garden, planting trees and cultivating flowers. It was a matter of pride and consolation to her, she added, that they left the regency poorer than when they entered it. I was pleased to see that she spoke without acrimony of those political rivals who had effected the downfall of her husband, but with deep feeling of the conduct of some who had always professed devotion to him, who had risen by his friendship, and who had betrayed him. "This," said she, "is the severest blow of all, for it destroys our confidence in humankind." I could not but admire the discrimination of her conduct with respect to the two great leaders of the present Government, Generals Narvaez (Commander-in-Chief) and Serrano (the Minister of War). They both sent her offers of escort, and of any other service and facility. "As to General Narvaez," said she, "he has always been the avowed enemy of my husband, but an open and frank one; he practised nothing but what he professed; I accept his offers with gratitude and thanks. As to Serrano, he professed to be my husband's friend; he rose by his friendship and favors, and he proved faithless to him; I will accept nothing at his hands, and beg his name may not again be mentioned to me."

The Duchess has set off for England by the way of France, and an escort was furnished her by Narvaez to protect her on her journey through Spain. I have no doubt she will be well received in England, and will feel a tranquillity of mind there to which she has long been a stranger. "Oh!" said she, drawing a long breath, "how glad I shall be to find myself once more at complete liberty, where I can breathe a freer air, and be out of this atmosphere of politics, trouble, and anxiety."

CHAPTER XVI.

LEAVES MADRID FOR CHANGE OF AIR—EXCURSION TO VERSAILLES AND PARIS—GRISI IN NORMA—BORDEAUX—LETTER TO HENRY BREVOORT—REGRETS ABOUT THE INTERRUPTION OF HIS LITERARY PLANS—ALLUSION TO THE DIPLOMATIC INTERVENTION FOR THE SAFETY OF THE QUEEN—MEETING WITH ROGERS—RETURN TO MADRID—LETTER TO MRS. PARIS—THE YOUNG QUEEN'S ACCESSION TO THE THRONE—MADAME CALDERON—PASSAGES FROM A LETTER TO MRS. GRINNELL.

BEING strongly urged by his physician to try the effects of travel and a change of air for the inflammation in his ankles, which had now harassed him, more or less, for seven months past, confining him for a great part of the time to the house, and sometimes to his bed, Mr. Irving left Madrid on the 7th of September, to make an excursion into France, leaving the legation in the hands of the Secretary, Mr. Hamilton. He was accompanied by his faithful servant, Lorenzo, and from Bordeaux, where he stopped to pass a few days among his friends, the Guestiers and Johnsons, writes to his niece, Mrs. Storrow, then quartered at Versailles:

I hope you will retain your apartments at Versailles. I would vastly prefer visiting you there, than at Paris.

I must tell you that I have thus far enjoyed my journey extremely. I do not know when scenery had a more vivifying effect on my feelings than in passing from the dreary, parched wastes of the Castiles, to the green mountains and valleys of the Basque provinces. The nights were superb, a full moon lighting up splendid mountain scenery; the air bland and fresh and balmy, instead of the parching airs of Madrid. The first sight of the sea, too, and the inhaling of the sea breeze, brought a home feeling that was quite reviving. You cannot imagine how beautiful France looks to me, with her orchards and vineyards and groves and green meadows, after naked, sterile Spain. I feel confident I shall return from this excursion with a stock of health and good spirits to carry me through the winter.

He left Bordeaux on Wednesday, the 13th, and, travelling day and night, arrived at Versailles at three o'clock on Friday (15th). "I need not tell you," he writes to the mother the day after his arrival, "what a joyful meeting it has been to Sarah and myself. I am sure this visit will effect my perfect restoration. * * * After so long a separation from kith and kin, and so much time passed in loneliness and sickness, it is a heartfelt satisfaction to be with one kindred in heart as well as blood."

Mr. Irving remained at Versailles nearly two weeks without coming to Paris, and, indeed, without leaving the house, excepting in a carriage to take the air, the journey from Madrid having brought on a temporary irritation of the lingering symptoms of his malady.

We came to Paris the day before yesterday [he writes to his brother, September 30th], but I have not yet been out of the house. I am gradually, however, getting over this transient access of my complaint, and hope in a few days to be again able to go about on foot. I intend consulting the ablest physician on the subject. I am anxious to get well, so as to be able to return to Madrid before the cold weather sets in. I do not like to be away from my post in these critical times. * * * I have full confidence in the ability of Alexander Hamilton to carry on the ordinary business of the legation, but questions may arise, and claims to sovereignty between warring parties in these revolutionary times, in respect to which I wish to take upon myself the responsibility of deciding.

Thirteen days later, he writes to his sister (October 12th):

I have now been two weeks in Paris, but am still confined very much to the house, excepting when I go out in a carriage. The least exercise on foot produces an irritation of the malady which still lingers about my ankles, and thus retards my cure. I begin to think it will yet take a considerable time to conquer it, and that I shall have to return to Madrid before my cure is completed. My general health, however, is good, my appetite excellent, and I am growing as stout a gentleman as formerly. My time passes pleasantly in the house, having the "babe" for a playmate, and a delightful one she is, I can assure you. She is very intelligent for so young a creature, and has a thousand winning and amusing ways. We now understand each other perfectly, and have a great many jokes together. She relishes my jokes greatly, and enters into the spirit of them completely, which makes me think she has a great perception of wit and humor.

The ways and whims of children were to Mr. Irving an endless source of amusement. Kate, the little playmate here alluded to—"dear, darling, restless little Kate," as he calls her in one letter, "that pebble-hearted little woman," in another—was not yet two years of age.

The next day (October 13th) he writes to me from Paris:

I am leading a very quiet life in the very centre of all that is gay and splendid. My obstinate malady, which still clings to me just sufficiently to fetter me, prevents my sallying forth excepting in a carriage, so that I pass most of the time in the house. Last night, however, I managed to visit the opera, and saw Grisi in Norma. She is one of the finest actors I have ever seen, quite worthy of being classed with the Siddonses, Pastas, &c. I had scarcely expected ever again to have seen such a glorious combination of talent and personal endowment on the stage.

November 22d, in a letter to me, he reports himself as being on the point of setting off in the *malle poste* for Bordeaux, in very good travelling condition; and, four days later, after a comfortable journey, he writes to his old friend, Brevoort, from that city, as follows, giving, as will be seen, a glance at his own private affairs, the public concerns of his mission, and an amusing sketch of an encounter with Rogers, while at Paris:

BORDEAUX, NOV. 26, 1843.

MY DEAR BREVOORT:

I received your most kind and welcome letter some short time before leaving Paris, and should have answered it immediately, but I was in one of those moods when my mind has no power over my pen. Indeed, I have long owed you a letter, and have intended to write to you; but correspondents multiplied fearfully upon me, and my pen was tasked, diplomatically and otherwise, on my arrival at Madrid, to such a degree as to fag me out, and to produce the malady which has harassed me for nearly a year past. I am now on my way back to my post, after between two and three months' absence. I set out in pursuit of health, and thought a little travelling and a change of air would "make me my own man" again; but I was laid by the heels at Paris, by a recurrence of my malady, and have just escaped out of the doctor's hands, sufficiently recovered to get back to my post, where I hope, by care and medical treatment, to effect my cure.

This indisposition has been a sad check upon all my plans. I had hoped, by zealous employment of all the leisure afforded me at Madrid, to accomplish one or two literary tasks which I have in hand. * * * A year, however, has now been completely lost to me, and a precious year, at my time of life. The Life of Washington, and, indeed, all my literary tasks, have remained suspended; and my pen has remained idle, excepting now and then in writing a despatch to Government, or scrawling a letter to my family. In the mean time, the income which I used to derive from farming out my writings has died away, and my moneyed investments yield scarce any interest. * * * However, thank God, my health, and with it my capacity for working, are returning. I shall soon again have pen in hand, and hope to get two or three good years of literary labor out of myself. Times are improving in America, and with them may improve the landed property which I hold. * * *

Carson will give you an account of diplomatic and household affairs at Madrid. I was extremely sorry to part with him; but I could not advise him to stay, where there was no career nor regular pursuit opening to him. * * *

I do not know whether you speak in jest or earnest about the popular view of my conduct on the occasion of the diplomatic intervention for the safety of the little Queen, during the late siege of Madrid. My conduct was dictated at the time by honest and spontaneous impulse, without reference to policy or politics. I felt deeply for the situation of the Queen and her sister, and was anxious that their persons should be secured from the civil brawls and fightings which threatened to distract the city, and invade the very courts of the royal palace. In all my diplomacy, I have depended more upon good intentions and frank and open conduct, than upon any subtle management. I have an opinion that the old maxim, "Honesty is the best policy," holds good even in diplomacy!

Thus far I have got on well with my brother diplomatists, and have met with very respectful treatment from the Spanish Government in all its changes and fluctuations. I have endeavored punctually to perform the duties of my office, and to execute the instructions of Government; and I believe that the archives of the legation will testify that the business of the mission has never been neglected. I have not suffered illness to prevent me from keeping everything in train; and, indeed, my recovery has been retarded by remaining at my post during the revolutionary scenes of last summer, though urged by my physicians to spend the hot months at the watering places in the mountains. I do not pretend to any great skill as a diplomatist; but in whatever situation I am placed in life, when I doubt my skill, I endeavor to make up for it by conscientious assiduity.

While I was in Paris, in driving out, one day, with my niece in the Champs Elysées, we nearly ran over my old friend Rogers. We stopped, and took him in. He was in one of his yearly epicurean visits to Paris, to enjoy the Italian opera and other refined sources of pleasure. The hand of age begins to bow him down, but his intellect is clear as ever, and his talents and taste for society in full vigor. He breakfasted with us several times, and I have never known him more delightful. He would sit for two or three hours continually conversing, and giving anecdotes of all the conspicuous persons who have figured within the last sixty years, with most of whom he has been on terms of intimacy. He has refined upon the art of telling a story, until he has brought it to the most perfect simplicity, where there is not a word too much or too little, and where every word has its effect. His manner, too, is the most quiet, natural, and unpretending that can be imagined. I was very much amused by an anecdote he gave us of little Queen Victoria and her nautical vagaries. Lord Aberdeen has had to attend her in her cruisings, very much against his will, or, at least, against his stomach. You know he is one of the gravest and most laconic men in the world. The Queen, one day, undertook to reconcile him to his fate. "I believe, my lord," said she, graciously, "you are not often seasick." "*Always*, madam," was the grave reply. "But," still more graciously, "not *very* seasick." With profounder gravity, "VERY, madam!" Lord Aberdeen declares, that if her Majesty persists in her cruisings, he will have to resign.

I rejoice to hear of Mrs. Brevoort's improved health, and think you are right, should you find the seacoast of Long Island favorable to the health of your family, to set up a retreat there. I can say from experience, that a man has tenfold more enjoyment from any rural retreat that belongs to himself, than from any that he hires as a temporary sojourn.

During his absence in Paris, the declaration of the majority of the Queen had been made by the *Cortes*, and she had taken the oath to support the constitution; an imposing ceremonial, at which the diplomatic body were present. Soon after his return to Madrid, he writes as follows:

[*To Mrs. Paris.*]

MADRID, Dec. 10, 1843.

MY DEAR SISTER:

I received, yesterday, your letter dated about the middle of last month. It was extremely gratifying to me, for I was longing for domestic news from home, and your letters always place home completely before me. I have not time to write you a long letter, for I have been writing despatches to Government, and am fatigued, and the courier is soon to set off.

I arrived safe in Madrid about ten days since, after a somewhat rapid journey; but I had the mail carriage to myself, and was enabled to make myself comfortable. On approaching Spain, I heard of the mail having been robbed between Bayonne and Madrid, and the passengers extremely maltreated, and was advised not to go until I could be well escorted; but I knew that highway robberies seldom occurred twice in any neighborhood, unless at long intervals, so I pushed forward. It had been advertised that the mail would be doubly guarded, in consequence of the late robberies, but the promise was not fulfilled. We passed through the robber region in the night, with only two musketeers to guard the carriage, both of whom went to sleep. As I did not care to keep watch myself, and alarm myself with shadows, I arranged myself comfortably, and fell asleep likewise, and continued napping through all the dangerous part of the road. I arrived in Madrid just in time to witness the three days of public rejoicing for the young Queen's accession to the throne. All the houses were decorated, the balconies hung with tapestry; there were triumphal arches, fountains running with milk and wine, games, dances, processions, and parades by day, illuminations and spectacles at night, and the streets were constantly thronged by the populace in their holiday garb. * * * The *Moderados* have the government at present, and are determined to maintain their sway by military means. General Narvaez is with them, and, under his military vigilance, the capital gleams with the bayonet as in time of war.

Ten days later, he writes to his niece, at Paris: * * * "I found Mr. Hamilton in good health and good looks on my return. He has conducted the legation extremely well during my absence, and given it up into my hands in complete order." * * * "I was cordially welcomed back by my brother diplomatists, and really had a home feeling on finding myself once more among them. I miss my old crony, Mr. Asten, however, sadly, and fear it will be difficult to supply his loss."

Mr. Asten, the British Minister, was succeeded by Henry Lytton Bulwer, who had not yet made his appearance in the diplomatic circle. After mentioning some accessions to that body during his absence, he adds:

We have here, also, Mr. Calderon, formerly Minister to the United States, and his wife. The latter recently wrote a very lively work on a residence in Mexico. She is originally Scotch, but has resided for some time in the United States. I am highly pleased with her. She is intelligent, sprightly, and full of agreeable talent. I fear, however, she will not remain here long, as Mr. Calderon is likely to be appointed to some diplomatic post. Madame Calderon is a constant correspondent of Mr. Prescott. By the by, she has just lent me a copy of his Conquest of Mexico, in sheets. I have read a great part of the introductory chapters, treating of Aztec manners, customs, &c., and am deeply interested in it.

I close the year with a few extracts from a letter, dated December 29th, to Mrs. Moses H. Grinnell, in answer to some account of changes and improvements in her residence in the city of New York:

Your account of the wonderful additions and alterations in the house in College Place quite astonishes me. Grinnell certainly must have the bump of constructiveness strongly developed, particularly in that department of architecture which appertains to dining rooms, butlers' pantries, and wine cellars.

I have no doubt that, in consequence of his increased facilities, he now gives two dinners where he formerly gave one; though that can hardly be, as he formerly, in general, gave one dinner and a half per diem, the latter being smuggled into the household economy under the name of a supper. * * * God bless his bounteous heart! I have no doubt that, had he been in the place of his great namesake of holy writ, when he smote the rock, there would have spouted out wine instead of water.

* * * * * *

I perfectly agree with you in your idea of ——— and ———. I feel deeply my separation from them; they both seemed to take the place of others dear to my heart, whom I had lost and deplored. ——— came to my side, when I was grieving over the loss of my dear brother Peter, who had so long been the companion of my thoughts, and I found in him many of the qualities which made that brother so invaluable to me as a bosom friend; * * * while ———, in the delightful variety of her character, so affectionate, so tender, so playful at times, and at other times so serious and elevated, and always so intelligent and sensitive, continually brought to mind her mother, who was one of the tenderest friends of my childhood, and the delight of my youthful years. God bless and prosper them both! * * *

The letter concludes with a fervent wish that he could return and be once more with his "little flock":

My heart yearns for home; and as I have now probably turned the last corner in life, and my remaining years are growing scanty in number, I begrudge every one that I am obliged to pass separated from my cottage and my kindred.

CHAPTER XVII.

EXTRACTS FROM VARIOUS LETTERS—THE PAST YEAR A LITERARY BLANK—THE QUEEN'S ENTRANCE UPON HER REIGN—EXPLANATION OF A SCENE IN THE CABINET—ROYALTY ON ITS BED OF DEATH—PREPARATION FOR THE ARRIVAL OF THE QUEEN MOTHER—HER RETURN—LETTER TO MARY IRVING—LETTER TO MRS. PARIS—THE ROYAL MEETING—ENTRANCE OF QUEEN CHRISTINA INTO MADRID—DEATH OF ARGUELLES.

THOUGH Mr. Irving had the advantage of one of the most eminent physicians in Paris, he still brought back to Madrid the malady with which he had been so long tormented; a malady the more annoying, as it robbed him of the free use of his pen, and prevented him from being agreeably employed. The following extracts from various letters at this period are all more or less tinged with a depression arising from this drawback upon his literary plans:

[*To Mrs. Storrow.*]

January 7th, 1844.— * * * Madame A——— says my visit to Paris has done me no good in one respect, that I am less content with Madrid since my return; but, in fact, I am at times disheartened by the continuance of my malady, which obliges me to abstain from all literary occupations, and half disables me for social intercourse. If I could only exercise my pen, I should be quite another being. * * *

I am preparing to give a diplomatic dinner, which is something of an undertaking in my present nerveless condition.

[*To the Same.*]

January 14*th.*— * * * I fear I am growing miserly over the remnant of existence, and cannot bear to have any of the few years that remain to me wasted as the last has been. I hope this year I may live more to the purpose; otherwise it is a heavy tax to pay for mere existence.

To his niece, Sarah Irving, at the cottage, he writes:

January 19*th.*— * * * I hope you will all make your contemplated visits to New York in the course of the winter; it will serve to break up the monotony of the season, though, for my part, if I could only be in my little cottage, looking out from its snug, warm shelter, upon the broad expanse of the Tappan Sea, all brilliant with snow and ice and sunshine, I think I should be loth to leave it for the city; but then, what would suit a philosophic old gentleman, who has seen enough of the world, and grown too wise for its gayeties, would hardly be to the taste of a bevy of young ladies, for whom the world has still some novelty.

[*To Pierre M. Irving.*]

January 20*th*, 1844.— * * * I feel sadly the loss of the past year, which has disconcerted all those literary plans I formed on leaving home. However, I still hope the opening year, or at least a part of it, may be more profitably employed.

Give my love to my dear Helen, whose letters are perfect balm to me when I am in a moody fit, as I am apt to be sometimes, when my cure does not go on as well as I could wish. I will write to her before long, so beg her to send the answer in advance.

Though much depressed in spirit at this recurrence, or rather aggravation of his blighting malady, after such a long course of assiduous treatment, he still makes the exertion to continue to his sister, Mrs. Paris, an account of the affairs of the palace, in which she had taken great interest. His letter is dated January 20th, 1844. I quote the part which gives his version of the abrupt dismissal by the Queen of her Minister of State, Olozaga, a chief of the *Progresista* party:

The papers will have shown you that the entrance of the poor little Queen upon her reign has been the commencement of troubles. Mr. Olozaga, the Minister of State, and one of the leading men of the coalition that overthrew Espartero, was suddenly dismissed from office, and accused by the Queen with having, when alone with her in her cabinet, treated her in an arrogant and imperious manner, insisting on her signing a decree dissolving the *Cortes*, and actually bolting the doors and preventing her leaving the room until she had so given her signature. This accusation has produced a prodigious effect in the political world. Mr. Olozaga has defended himself in the Chamber of Deputies, declaring that the Queen signed the decree voluntarily, that the accusation was dictated to the Queen by a *camarilla*, or knot of court intriguers who surround her, and that the whole was a palace intrigue, designed to produce his downfall. The whole party of *Progresistas*, who had been in league with the *Moderados*, broke from the coalition, and espoused the side of Mr. Olozaga; and the members of the Cabinet who were of that party resigned their posts, and came out in defence of the fallen Minister. A commission was appointed to examine into the circumstances of the case, and to ascertain whether there were grounds for criminal proceedings against Mr. Olozaga. In the mean time, the latter secretly fled to Portugal, declaring, by letter, that he did so in consequence of finding himself waylaid and threatened with assassination, but that he was ready to return and appear before the commission whenever the investigation should be commenced, and his presence required.

The misfortune of all this is, that it places the veracity of the Queen in the balance with that of a subject, and that the public seem inclined to decide in favor of the latter; since, in a recent election to supply vacancies in the Chamber of Deputies, Mr. Olozaga has been placed at the head of the list of opposition candidates, and elected by a large majority. This is hailed as a great triumph by the *Progresista* party; but it appears to me ominous to the throne, and shows that the prestige which so lately surrounded the youthful Queen is already impaired by party rancor.

My idea is, that this famous scene in the cabinet of the Queen has not been fairly stated by either party, each having, perhaps unconsciously, given it an after-coloring. A jealousy evidently existed between Olozaga and those in the palace who were daily about the Queen. He suspected them of seeking his downfall. When the Queen hesitated to sign the decree dissolving the *Cortes*, he no doubt supposed that she acted, not from her own judgment or inclination, but from the instigations of others, his enemies. Accustomed, in his former office as tutor, to treat her with great familiarity, and to look upon her as a child, rather than as his sovereign, and vexed that his present measures of state policy should be impeded by the mere wilfulness of an inexperienced girl, he probably became authoritative and peremptory, like a tutor enforcing a necessary task upon his pupil, and the Queen acquiesced as a matter of course, without probably feeling outraged by his dictatorial conduct. It may not have been until afterward, when her palace advisers exclaimed against the dangerous nature of the decree which she had signed, that, like a child, she sought to excuse herself by saying Mr. Olozaga made her sign it; and then was made aware, by those experienced courtiers, of the terrible infraction of sovereign dignity perpetrated by Mr. Olozaga, and of the gross outrage she had unconsciously sustained. Of course, she then saw the whole affair in a different light; her ire was kindled, and, in her subsequent accounts, facts were colored and exaggerated by her feelings. Such would commonly be the case with the statements of a child under similar circumstances; and, after all, the poor little Queen, though the *Cortes* has solemnly declared her of age, is but a child. I cannot explain this matter to myself in any other manner, without thinking either that the little Queen has been guilty of a wanton and unprofitable falsehood, or that Mr. Olozaga has acted like a *fool* as well as a brute. I have no great opinion of Mr. Olozaga's principles or manners. He has been a shifting, intriguing politician, and, during his elevation to office, which brought him in immediate proximity with the sovereign, he displayed a forward, and, at times, jocose familiarity, which showed he was unaccustomed to the etiquette of courts, unconscious of the high decorum and almost sanctity which should surround the royal person, and incapable of the dignified yet modest self-command and self-respect proper to a statesman in his elevated position. He is, however, a shrewd, able man, and could scarcely have been *intentionally* guilty of such an outrage upon the royal will and dignity, as might be inferred by a rigorous view of his conduct in this transaction. He probably was not aware of the construction of which his conduct was susceptible, nor thought that, while he was exercising the authority of a tutor over a refractory pupil, he, as a Minister, was outraging the dignity of a sovereign.

You now see in what a critical situation the poor little Queen is placed by being declared of age. She has now to exercise the functions of a sovereign, while her mind is immature, her character unfixed; where she has no one at hand of talent, integrity, and disinterested devotion, to whom she can look for counsel; where she is surrounded by court flatterers and court intriguers of both sexes, and where even her ministers are faithless. Already she is becoming an object of party hostility, though it is not openly avowed; and the late triumphant reëlection of Olozaga, in thus returning him to the *Cortes*, to confront his sovereign, as it were, in her own capital, before the charges against him are investigated, shows the disposition of the opposition party to prejudge the case in his favor. * * *

Twenty days later, we have the following picture of a royal princess on her bed of death:

MADRID, Feb. 9, 1844.

MY DEAR SISTER:

* * * * * *

The Spanish Court has recently been put into mourning by the sudden death of the Infanta Luisa Carlota, wife to the Infante Don Francisco, and aunt to the Queen. She was a woman of strong passions and restless ambition. For some time past she has been scheming and intriguing to effect a marriage between her son, the Duke of Cadiz, and his cousin, the youthful Queen, and had embroiled herself with all parties, and impoverished her husband and herself in the prosecution of her plans. Their failure mortified her pride and exasperated her temper, and of late she had been extremely ungracious in looks and manners. Her illness was preceded by a kind of fever of the mind. "I know not what is the matter with me," said she to one of her attendants; "wherever I am, and wherever I go, I am in a constant state of irritation; at the theatre, on the Prado, at home, it is still the same—I am in a passion (*je m'enrage*"). In this state of mind she was attacked by measles and *pulmonia* (a kind of inflammation of the lungs), which, acting upon an extremely full, plethoric habit, hurried her out of existence in the course of two or three days, and in the thirty-ninth year of her age. The body lay in state for three days, and the populace were admitted to see it, according to Spanish custom. I called to inscribe my name on the list of visitors, as is the etiquette, and suffered myself to be carried by the throng through a suite of rooms decked out with escutcheons, funeral hatchments, lighted tapers, and files of mute attendants. The corpse was on a bed of state, and arrayed in a gala dress—white brocade and gold, with a royal coronet—the face livid, and bloated with disease.

I have given you, my dear sister, some features of royalty in its grandeur: here you have it brought down to the dusty level of mere mortality. But a few days previously I had beheld this proud-hearted Princess walking the Prado with her family, with sullen and almost disdainful air, scarce noticing the salutations of the well-dressed throngs which bowed, with uncovered head, as she passed. Here she was, on her bed of death, exposed to the gaze of the unmannered populace, some of whom even whispered jests to each other, and sneered and laughed as they criticized the corpse and the funeral pageant!

We are again in the midst of popular commotions. Insurrections have broken out in Alicante and Carthagena, and Government are taking strong measures to nip them in the bud. The whole kingdom is put under martial law; all political offences are to be tried by military tribunals, and all officers and subaltern officers taken in rebellion are to be shot on the mere identification of their persons. The Government is evidently determined to rule by the sword. Unfortunately, some of these sanguinary decrees are worded as if proceeding from the immediate will and wish of the Queen, who, poor child, is little conscious of the force and nature of the papers she is signing. They have produced a great sensation, and, I fear, will contribute to involve the innocent little Queen in the party odium which the opposition is endeavoring to excite against the Government. Important arrests have taken place of persons suspected of participation in the new conspiracies. Among these are some of those political leaders who were active, last summer, in effecting the downfall of Espartero, and who are now proscribed by their late confederates, whom they helped up into power. Such is the continual succession of plot and counterplot in this unhappy country. It is probable the strong measures taken by Government will check the present insurrection, and that the *Moderados* (or aristocratical party) may maintain the sway for a time. If not, their case will be desperate; for their strong measures have awakened the most deadly enmity in the opposition, and a new revolution, I fear, would be sanguinary and vindictive in the extreme.

March 15th, he writes to a niece at Sunnyside, yet in her teens, a letter, of which one or two extracts may amuse. The Countess of Montijo, whose name occurs in the letter, is the mother of the present Empress of France.

[*To Miss Mary Irving.*]

MADRID, March 15, 1844.

MY DEAR MARY:

I am told you want me to write you again, "if it is only a few lines;" so, my dear, good little girl, I will give you a small letter, which is all I can afford for the present, having to write not merely to your aunt, in New York, but to "Uncle Sam," at Washington, who generally expects pretty long letters.

We are on the eve of great fêtes and ceremonies, to greet the arrival of the Queen Mother, who is on her way once more to embrace her children. I wish you could be here to enjoy these sights and festivities; I think they would delight you. They are rather thrown away upon me. I am not well enough to enter into them with spirit, and then, I have grown so wise!

I was, a few mornings since, on a visit to the Duchess of

Berwick. She is the widow of a grandee of Spain, who claimed some kind of descent from the royal line of the Stuarts. She is of immense wealth, and resides in the most beautiful palace in Madrid (excepting the royal one). I passed up a splendid staircase, and through halls and saloons without number, all magnificently furnished, and hung with pictures and family portraits. This Duchess was an Italian by birth, and brought up in the royal family at Naples. She is the very head of fashion here. Well, this lady, of almost princely state, will be one of the ladies-in-waiting on the little Queen when she receives her mother. She will stand behind the Queen at the foot of the staircase of the royal palace, and perhaps bear her Majesty's train. Think of that, my dear; think how grandly these little queens of thirteen years of age are waited upon.

* * * A grand wedding took place, shortly since, between the eldest son of the Duchess (the present Duke of Alva, about twenty-two years of age) and the daughter of the Countess of Montijo, another very rich grandee. The *corbeille*, or wedding presents of the bride, amounted to one hundred and twenty thousand dollars, all in finery. There were lace handkerchiefs worth a hundred or two dollars, only to look at; and dresses, the very sight of which made several young ladies quite ill. The young Duchess is thought to be one of the happiest and best-dressed young ladies in the whole world. She is already quite hated in the *beau monde.*

After all this magnificent detail, I shall expect, in return, an account of cousin Julia's ball, and how you all enjoyed yourselves, and how you were all dressed. Between you and I, I would not give little Sunnyside for the grandest duke's palace in Spain; and as to the bride and her fine dresses, when you and Julia get on your spring dresses and spring bonnets, I should not be afraid to challenge a comparison.

And now, my dear little girl, I have scribbled for you a very rigmarole letter, but it was the best I could furnish in this hurried moment. I hope it may find you bright and happy at our dear little cottage, where it will be the happiest moment of my life once more to join you.

Give my best love to all the family, and believe me ever, my dear, dear Mary, your affectionate uncle,

WASHINGTON IRVING.

The following letter unfolds another page in Spanish affairs:

[*To Mrs. Paris.*]

MADRID, March 16, 1844.

MY DEAR SISTER:

We are preparing for great ceremonies and festivities on the arrival of the Queen Mother, who has lately entered from France, and is slowly making her way to the capital, to be restored to her children. The little Queen and her sister departed from Madrid some time since, to meet her mother on the road, according to Spanish usage. The meeting is to take place a little beyond the royal *sitio*, or country residence of Aranjuez, between that place and Ocaña. A temporary structure has been put up in the road for the purpose. The *corps diplomatique*, and all the court and nobility, are invited to attend on the occasion, and Aranjuez is already crowded. This place is about twenty-seven miles from Madrid, situated in a narrow valley watered by the Tagus. It is a small town, or rather village, in which are some indifferent hotels, and large barracks of houses, and is almost deserted, excepting when visited by the sovereign in the spring. The royal palace is spacious, but not magnificent. The great attractions are delicious gardens, with shady walks and bowers, refreshing fountains, and thousands of nightingales; also noble avenues of trees, and fine, shady drives. All these render it a paradise in this arid, naked country; and you come upon it by surprise, after traversing dreary plains, for it lies sunk in a narrow, green valley scooped out of the desert by the Tagus. As I have not yet sufficiently the use of my legs to enjoy the gardens and promenades, I shall not go to Aranjuez, this time, until the day before the Queen is expected to arrive.

* * * * * *

The return of the Queen Mother is quite an event in the royal romance of the palace, and the circumstances of her journey have really a touching interest for me. She returns by the very way by which she left the kingdom in 1840, when the whole world seemed to be roused against her, and she was followed by clamor and execrations. What is the case at present? The cities that were then almost in arms against her, now receive her with fêtes and rejoicings. Arches of triumph are erected in the streets; *Te Deums* are chaunted in the cathedrals; processions issue forth to escort her; the streets ring with shouts and acclamations; homage and adulation meet her at every step; the meanest village has its ceremonial of respect, and a speech of loyalty from its alcalde. Thus her progress through the kingdom is a continual triumph. * * *

In the following, to the same correspondent, he gives a picture of the restoration of the Queen Mother to her children:

MADRID, March 23, 1844.

MY DEAR SISTER:

I have just received your long letter of February 25th to 29th, and feel how kind it is in you to give me such frequent budgets from home. Your letters are full of matter, and, being written from day to day, give me an everyday peep into domestic affairs. I have a letter, also, from Pierre M. Irving, giving me a very satisfactory statement of my affairs, which he has managed with great judgment.

* * * * * *

I must now give you a chapter of the romance of the palace. I set off, the day before yesterday, for Aranjuez, to be present at the meeting of the little Queen and her mother. I started at six o'clock in the morning, in my carriage, with old Pedro the coachman, and my faithful Lorenzo. Mr. Valdevielso, the Mexican Minister, accompanied me, having sent on his four horses to be stationed on the road as relays. We had a beautiful morning, and enjoyed our drive to the old village of Valdemoro, where we left Pedro and the horses to await our return, and took the first pair of Mr. Valdevielso's horses, with his coachman. With these we drove to Aranjuez, not finding occasion to use the second relay, which followed us. We arrived at Aranjuez at half-past eleven, and found the meeting was expected to take place about five o'clock in the afternoon, about three miles from Aranjuez, on the road to Ocaña, a royal tent having been put up for the occasion. Aranjuez was crowded with company—all the nobility from Madrid, the military, and official characters of all sorts, not to mention office hunters, and the countless crowd that courts the smiles of royalty.

Every vehicle at Madrid had been engaged at high prices

to bring on the multitude; every lodging, good or bad, at Aranjuez, had been taken up beforehand. I had comfortable quarters with my good friends the Albuquerques, and found myself the inmate of quite a diplomatic commonwealth, occupying a huge house hired for the occasion. It was two stories high, built around a square courtyard. You may imagine the size of the Spanish houses, when I tell you that in this were accommodated the French ambassador and his lady, with two young gentlemen of the embassy; the Albuquerques and their family; the Prince and Princess de Carini; the Count Marnex, Belgian *chargé d'affaires;* Mr. D'Alborgo, *chargé d'affaires* of Denmark; the Mexican Minister and myself; and that each family had a distinct apartment to itself, with sitting room, antechamber, &c. We all dined together, and a pleasant dinner we had; while, throughout the day and evening, Madame Albuquerque's saloon was a general resort. Here I had a comfortable sofa to lounge upon, and was quite petted by the good people. This gathering together of the diplomatic corps had, indeed, a most sociable, agreeable effect; we seemed like one family. I became great friends with the Princess Carini, who is full of good humor and good spirits, and disposed to take the world cheerfully. Her husband was quite the life of the house, ever ready for anything that may amuse; a man of varied talent—a musician, a painter, &c., &c.

In the course of the afternoon, I drove out, with Mr. Valdevielso, to the place where the royal meeting was to take place. The road was full of carriages and horsemen, hastening to the rendezvous, and was lined with spectators, seated by the roadside in gaping expectation. The scene of the rendezvous was quite picturesque. In an open plain, a short distance from the road, was pitched the royal tent—very spacious, and decorated with fluttering flags and streamers. Three or four other tents were pitched in the vicinity, and there was an immense assemblage of carriages, with squadrons of cavalry, and crowds of people of all ranks, from the grandee to the beggar. We left our carriage at a distance from the tent, and proceeded on foot to the royal presence. The impatience of the little Queen and her sister would not permit them to remain in the tent; they were continually sallying forth among the throng of courtiers, to a position that commanded a distant view of the road of Ocaña, as it sloped down the side of a rising ground. Poor things! they were kept nearly a couple of hours in anxious suspense. * * * At length the royal cortege was seen descending the distant slope of the road, escorted by squadrons of lancers, whose yellow uniforms, with the red flag of the lance fluttering aloft, made them look at a distance like a moving mass of fire and flame. As they drew near, the squadrons of horse wheeled off into the plain, and the royal carriage approached. The impatience of the little Queen could no longer be restrained. Without waiting at the entrance of the tent to receive her royal mother, according to etiquette, she hurried forth, through the avenue of guards, quite to the road, where I lost sight of her amidst a throng of courtiers, horse guards, &c., &c. * * * The reception of the Queen Mother was quite enthusiastic. The air resounded with acclamations. * * * The old nobility, who have long been cast down and dispirited, and surrounded by doubt and danger, look upon the return of the Queen Mother as the triumph of their cause, and the harbinger of happier and more prosperous days.

After witnessing this meeting, I hastened back to Aranjuez, to dine and get some repose before the reception of the *corps diplomatique*, which was to take place at the palace at half-past nine o'clock. We were received in plain clothes, the Queen Mother wishing to avoid the necessity of putting on a court dress. The royal palace was illuminated, and was surrounded by a crowd. We were received in a very beautiful saloon, furnished in the style of the "Empire;" that is to say, the classic style prevalent during the reign of Napoleon. Our diplomatic circle has quite increased of late, since the Queen has been recognized by different courts. The ambassador of France takes precedence in it, from his diplomatic rank; then come the Ministers, &c., according to the date of their residence: first the Portuguese Minister, then myself, then the Mexican Minister, &c. The little Queen entered the room, followed by her mother and her sister, and the Minister of State. The Ambassador of France made her a congratulatory address in the name of the corps, to which she read a brief, written reply. She then, followed by her mother and sister, passed along the line, addressing some words, of course, to each member of the diplomatic corps; after which the royal party courtesied themselves out of the room.

* * * * * *

I was glad to get to bed that night, for my poor ankles fairly ached with having to be so much on my legs that day. The next morning Mr. Valdevielso and myself returned to Madrid, as did most of the diplomatic corps, so as to be ready to see the royal entrance into the capital. It will take place between three and four o'clock this afternoon, and I will keep my letter open to give you a word or two about it.

* * * * * *

I have just returned from witnessing the entrance of Queen Christina, but have no time to give particulars, as it is dinner time, and the courier is about to depart. There was a great parade of military, and the streets were filled with a countless multitude. The Queen Mother sat in an open carriage, on the left hand of her daughter. The houses were all decorated with tapestry hung out of the windows and balconies. The reception of the Queen by the populace was not very animated. She is popular with the *Moderados*—that is to say, the aristocracy.

I must close my letter abruptly, with love to "all bodies."

Your affectionate brother,

WASHINGTON IRVING.

The excellent Arguelles died the very morning of the day on which the Queen Mother entered Madrid.

His health had been broken for some time [writes Mr. Irving, in giving the account, under date of March 20th], and the agitations through which he has passed, of late, may have hastened his end, which, however, was somewhat sudden. He was a good man, a true patriot, and an able statesman, but ardent and anxious as a politician. His life had been a life of trial and vicissitude; he had borne all kinds of reverses of fortune—one time in power, another in exile or in prison; but, through every trial, has passed pure and unsullied. When he had the guardianship of the young Queen, he was entitled to a salary of about seventy thousand dollars; he only accepted one tenth. On the triumph of the *Moderado* party, last year, he retired from office poor. When he died, but twenty-two dollars were found in his house, and he left debts to the amount of nearly five thousand dollars. He was faithful in his guardianship of the little Queen and her sister, and was strongly attached to them. He was represented by his political opponents as an enemy of the Queen Mother; but, though he may have disapproved of her political course when in power, he did justice to the amiableness of her character, and, in a conversation with me, lamented that she was separated from her daughters, as her presence would have been of vast advantage to them, especially to the young Queen. When the Queen Mother was entering Madrid in state, in company with the little Queen and her sister, an officious courtier rode up to the carriage, and announced to her, with congratulation, the death of her enemy, Arguelles! "Hush!" said the Queen Mother; "do not let the children hear you, *for they loved the old man!*" Poor Arguelles! few men who have figured in the political affairs of Spain for the last thirty years will leave so honest a name behind.

CHAPTER XVIII.

LETTER TO PIERRE MUNRO IRVING — OCCUPIED IN LITERARY REVISION — HIS DOUBTS ABOUT THE KING WHO FIRST MADE MADRID A COURT RESIDENCE—LETTER TO MRS. PARIS—BESA MANOS AT THE ROYAL PALACE—SURVEY OF THE SCENE—HIS MEDITATIONS—APPROACHING DEPARTURE OF HIS SECRETARY OF LEGATION—LETTER TO MRS. STORROW—LETTER TO MRS. P. M. IRVING—BESAMANOS AT THE QUEEN MOTHER'S—A SUCCESSION OF DIPLOMATIC DINNERS—A BLESSING INVOKED ON SURGEONS AND DENTISTS.

IN the letter from which I am about to quote, Mr. Irving informs me that he had just received from Mr. Prescott a copy of his History of the Conquest of Mexico, which, we have seen, he had previously read in sheets furnished him by Madame Calderon de la Barca, a correspondent of the historian. As I have already given the passages relative to the work in another connection, when speaking of his surrender of the theme, I content myself with the following opening allusion to his affairs:

MADRID, March 24, 1844.

MY DEAR PIERRE:

I have received your letter of the 29th February, containing the account current and the statement, both of which are highly satisfactory. I am glad to find that you have concluded the Green Bay transfer, and raked twenty-one hundred dollars for me out of the ashes and cinders of that once sanguine speculation. It is so much money that will yield me interest during my lifetime, instead of producing a possible profit after my death. I trust my other investments will turn out more productive, but shall be glad to get them in such a train as to yield me income. I watch with an anxious eye the gradual growth of my productive funds at home. * * *

The cruel malady which has afflicted me for nearly fourteen months past, has marred those literary plans on which I calculated so sanguinely when I set off upon my mission. I have lately resumed my pen, and occupied myself occasionally with revising some of my works for a new edition; but I have to exercise the pen sparingly, as I find literary excitement produces irritation in my complaint. My correspondence, too, is a heavy tax upon my pen, and occupies most of the time I can venture to devote to it; yet I cannot give it up; it is the only mode I have now of keeping up an intercourse with my family and friends.

To Mrs. Storrow he writes, six days after (March 30th), when he was looking forward sorrowfully to the approaching departure of his Secretary of Legation, Mr. Hamilton, after mentioning the call of two American gentlemen the day before, without leaving their names:

Madrid is becoming much more a place of visitation of the Americans than it used to be, though still an immeasurable distance behind Paris in this particular. Colonel W———, when he was here, told me he was one of, I think, *forty-six*, presented at one time to Louis Philippe. What a task for a

Minister to have to present such a regiment! I never could stand it.

* * * Our spring is backward, not from cold, but from drought. Vegetation needs more moisture to bring it forth, and there has been very little rain for months past. My drives, therefore, in the neighborhood of the city, continue to be somewhat dull and dreary, but I hope soon to find the meadows along the Manzanares once more green, the groves in leaf, and the nightingales in song. I doubt if the king who first made Madrid a court residence has yet got out of purgatory for this monstrous evil inflicted upon the nation and its visitors. I hope he may be kept there as long as I am obliged to sojourn here—so there's Christian charity for you.

In the following letter to Mrs. Paris, he takes up the thread of his diplomatic themes. His elation, at the close, at being restored to the free use of his legs, from which he had been so long debarred, is quite in character:

[*To Mrs. Paris, New York.*.]

MADRID, April 17, 1844.

MY DEAR SISTER:

My last letter concluded with the entrance of the Queen and Queen Mother into Madrid. Various fêtes and ceremonies, civil and religious, have since taken place in honor of the return of Maria Christina. I have been obliged to absent myself from most of them on account of my indisposition. I was present, however, at the *Besa manos* (or hand kissing) at the royal palace. This is the grand act of homage to the sovereign and the royal family. The day was bright and propitious. The place in front of the royal palace was thronged with people waiting to see the equipages drive up; while the avenues were guarded by horse and foot, and the courts and halls echoed with military music. On entering the palace, the grand staircase and the antechambers were lined with the officers, halberdiers, and attendants of the royal household, and thronged with a gorgeous multitude, civil and military, glittering with gold lace and embroidery. I made my way into the Hall of Ambassadors, where the throne is situated, and which I found already filled with grandees and high functionaries, and a number of the *corps diplomatique.* I have already noticed this hall in my former letters; it is very magnificent, though somewhat *sombre,* the walls being covered with crimson velvet. It has a great number of large mirrors, immense chandeliers of crystal, and the vaulted ceiling is beautifully painted, representing, in various compartments, the people and productions of the various countries and climates of the Spanish empire, as it existed before its dismemberment. The throne is on the side of the hall opposite to the windows, just midway. It is raised three or four steps, and surmounted by a rich canopy of velvet. There were two chairs of state thus elevated, one on the right hand for the Queen, and on the left for the Queen Mother; at the foot of the throne, to the left, was a chair of state for the Queen's sister. As everybody is expected to stand in the royal presence, there are no other seats provided. I began to apprehend a severe trial for my legs, as some time would probably elapse before the entrance of the Queen. The introducer of ambassadors, however (the Chevalier de Arana), knowing my invalid condition, kindly pointed out to me a statue at the lower end of the hall, with a low pedestal, and advised me to take my seat there until the opening of the court. I gladly availed myself of the suggestion, and, seating myself on the edge of the pedestal, indulged myself in a quiet survey of the scene before me, and a meditation on the various scenes of the kind I had witnessed in this hall in the time of Ferdinand VII, and during the time of my present sojourn at this court, and in calling to mind the rapid vicissitudes which had occurred, even in my limited experience, in the gilded and anxious throngs which, each in their turns, have glittered about this hall. How brief has been their butterfly existence! how sudden and desolate their reverses! Exile, imprisonment, death itself, have followed hard upon the transient pageants of a court; and who could say how soon a like lot might befall the courtier host before me, thus swarming forth into sudden sunshine? They all seemed, however, secure that their summer was to last, and that the golden days of monarchical rule had once more returned. The arrival of the Queen Mother has been regarded by the aristocracy as the completion and consolidation of their triumph. They have crowded, therefore, to do homage to the throne, and the Spanish Court has once more resumed something of its ancient splendor. Indeed, I had never seen the royal palace so brilliantly attended; and the whole ceremonial had an effect even upon the French Ambassador, who has been slow to see anything good at Madrid, but who acknowledged that the splendor of the court quite surpassed his expectations.

After we had been for some time assembled, the Queen was announced, and every one immediately ranged himself in order. The grandees take their station on the right hand of the throne; the diplomatic corps forms a line directly in front of it, with the French Ambassador at the head. The Queen entered first, followed by her mother and the Princess Royal, and a long train of ladies of the highest nobility, magnificently dressed. The Queen and the Queen Mother took their seats on the throne, the latter on the left hand. The Princess was seated in a chair of state to the left of the throne, and the ladies in attendance ranged themselves from the left of the throne to the lower end of the hall. Among them were some of the most beautiful ladies of the nobility; they were all in court dresses, with lappets and trains, and as fine as silk, and plumes, and lace, and diamonds could make them. I doubt whether even the lilies of the valley, though better arrayed than King Solomon in all his glory, could have stood a comparison with them. (I hope it is not wicked to say so.)

The little Queen and her sister were each dressed in white satin, richly trimmed with lace; they had trains of lilac silk, and wreaths of diamonds on their heads, the only difference in their dress being the superior number of diamonds of the Queen. The Queen Mother had a train of azure blue, her favorite color. I like to describe dresses, having a knack at it; but I absolutely forget the rest of her equipments. The little Queen, who, by the by, will soon cease to deserve the adjective of *little*, looked rather full and puffy on the occasion, being perhaps rather too straitly caparisoned; the Infanta, too, looked pale, and, I was told, was in bad health. The Queen Mother, on the contrary, was in her best looks; no longer fatigued and worn by a long and anxious journey, as when I saw her at Aranjuez, but cheerful and animated. I think, for queenly grace and dignity, mingled with the most gracious affability, she surpasses any sovereign I have ever seen. Her manner of receiving every one, as they knelt and kissed her hand, and the smile with which she sent them on their way rejoicing, let me at once into the secret of her popularity with all who have frequented her court.

I remained but a short time after the *Besa manos* had commenced. It was likely to be between two and three hours before the immense crowd of courtiers, clergy, military, municipality, &c., could pay homage, and it was impossible for me to remain standing so long. I beat a retreat, therefore, in company with the *chargé d'affaires* of Denmark, the veteran D'Alborgo—a thoroughgoing courtier, who had risen from a sickbed to be present on the occasion. I have since written a note to the Minister of State, requesting him to explain to the Queen and Queen Mother the cause of my absence from most of the court ceremonies on the recent joyful occasion; and have received a very satisfactory note in reply, with kind expressions on the part of the sovereigns. There is to be another grand *Besa manos* on the twenty-seventh of this month, by which time I hope to be sufficiently recovered from my long indisposition to resume my usual station in the diplomatic corps.

I am happy to tell you that I am getting on prosperously in my cure by the aid of baths, which I take at home. Indeed, I expect, in a very little time, to be able to go about on foot as usual, and only refrain from doing so at present lest, by any over exercise, I might retard my complete recovery. When I drive out and notice the opening of spring, I feel, sometimes, almost moved to tears at the thought that in a little while I shall again have the use of my limbs, and be able to ramble about and enjoy these green fields and meadows. It seems almost too great a privilege. I am afraid, when I once more sally forth and walk about the streets, I shall feel like a boy with a new coat, who thinks everybody will turn round to look at him. "Bless my soul, how that gentleman has the use of his legs!"

I want some little excitement of the kind, just now, to enliven me, for Alexander Hamilton is packing up, and preparing for his departure, which will probably take place in the course of three weeks. It will be a hard parting for me, and I shall feel his loss sadly, for he has been everything to me as an efficient aid in business, a most kind-hearted attendant in sickness, and a cheerful, intelligent, sunshiny companion at all times. He will leave a popular name behind him among his intimates and acquaintances in Madrid, who have learned to appreciate his noble qualities of head and heart. What makes his departure very trying to me, is, that he is in a manner linked with my home, and is the last of the young companions who left home with me. God bless him! he will carry home sunshine to his family.

And now, with love to "all bodies," I must conclude.

Your affectionate brother,

WASHINGTON IRVING.

On the 27th of April, Mr. Irving informs his niece, at Paris, that he had given two diplomatic dinners lately, and should give a third the next day. "You will think," he says, "I am quite 'breaking forth' with dinner parties; but, in truth, I have for a long time been so much depressed and out of social mood with my tedious malady, that I fell quite in arrears; and one of the first impulses, on finding myself really getting better, was to call my friends about me and make good cheer."

The following is written under the same auspicious improvement in the state of his health, and after some encouraging news as to the condition of his investments at home:

[*To Mrs. Pierre M. Irving.*]

MADRID, April 28, 1844.

MY DEAR HELEN:

* * * I have been rather lighthearted of late, at being in a great degree relieved from the malady which has so long kept me, as it were, in fetters. Yesterday I was at a *Besa manos*, or royal levee, at the palace, in honor of the birthday of the Queen Mother, where all the nobility and people of official rank have the honor of kissing the hands of the Queen and royal family; and though the ceremonial lasted between two and three hours, I stood through the whole of it without flinching. I have also taken a walk in the green alleys of the Retiro, for the first time in upward of fifteen months, and performed the feat to admiration. I do not figure about yet in the streets on foot, lest people should think me proud; I continue, therefore, to drive out in my carriage. Indeed, I endeavor to behave as humbly and modestly as possible under "so great a dispensation;" but one cannot help being puffed up a little on having the use of one's legs.

* * * In consequence of the flourishing accounts Pierre has lately written of the state of my investments, I have just given a succession of diplomatic dinners, and am looking forward with impatience to the arrival of an American party of travellers, to have a pretence for giving more. I am terribly afraid my purse will get ahead of me under Pierre's accumulating management, and I shall grow rich and stingy. However, I'll have a "hard try" for the contrary.

May 3d.—We have beautiful weather, and yesterday, for he first time in upward of a year, I took a walk on the Prado among all the gay world, and then seated myself under one of the trees, and looked on. The delightful temperature of the air, the sight of verdure, and the sound of fountains, made me feel quite young again, and I presume that was the reason why all the ladies looked so beautiful. I do not think I have seen so many pretty faces in the course of a morning since I was a young man. In fact, I have now and then thought that the world was growing old, and all the beauty dying out; but yesterday's walk in the Prado convinced me that I was mistaken.

In the same cheerful mood he writes, a few days after, to his brother, who had informed him that General George P. Morris had requested permission to publish his story of "The Wife," from the Sketch Book, in a periodical of which he was proprietor: "Give my regards to General Morris, and tell him he is quite welcome to my 'Wife,' which is more than most of his friends could say."

In another letter, written near the same period, we have, perhaps, the most curiously whimsical and original benediction that ever was invoked. It is in reply to information that one of his friends had submitted to a surgical operation, which had ended favorably:

God bless these surgeons and dentists! May their good deeds be returned upon them a thousandfold! May they have the felicity, in the next world, to have successful operations performed upon them to all eternity!

CHAPTER XIX.

DEPARTURE OF HAMILTON — LONELINESS — THE NEW AMERICAN MINISTER AT PARIS — HEARTSICK WITH THE POLITICS OF SPAIN—THE RETIRO — A NEW SECRETARY OF LEGATION—LETTER FROM BARCELONA—THE TURKISH MINISTER—AUDIENCE OF THE QUEEN—REMINISCENCE OF THE PALACE—ITS PECULIAR INTEREST TO HIM—COUNT DE ESPAGNE—LETTER TO PIERRE M. IRVING TEMPORARY LEAVE OF ABSENCE GRANTED HIM—INTENDS TO VISIT PARIS.

THE day after the departure of Mr. Hamilton, the last of the three young companions who had embarked with him in his mission, and were linked to him by home affinities, Mr. Irving writes to Mrs. Storrow (May 15th):

To-day there is an inexpressible loneliness in my mansion, and its great saloons seem uncommonly empty and silent. I feel my heart choking me, as I walk about, and miss Hamilton from the places and seats he used to occupy. The servants partake in my dreary feelings, and that increases them. Juana cannot speak of the *Senorito*, without the tears starting in her eyes. * * *

I am scrawling this, because it is a relief to me to express what I feel, and I have no one at hand to converse with. The morning has been rainy, but it is holding up, and I shall drive out and get rid of these lonely feelings. To-day I dine with the Albuquerques, of which I am glad.

All this will soon pass away, for I have been accustomed,

for a great part of my life, to be much alone; but I think, of late years, living at home, with those around to love and cherish me, my heart has become accustomed to look around for others to lean upon; or, perhaps, I am growing less self-dependent and self-competent than I used to be. However, thank God, I am getting completely clear of my malady, and in a train to resume the occasional exercise of my pen; and when I have that to occupy and solace me, I am independent of the world.

I select some further passages from letters to Mrs. Storrow, addressed to her at Paris:

May 18*th.*—I am wearied and at times heartsick of the wretched politics of this country, where there is so much intrigue, falsehood, profligacy, and crime, and so little of high honor and pure patriotism in political affairs. The last ten or twelve years of my life * * * has shown me so much of the dark side of human nature, that I begin to have painful doubts of my fellow men, and look back with regret to the confiding period of my literary career, when, poor as a rat, but rich in dreams, I beheld the world through the medium of my imagination, and was apt to believe men as good as I wished them to be.

May 24*th.*—I see that a new Minister has been appointed for Paris, Mr. William King, of Alabama, who for many years has been in the Senate of the United States. He is an old acquaintance of mine, a very gentleman-like man. I first knew him about the year 1817, when I was residing with your uncle Peter, in Liverpool. He was then on his way home from Russia, having been attached to the legation in that court. He remained a week or two at Liverpool, and dined alternately with us, with a Mr. Kirwan, of Philadelphia, and Mr. Haggerty, of Virginia, so that we were every day the same party of five, though at different houses. We supposed he would give a good account of Liverpool, on his return home, as a very hospitable place, but with *only five inhabitants.* I believe he is still a bachelor, in which case I should not be surprised if he were an old one.

I have enjoyed myself greatly in the Retiro of late. It is such a delight to be able once more to ramble about the shady alleys, and to have the companionship of nightingales, with which the place abounds at this season of the year. There is a beautiful prospect, too, of the distant Guadarrama mountains, seen rising above the treetops, tinted with hazy purple, and crowned with snow. The Retiro is one of the few pleasant haunts that cheer the surrounding sterility of Madrid.

* * * I am rejoiced to find, by my family letters, that Mr. Grinnell has taken Mr. George Jones's house for the present year, and that Mr. Minturn continues to occupy Mrs. Colford Jones's. What delightful arrangements these will be for the cottage! I feel homesick at the very idea! It will be a gay, social neighborhood, with gayety of the right kind. Grinnell will be a famous hand for yachting with the jovial mariners of Nevis. Tell Alexander Hamilton I envy him the merry cruisings there will be this summer on the Tappan Zee.

* * * Give my kind remembrances to Mr. Storrow, and kiss my darling little Kate for me, who, I fear, has quite forgotten the "Unty" from whom she receives so many remittances of the kind.

Your affectionate uncle,

WASHINGTON IRVING.

Alexander Hamilton, to whom the message toward the close of this extract is sent, was his late Secretary of Legation, then at Paris, on his way homeward. Nevis was the name of the family homestead on the Hudson, about a mile south of Sunnyside.

The following extract from a letter to his sister, Mrs. Paris, announces the arrival of his new Secretary of Legation, Mr. Jasper H. Livingston, a son of Brockholst Livingston, Judge of the Supreme Court of the United States, with whom, as has been noted, Mr. Irving had passed a part of his novitiate as a student at law:

June 15*th.*—I am now preparing for a journey to Barcelona, where I have to go to deliver two letters from the President to the Queen: one congratulatory on her accession to the throne, the other of condolence on the death of her uncle. They have been a long time on the way, and did not reach us until long after the Queen's departure; otherwise I should have delivered them here, and have endeavored to dispense with this journey to Barcelona. It is a long journey to make in this hot weather, and I fear I shall find Barcelona crowded, and comfortable quarters not to be had.

Mr. Livingston, who takes the place of Mr. Hamilton, arrived here about a week since, with a nephew, a fine boy about thirteen years of age. They have taken up their abode with me, and have quite enlivened my house.

Mr. Irving left Madrid for Barcelona on the 26th of June. The following is written about a week after his arrival in that "beautiful city, which," he writes to me, "appears to me to be one of the favored spots of the earth; surrounded by a rich and fruitful country, magnificent prospects of land and sea, and blessed with a sweetly tempered southern climate."

[*To Mrs. Paris.*]

BARCELONA, July 5, 1844.

MY DEAR SISTER:

I presume Sarah Storrow has forwarded to you the letter I wrote to her on my arrival at this city, giving some account of my journey from Madrid, through the wild, mountainous region of Arragon. It was very fatiguing, very hot, and very dusty, yet I am glad I have made it, as it took me through a great part of what was a distinct kingdom before the marriage of Ferdinand with Isabella, by which the crowns of Arragon and Castile became united. We travelled almost constantly, day and night. In some of the mountainous parts the diligence was drawn by eight, and occasionally ten mules, harnessed two and two, with a driver on the box, a *zagal*, or help, who scampered for a great part of the way beside the mules, thwacking them occasionally with a stick, and bawling out their names in all kinds of tones and inflections; while a lad of fifteen years of age was mounted on one of the leaders, to act as pilot. This lad kept on with us for a great part of the journey. How he bore the fatigue, I can hardly imagine; and more especially the want of sleep, for we only paused about six hours each evening to dine and take repose. He, however, I found, could sleep on horseback; and repeatedly, when our long line of mules and the lumbering diligence were winding along roads cut around the face of mountains, and along the brink of tremendous precipices, the postilion was sleeping on his saddle, and we were left to the caution and discretion of the mules. However, we accomplished our journey in safety, in defiance of rough roads and robbers, and arrived here, after three days and a half of almost continual travel.

My first care was to get into comfortable quarters, every hotel being crowded, and all furnished apartments being taken up since the arrival of the court. For a few days I was stowed away in a small room in the upper part of a hotel, and recollected, with regret, my spacious and cool saloons at Madrid. While thus lodged, I received a visit from a Mr. or Don Pablo Anguera, who formerly acted here as American Consul, and who is an old customer and intimate of Mr. Van Wart, having a mercantile establishment in Havana, where he has made his fortune. He and his wife have resided for a couple of years in England, in the neighborhood of Mr. Van Wart, and have been extremely intimate with the family.

Finding I was so indifferently lodged, nothing would suit this worthy man but I must accept of a part of his house. It was very spacious, he said, and his family was very small, and I could have a distinct apartment entirely to myself. In fine, I was easily compelled to avail myself of his hospitality, and, accordingly, here I am, most capitally accommodated. I have the front part of the house, which looks on the street, to myself, while the family occupy the apartments in the rear, which look on a very pretty garden, with fountains, statues, &c. I have a spacious and beautiful saloon, richly gilded, the ceilings painted in fresco, the furniture fashionable and commodious, adjoining which is a cabinet in similar style, where I write, receive visitors, &c.; and a noble alcove, in which is a bed ample enough for the seven sleepers, and so luxurious, that, had they once been tucked into it, they would have slept on until doomsday. Lorenzo has a room adjoining, so as to be completely within call. My breakfasts are served to me in the cabinet, and I dine with the family, or dine abroad, as I may find pleasant or convenient. * * *

I am delighted with Barcelona. It is a beautiful city, especially the new part, with a mixture of Spanish, French, and Italian character. The climate is soft and voluptuous, the heats being tempered by the sea breezes. Instead of the naked desert which surrounds Madrid, we have here, between the sea and the mountains, a rich and fertile plain, with villas buried among groves and gardens, in which grow the orange, the citron, the pomegranate, and other fruits of southern climates. We have here, too, an excellent Italian opera, which is a great resource to me. Indeed, the theatre is the nightly place of meeting of the diplomatic corps and various members of the court, and there is great visiting from box to box. The greatest novelty in our diplomatic circle is the Turkish Minister, who arrived lately at Barcelona on a special mission to the Spanish Court. His arrival made quite a sensation here, there having been no representative from the Court of the Grand Sultan for more than half a century. He was for a time quite the lion; everything he said and did was the theme of conversation. I think, however, he has quite disappointed the popular curiosity. Something oriental and theatrical was expected —a Turk in a turban and bagging trousers, with a furred robe, a long pipe, a huge beard and moustache, a bevy of wives, and a regiment of black slaves. Instead of this, the Turkish Ambassador turned out to be an easy, pleasant, gentleman-like man, in a frock coat, white drill pantaloons, black cravat, white kid gloves, and dandy cane; with nothing Turkish in his costume but a red cap with a long, blue silken tassel. In fact, he is a complete man of society, who has visited various parts of Europe, is European in his manners, and, when he takes off his Turkish cap, has very much the look of a well-bred Italian gentleman. I confess I should rather have seen him in the magnificent costume of the East; and I regret that that costume, endeared to me by the Arabian Nights' Entertainments, that joy of my boyhood, is fast giving way to the levelling and monotonous prevalence of French and English fashions. The Turks, too, are not aware of what they lose by the change of costume. In their oriental dress, they are magnificent-looking men, and seem superior in dignity of form to Europeans; but, once stripped of turban and flowing robes, and attired in the close-fitting, trimly cut modern dress, and they shrink in dimensions, and turn out a very ill-made race. Notwithstanding his Christian dress, however, I have found the Effendi a very intelligent and interesting companion. He is extremely well informed, has read much and observed still more, and is very frank and animated in conversation. Unfortunately, his sojourn here will be but for a very few days longer. He intends to make the tour of Spain, and to visit those parts especially which contain historical remains of the time of the Moors and Arabs. Granada will be a leading object of curiosity with him. I should have delighted to visit it in company with him.

I know, all this while you are dying to have another chapter about the little Queen, so I must gratify you. I applied for an audience shortly after my arrival, having two letters to deliver to the Queen from President Tyler; one congratulating her on her majority, the other condoling with her on the death of her aunt. The next day, at six o'clock in the evening, was appointed for the audience, which was granted at the same time to the members of the diplomatic corps who had travelled in company with me, and to two others who had preceded us. It was about the time when the Queen drives out to take the air. Troops were drawn up in the square in front of the palace, awaiting her appearance, and a considerable crowd assembled. As we ascended the grand staircase, we found groups of people on the principal landing places, waiting to get a sight of royalty. This palace had a peculiar interest for me. Here, as often occurs in my unsettled and wandering life, I was coming back again on the footsteps of former times. In 1829, when I passed a few days in Barcelona, on my way to England to take my post as Secretary of Legation, this palace was inhabited by the Count de Espagne, at that time Captain General of the province. I had heard much of the cruelty of his disposition, and the rigor of his military rule. He was the terror of the Catalans, and hated by them as much as he was feared. I dined with him, in company with two or three English gentlemen, residents of the place, with whom he was on familiar terms. In entering his palace, I felt that I was entering the abode of a tyrant. His appearance was characteristic. He was about forty-five years of age, of the middle size, but well set and strongly built, and became his military dress. His face was rather handsome, his demeanor courteous, and at table he became social and jocose; but I thought I could see a lurking devil in his eye, and something hardhearted and derisive in his laugh. The English guests were his cronies, and, with them, I perceived his jokes were coarse, and his humor inclined to buffoonery. At that time, Maria Christina, then a beautiful Neapolitan princess in the flower of her years, was daily expected at Barcelona, on her way to Madrid to be married to

Ferdinand VII. While the Count and his guests were seated at table, after dinner, enjoying the wine and cigars, one of the petty functionaries of the city, equivalent to a deputy alderman, was announced. The Count winked to the company, and promised a scene for their amusement. The city dignitary came bustling into the apartment with an air of hurried zeal and momentous import, as if about to make some great revelation. He had just received intelligence, by letter, of the movements of the Princess, and the time when she might be expected to arrive, and had hastened to communicate it at headquarters. There was nothing in the intelligence that had not been previously known to the Count, and that he had not communicated to us during dinner; but he affected to receive the information with great surprise, made the functionary repeat it over and over, each time deepening the profundity of his attention; finally he bowed the city oracle quite out of the saloon, and almost to the head of the staircase, and sent him home swelling with the idea that he had communicated a state secret, and fixed himself in the favor of the Count. The latter returned to us laughing immoderately at the manner in which he had played off the little dignitary, and mimicking the voice and manner with which the latter had imparted his important nothings. It was altogether a high farce, more comic in the acting than in the description; but it was the sportive gambolling of a tiger, and I give it to show how the tyrant, in his hours of familiarity, may play the buffoon.

The Count de Espagne was a favorite general of Ferdinand, and, during the life of that monarch, continued in high military command. In the civil wars, he espoused the cause of Don Carlos, and was charged with many sanguinary acts. His day of retribution came. He fell into the hands of his enemies, and was murdered, it is said, with savage cruelty, while being conducted a prisoner among the mountains. Such are the bloody reverses which continually occur in this eventful country, especially in these revolutionary times.

I thought of all these things as I ascended the grand staircase. Fifteen years had elapsed since I took leave of the Count at the top of this staircase, and it seemed as if his hard-hearted, derisive laugh still sounded in my ears. He was then a loyal subject and a powerful commander; he had since been branded as a traitor and a rebel, murdered by those whom he had oppressed, and hurried into a bloody grave. The beautiful young Princess, whose approach was at that time the theme of every tongue, had since gone through all kinds of reverses. She had been on a throne, she had been in exile, she was now a widowed Queen, a subject of her own daughter, and a sojourner in this palace.

On entering the royal apartments, I recognized some of the old courtiers whom I had been accustomed to see about the royal person at Madrid, and was cordially greeted by them, for at Barcelona we all come together sociably as at a watering place. The "introducer of ambassadors" (the Chevalier de Arana) conducted my companions and myself into a saloon, where we waited to be summoned into the royal presence. I, being the highest in diplomatic rank of the party present, was first summoned. On entering, I found the little Queen standing in the centre of the room, and, at a little distance behind her, the Marchioness of Santa Cruz, first lady in attendance. Unfortunately, I forgot to take notice how the Queen was dressed, and, for this time, cannot give you accurate information on this important point. I only know that she was dressed to take her evening drive. She had a pinkish bonnet, with pinkish flowers, and, altogether, her whole dress has left a kind of pinkish idea in my mind. She had even a slight pinkish bloom in her face, which is usually pale. Indeed, her whole appearance is improved; it is more healthful. She is growing more and more womanly, and more and more engaging. The expression of her countenance was extremely amiable. She received me in a quiet, graceful manner, with considerable self-possession, expressing, in a low voice, the hope that I had made a pleasant journey, &c. This must be the hardest task, for so young a creature, to have to play the Queen *solus*, receiving, one by one, the diplomatic corps, and beginning the conversation with each. Our interview was brief. I presented my two letters, expressed the satisfaction which I (really) felt at seeing, by her improved looks, that the sojourn at Barcelona had been beneficial to her, &c., after which I retired, to give place to my companions. We had afterward, one by one, an audience of the Queen Mother, who is looking very well, though, I am told, she is still subject to great anxiety and frequent depression of spirits, feeling the uncertainty of political affairs in Spain, and the difficulties and dangers which surround the throne of her youthful daughter. Nothing could be more gracious and amiable than her reception. Her smile is one of the most winning I have ever witnessed; and the more I see of her, the less I wonder at that fascination which, in her younger and more beautiful days, was so omnipotent, and which, even now, has such control over all who are much about her person.

July 7th.—Yesterday I made a very pleasant excursion into the country, two or three miles from Barcelona, toward the mountains, to a little rural retreat of the Brazilian Consul, who gave a dinner to about twenty-two persons, ladies and gentlemen, of the *corps diplomatique* and the consular corps. It was a very handsome and a very gay dinner. The saloon in which the table was laid looked out upon a garden, with fountains, the rich plain, the city of Barcelona in the distance, and the blue Mediterranean beyond; a splendid picture, seen under a southern sky, and with the enjoyment of the softest and most voluptuous temperature. The garden of the villa was shaded by fig trees, orange trees, citrons; and the hedges of the neighboring fields were of the aloes. Everything looked and felt and breathed of the sweet south. We returned for a great part of the way to town on foot, the evening was so delicious. The more I see of Barcelona and its environs, the more I am delighted with them. * * *

God bless you, my dear sister. Give my heart's love to all the dear inmates of sweet little Sunnyside.

Your affectionate brother,

WASHINGTON IRVING.

Eleven days after the date of the foregoing letter, to which he refers me, with a hint that he should have to "greatly retrench the epistolary prodigality of [his] pen," and in reply to a letter in which I informed him of my having taken advantage of a miraculous resuscitation of some long-barren stock of his to sell it, he writes me from Barcelona as follows:

July 18th.—Yesterday I received my letters by the steam packet of the 15th of June, among which is a despatch from Government, granting me the temporary leave of absence for the benefit of my health which I had solicited. I shall avail myself of the leave of absence toward the end of this month, to make an excursion to Paris previous to returning to Madrid. I shall thus escape the dry, parching summer heat of the Spanish capital, be enabled, if necessary, to consult the French physician who attended me last autumn, refresh and recruit myself by a pleasant tour and complete change of climate, and return to Madrid early in the autumn, fully prepared, I trust, to enter with vigor upon my literary as well as my diplomatic occupations. I feel quite obliged to President Tyler for enabling me to make this pleasant and healthful arrangement, and hope, in return, that, if he should succeed in annexing Texas, it may become an apanage in his family, for the benefit of his eldest son! However, this is a dangerous aspiration, and I beg you will not breathe it to any one but Helen.

By the same opportunity I have received the joint letter of yourself and Helen; or, rather, her letter with your postscript crowded into holes and corners. * * * Your postscript, however, is worth its weight in gold, as you tell me you have sold my ——— shares of ——— stock for ——— dollars a share. This is really so much money hauled out of the ashes. I shall now begin to think something may one day turn up for the girls, out of the dead and buried claim of Anaky Yanz.

Tell Helen this new and unlooked-for influx of wealth makes it indispensable for me to hurry to Paris, to prevent a plethora of the purse. Jupiter! how I will burn the candle at both ends when I get there! Don't tell your aunt, though, for I see she thinks I'm a wild, expensive young dog.

Your affectionate uncle, W. I.

P. S.—I have written to Mr. Livingston, my Secretary of

Legation, to have my old carriage vamped up and varnished, and a taller cockade put in Pepe's hat against I return to Madrid, for I am determined, now my pockets are so full, to strike out with unusual splendor. Not a word to your aunt, however.

The "aunt" to whom he alludes in this playful outbreak, was his sister, Mrs. Paris.

CHAPTER XX.

FROM BARCELONA TO PARIS—THE LIKENESS—MARSEILLES—AVIGNON—LYONS—VERSAILLES—FIVE DAYS WITH THE AMERICAN CONSUL AT HAVRE—LEAVES HAVRE FOR LONDON—SLIPS THROUGH LONDON QUIETLY—AT THE SHRUBBERY—BACK TO FRANCE—VISIT TO KING LOUIS PHILIPPE—LETTER TO MRS. PARIS—COURT GAYETIES—MUSINGS IN THE ROYAL PILE.

IN the following extract we have a pleasant picture of the author's wayfaring from Barcelona to Marseilles :

[*To Mrs. Paris.*]

BARCELONA, July 28, 1844.

MY DEAR SISTER :

To-morrow I embark in a Spanish steamer for Marseilles, on my way to Paris. I leave this beautiful city with regret, for my time has passed here most happily. Indeed, one enjoys the very poetry of existence in these soft southern climates which border the Mediterranean. All here is picture and romance. Nothing has given me greater delight than occasional evening drives with some of my diplomatic colleagues to those country seats, or *Torres*, as they are called, situated on the slopes of the hills, two or three miles from the city, surrounded by groves of oranges, citrons, figs, pomegranates, &c., with terraced gardens gay with flowers and fountains. Here we would sit on the lofty terraces overlooking the rich and varied plain; the distant city gilded by the setting sun, and the blue sea beyond. Nothing can be purer and softer and sweeter than the evening air inhaled in these favored retreats.

July 29th. On board of the Spanish steamer Villa de Madrid.—At seven o'clock this morning we left Barcelona, and have been all day gliding along a smooth summer sea, in sight of the Spanish coast, which is here very mountainous and picturesque. Old ruined castles are to be seen here and there on the summit of cragged heights, with villages gleaming along the shore below them. The Catalonian coast is studded with bright little towns, the seats of industry and enterprise, for Catalonia is the New England of Spain, full of bustle and activity. We have, as usual, a clear blue sky overhead; the air is bland and delightful, and the sea enlivened here and there by the picturesque Mediterranean vessels, with their tapering lateen sails. To-night we shall have delightful sailing by the light of the full moon—a light which I have peculiarly enjoyed, of late, among the orange gardens of Barcelona.

On board of the steamer we have a joyous party of Catalans, gentlemen and ladies, who are bound to St. Filian, a town on the coast, where there is to be held some annual fête. They have all the gayety and animation which distinguish the people of these provinces.

While I am writing at a table in the cabin, I am sensible of the power of a pair of splendid Spanish eyes which are occasionally flashing upon me, and which almost seem to throw a light upon the paper. Since I cannot break the spell, I will describe the owner of them. She is a young married lady, about four or five and twenty, middle sized, finely modelled, a Grecian outline of face, a complexion sallow yet healthful, raven black hair, eyes dark, large, and beaming, softened by long eyelashes, lips full and rosy red, yet finely chiselled, and teeth of dazzling whiteness. She is dressed in black, as if in mourning; on one hand is a black glove; the other hand, ungloved, is small, exquisitely formed, with taper fingers and blue veins. She has just put it up to adjust her clustering black locks. I never saw female hand more exquisite. Really, if I were a young man, I should not be able to draw the portrait of this beautiful creature so calmly.

I was interrupted in my letter writing, by an observation of the lady whom I was describing. She had caught my eye occasionally, as it glanced from my letter toward her. "Really, Señor," said she, at length, with a smile, "one would think you were a painter, taking my likeness." I could not resist the impulse. "Indeed," said I, "I am taking it; I am writing to a friend the other side of the world, discussing things that are passing before me, and I could not help noting down one of the best specimens of the country that I had met with." A little bantering took place between the young lady, her husband, and myself, which ended in my reading off, as well as I could into Spanish, the description I had just written down. It occasioned a world of merriment, and was taken in excellent part. The lady's cheek, for once, mantled with the rose. She laughed, shook her head, and said I was a very fanciful portrait painter; and the husband declared that, if I would stop at St. Filian, all the ladies in the place would crowd to me to have their portraits taken—my pictures were so flattering. I have just parted with them. The steamship stopped in the open sea, just in front of the little bay of St. Filian; boats came off from shore for the party. I helped the beautiful original of the portrait into the boat, and promised her and her husband, if ever I should come to St. Filian, I would pay them a visit. The last I noticed of her, was a Spanish farewell wave of her beautiful white hand, and the gleam of her dazzling teeth as she smiled adieu. So there's a very tolerable touch of romance for a gentleman of my years.

Marseilles, *July* 31*st*.—I arrived here yesterday morning, about eight o'clock, after a beautiful sail by moonlight, which kept me a great part of the night on the deck.

I entered the harbor of Marseilles between the forts that guard it like two giants. Just without the fort I recognized a little cove where I used to bathe when I was here, just forty years since. I landed on the quay where I had often walked in old times. It was but little altered, but the harbor, at that time, was nearly empty, being a time of war; it was now crowded with shipping. The city had nearly doubled in size, and had greatly improved in beauty, as have all European cities during this long peace. It is indeed a magnificent city, one of the stateliest in France.

On the afternoon of the 31st July, Mr. Irving, accompanied by his faithful Lorenzo, took the diligence for Avignon, and, after travelling all night, arrived early in the morning at that "ancient and picturesque town," which he had visited in his youthful days. He took another look at the old castle where the Pope resided for nearly a century, and a peep into the old church where once was the tomb of Petrarch's Laura, and then embarked in a steamer on the Rhone for Lyons. "I was delighted with the scenery of the river," he writes. "It is very varied, many parts wild, mountainous, and picturesque; some parts resembling the scenery of the Hudson, with the addition of old towns, villages, ruined castles, &c." From Lyons he continued his course in another steamer up the Saone, the scenery of which he did not find so striking as that of the Rhone, to Chalons, whence he took the diligence for Paris. After passing a week "of heartfelt pleasure" at Versailles with his niece, Mrs. Storrow, and her children, he set off, with Lorenzo, for Havre, to pay his "worthy friend Beasley a visit," who had written him to come down there before Captain Funck sailed, "that he might jollify a little with the magnanimous Captain and the Ledyards, who were to embark with him." From Havre, where he spent a few days "most pleasantly," he set off, at five o'clock in the afternoon of the 21st of August, in a steamer for London direct, whence he intended to make the best of his way to Birmingham, the residence of his sister. "Tell Mr. Storrow," he writes to his niece on the eve of his departure, "to send all letters for me in an envelope addressed to Mr. Van Wart. I do not want my name to appear in any way that may draw upon me invitations."

He slipped through London, only stopping to pass his trunks through the custom house; and, after a pleasant sojourn of about three weeks at Birmingham, where he found his sister, who had been an invalid, improved beyond his expectations, he shaped his course again for France.

The teasing remains of his malady still clung to his

ankles, and he continued to linger in Paris for some time, in hopes of getting in good travelling condition by the aid of baths. A few days before he set off on his long journey to his post, he sends his sister, Mrs. Paris, the following account of another visit to Louis Philippe:

I have been living so quietly for some time past, that I have nothing new to tell you excepting a visit which I paid to King Louis Philippe, about a week since. I made it in company with Mr. King, our Minister at the Court, and Mr. Wheaton, our Minister to Prussia, who is making a sojourn in this city. The royal family were at St. Cloud, a few miles from Paris. The King, while at the country seats, receives privileged visitors in the evenings, when they go in plain dress. We drove out to St. Cloud in Mr. King's carriage. I thought of Napoleon as we entered the gates and ascended the great marble staircase of this beautiful palace, for it was one of his favorite residences. The interior of the palace was brilliantly lighted up. We passed through spacious halls and antechambers, and caught vistas through long galleries superbly painted and gilded; all contrasting with the partial gloom of the royal palace at Madrid, on my last evening visit to it.

We found the royal family in a lofty square chamber, at the end of one of the saloons. As on my former visit (in 1842), the Queen and Madame Adelaide were seated at a round table, engaged in needlework or embroidery. The beautiful young Duchess de Nemours was likewise seated at the table, as were two or three ladies of rank. At another round table on the opposite side of the room, were seated two or three ladies of honor. The tea equipage was on the table, as in a private house. Several gentlemen, some in military uniforms, were in groups about the room. The Duke de Nemours was in one of the groups, and the King was conversing with a diplomatic personage in the embrasure of one of the windows. The King was in plain dress, and there was altogether an absence of form and ceremony. I paid my respects to the Queen and Madame Adelaide, both of whom recollected me and my previous visit, received me very amiably, inquired whether I was engaged on any literary work, &c. The Queen is always pale and thin, but appears still thinner than when I last saw her. You may recollect that it was but a few days after that visit, that her son, the Duke of Orleans, was killed by a fall from his carriage—a domestic blow which she has never ceased to deplore.

We had a long and varied conversation with the King. He appears to be in excellent health and spirits, and bears in his countenance and carriage the promise of a length of days. He converses very freely and copiously, and turned from one subject to another, varying his humor with his theme. He is fond of telling stories of his adventures in the backwoods in America, and gave us one or two in excellent style, laughing heartily. I was surprised to find how tenaciously he retains the names of places and persons, the relative distances, the nature of the country, &c., &c. Our conversation must have lasted for half an hour, and was more like the frank, social conversation of common life, than the diplomatic communications between a king and ambassadors. The King has been highly gratified by his late visit to England, and it has put him in wonderful good humor. He regretted that the ocean was so wide and the United States so far off, that he could not pay our country a visit with equal convenience.

The next letter from which I quote is addressed to the same correspondent, nine days after his arrival in Madrid, which he reached on the 17th of November, after a more comfortable journey from Paris than he had anticipated from the irritation that still hung about his ankles.

My return home was hailed with transports of joy by the whole household. Juana threw her arms round my neck. Old Pedro, the coachman, cut a most uncouth caper, and I had much ado to avoid the embraces of the cook's aide-de-camp and the footboy. I found everything prepared to make me comfortable for the winter: my bedroom fresh papered, curtained, and carpeted, and looking so cosey, that, were I an old bachelor (which you know I am not), I should have been tempted to nestle myself in it, and give up the world until spring time.

I find Madrid quite grand and gay under the domination of the *Moderados.* The nobility and the wealthy are vieing with each other in display, during this interval of political sunshine; and as many fortunes have been made by men in office and political speculators, all Madrid rattles and glitters with new equipages. One would hardly suspect, from the luxury of the capital, that the country was so wretchedly impoverished. The Court, too, is more gay and magnificent than I have ever known it to be. There had been a grand concert at the palace a few days before my arrival; and I came just in time for a *Besa manos* at the palace, and a ball at General Narvaez', on the young Queen's saint's day.

After some account of the crowded *Besa manos,* where the diplomatic corps were kept standing for a couple of hours in front of the throne, while the immense throng passed one by one, kneeling, and kissing the hands of the Queen and royal family, the letter proceeds:

In the evening was the ball at the hotel of General Narvaez, at which the Queen and royal family were present—a compliment rarely paid to a subject at this punctilious Court. Though the hotel of General Narvaez is of great size, built around an open court, with great saloons, yet it was exceedingly crowded, there being about fifteen hundred persons present. The General is of a swelling, magnificent spirit, and does not regard expense; and certainly nothing had been spared to make this entertainment worthy of the royal presence. An inner room, at the end of the principal saloon, was appropriated to the Queen and royal family, with such of the royal household as were in attendance on them, and to the members of the *corps diplomatique*, who are expected to be near the royal person. I had great difficulty in making my way through the crowded saloons to the royal presence. The young Queen had laid aside her state dress of the morning, and was arrayed simply, but becomingly, in white. Her principal ornament was a necklace of six rows of pearls with a splendid diamond clasp. She was in high glee. Indeed, I never saw a schoolgirl at a school ball enjoy herself more completely. A royal quadrille was formed in the saloon just in front of the presence chamber. In the first quadrille, General Narvaez danced with the Queen; Count Bresson (the French Ambassador) with the Queen Mother; the Portuguese Minister with the Infanta; others of the diplomatic corps and of the royal household with the princesses (daughters of Don Francisco), the Princess Carini, the French ambassadors, &c. There were blunders in the quadrille, which set the little Queen laughing; and queer, old-fashioned dancing on the part of the Portuguese Minister, which increased her risibility. She was at times absolutely convulsed with laughter, and throughout the whole evening showed a merriment that was quite contagious. I have never seen her in such a joyous mood, having chiefly seen her on ceremonious occasions, and had no idea that she had so much real *fun* in her disposition. She danced with various members of the diplomatic corps; and about four o'clock in the morning, when she was asked if she could venture upon another dance, Oh, yes! she said; she could dance eight more, if necessary. The Queen Mother, however, got her away between four and five. I was repeatedly asked to take a part in the royal quadrille, but pleaded my lameness as an excuse; for I do not know whether my *years* would have been a sufficient apology where royalty was in question. I left the ball about three o'clock in the morning; and, having been on my legs at that, and the *Besa manos*, almost ever since one o'clock in the preceding day, I expected to be laid up with inflammation of the ankles. To my great surprise and satisfaction, I have experienced no ill effects, and, ever since, the symptoms of my malady have been declining.

I have given you but the beginning of court gayeties. To-morrow, the *corps diplomatique* are invited to a royal dinner at the palace, which I am curious to see, having never been present on an occasion of the kind at this Court. There is a talk, also, of a succession of concerts and balls at the palace; of another ball at General Narvaez', and of other entertainments in the court circle, unless some conspiracy or insurrection should break out to throw everything in confusion. Everything is undertaken here with such a proviso; and a lady who was preparing for the grand ball of General Narvaez, expressed her fears to me that we should all be blown up there, a plot having been discovered, some months since, to blow the General up at his lodgings.

A few days later, he gives his sister a long account of the royal banquet, at which the number of guests was upward of a hundred, composed of the Cabinet Ministers, the principal dignitaries of the Government, the diplomatic corps, with their wives (such as had any), and the ladies in attendance on the royal family. His position at the table was to the left of the Queen Mother. In bringing his details to a close, he remarks:

Thus, my dear sister, I have endeavored to give you a familiar idea of a royal banquet, and the interior of a royal palace. I am afraid, if any strange eye should peruse these domestic scribblings, I should be set down as one infatuated with courts and court ceremonies; but these are intended only for your eye, my dear sister, and for the domestic little circle of the cottage, and to gratify that curiosity which those who live in the quiet and happy seclusion of the country have to learn the reality about kings and queens, and to have a peep into the interior of their abodes.

At the close of another letter addressed to Mrs. Storrow at Paris, in which he had indulged in some details of court entertainments, and other festivities, he observes:

You will conclude, from all these details of gayeties, that I am a very gay fellow; but I assure you I am often, in the midst of these brilliant throngs, the very dullest of the dull. Unless there should be some one or other of my few cordial intimates present to whom I can link myself, I am apt to gaze on the crowd around me with perfect apathy, and find it very difficult, and at times impossible, to pay those commonplace attentions, and make those commonplace speeches to scores of half acquaintances, required in the wide circulation of fashionable society. I have grown too old or too wise for all that. I hope those who observe my delinquency attribute it to the latter cause. How different my feelings are at these court fêtes and fashionable routs, from what they were at our cordial little American *soirées* at Paris!

I take the following from a letter to Mrs. Paris, dated Madrid, February 19th, 1845:

Madrid has been uncommonly gay this winter. The aristocracy, having got the Government in their hands, and feeling confident of continuing in power, have resumed somewhat of their old state and splendor. The Court has been quite magnificent. * * *

I have been particularly pleased with two concerts given at the palace. One was an amateur concert, at which several ladies of the court circle acquitted themselves in a manner that would have done credit to first-rate artistes. On these occasions an immense range of saloons and chambers was thrown open, different from those in which the banquet was given, or in which the *Besa manos* are held. The concert was given in a splendid saloon, where seats were provided for a great part of the company; many, however, had to stand the whole time. The seats assigned to the diplomatic corps were in front, close to those of the Queen and royal family; there was no stirring, therefore, from one's place. After the first part of the concert, however, we all adjourned to a distant apartment fitted up in the style of a grotto, where tables were set out with a cold supper, confectionery, ices, &c., &c. * * *

When the company returned to the concert room, I did not return to my place, but passed through, to the range of apartments beyond. Here I enjoyed myself in my own way: loitering about a long suite of magnificent rooms brilliantly lighted up, decorated with all the luxuries of art, hung with paintings of the great masters, and with historical portraits. These I had, in a manner, all to myself, for, excepting here and there a domestic in royal livery, or a couple of courtiers who had stolen out to whisper secrets in a corner, the whole range was deserted. All the embroidered throng had crowded into the concert room to be in the presence of majesty. I wandered about, therefore, musing, and weaving fancies, and seeming to mingle them with the sweet notes of female voices, which came floating through these silken chambers from the distant music room. And now and then I half moralized upon the portraits of kings and queens looking down upon me from the walls, who had figured for a time in the pageants of this royal pile, but, one after another, had "gone down to dusty death." Among them was Ferdinand VII, and his wife, Amelia of Saxony, who had presided in this palace during my first visit to Spain, and whom I had often seen objects of the adulation of its courtiers—Amelia, whose death knell I heard rung from the cathedral towers of Granada, at the time I was a resident in the Alhambra. Talk of moralizing among the tombs! You see one may moralize even in a palace, and within hearing of the revelry of a court.

CHAPTER XXI.

EXTRACT FROM A LETTER TO MRS. PARIS—NARVAEZ—PASSAGES FROM LETTERS TO MRS. STORROW—LETTER TO MRS. PARIS—TRANSFER OF HIS ESTABLISHMENT, INTENDING TO SEND IN HIS RESIGNATION—RESOLVES ON A BRIEF VISIT TO PARIS—LINGERS THERE TO SEE MR. McLANE, THE AMERICAN MINISTER AT THE COURT OF ST. JAMES—TRANSMITS HIS RESIGNATION—VISITS LONDON—THE OREGON DISPUTE—LETTER TO PIERRE M. IRVING—RETURN TO MADRID.

I CONTINUE the picture of Mr. Irving's life at Madrid, and the changing scenes in which he was mingling, with some extracts from a letter to the sister to whom he was accustomed to write so copiously on Spanish affairs :

* * * General Narvaez, you perceive, is quite the lord of the ascendant. There appears to be more court paid to him even than to the sovereign. Wherever he goes he is the object of adulation, not merely among men but among women. He is a great admirer of the sex, and received by them everywhere with smiles; and he has a quick, inflammable temper, that makes men stand in awe of him. He is, in fact, a singular compound: brave, high spirited, proud, and even vain, generous to profusion, very punctilious, excessively sensitive to affronts, but passionate rather than vindictive; for, though in the first moment of passion he is capable of any excess, yet, when passion is past, he can forgive anything but an insult.

* * * * * *

While thus at the height of power as a subject, and apparently basking in the sunshine of royal favor, I look on the position of Narvaez as perilous in the extreme, and I should not be surprised at seeing him suddenly toppled down by some unlooked-for catastrophe. A schism has gradually taken place between him and the Queen Mother, which is daily widening, though still they wear the external appearance of good will. The Narvaez Cabinet has pushed the reform of the constitution to a great extent, so as to take a vast deal of the power out of the hands of the people, and invest it in the crown. It has stopped short, however, of what is desired by some of the Absolutists, who are for restoring an absolute monarchy; and it has stopped short of the wishes of the clergy. During the revolution, the clergy were stripped of their immense landed possessions, which gave the Church such power in Spain; and all the convents of monks, and most of those of nuns, were suppressed. A great part of the lands thus confiscated have been sold and resold, and have passed into the hands of persons of all ranks and conditions. One great object of the Queen Mother, since her return to Spain, has been to replace the clergy, as much as possible, in their former state. To this she is urged by the Court of Rome, and it is made a condition for her being taken into favor with the Pope, receiving absolution for her sins, and for her daughter, Isabella II, being recognized by the Pope as the legitimate sovereign of Spain. The Narvaez Cabinet, in compliance with these views and wishes, have suspended the sale of the Church property, and have determined that all that remained unsold should be devoted to the benefit of the clergy. This, however, is not considered enough by a number of hot-headed priests, who have recently denounced from their pulpits all those who should purchase or hold property that had been wrested from the Church. An alarm has spread through all ranks of society, as this rendered all property insecure, and threatened to unsettle society. The Queen Mother, being a little tender in conscience, and under the influence of some of the most bigoted of the priesthood, is thought to incline to ultra-monarchical and apostolical measures. Narvaez has come out bravely in opposition to any measures of the kind, and has declared his determination to stand by the constitution as at present reformed, defending it equally against absolute Monarchists and ultra Apostolicals on the one side, and Revolutionists, or Radicals, on the other. He says the Cabinet are all strictly united, and determined to stand or fall together; and he trusts to the fidelity of the army to check any attempts at insurrection. Thus you see how critical a stand he takes—how full of danger. The whole Cabinet may be upset by a *coup d'état* brought about by the policy of the Queen Mother; or Narvaez may be shot down by a secret enemy or rival (as had nearly been the case last year); or the army may be corrupted, as it was under Espartero, and then we shall have confusion and bloodshed. Even within these two days a conspiracy has been discovered in Vittoria, among the troops stationed there; and this day's *Gazette* gives the names of three captains, several lieutenants, and about twenty sergeants arrested, of whom a number will no doubt be promptly shot. * * *

Narvaez has great faults, but he has also great merits. He has risen to the level of his situation, and displays a tact and capacity in the various concerns of government quite beyond what was expected from him. He is extremely vigilant, prompt in action, and possesses the true spirit of command. Altogether, he appears to me to be one of the most striking characters, if not the most striking, that has risen to power in Spain during the long course of her convulsions.

The epistolary passages which follow, present some interesting touches of self-portraiture:

[*To Mrs. Storrow.*]

MADRID, March 27, 1845.

* * * The spring has suddenly broken upon us with all its splendor; that is to say, as far as weather is concerned, for the vicinity of Madrid affords but little opportunity for the spring to put on its gala dress. The weather, however, is exquisite. Such bright sunshine, such a deep blue sky, and such bland temperature! The Prado is gay with equipages, and the promenade crowded with all the beauty and fashion of Madrid. I confine my drives, at present, to this popular resort, which is somewhat like the Champs Elysées, and amuse myself by observing the passing throngs. In this way, though alone, I am not lonely. Indeed, I have been for so much of my life a mere looker on in the game of society, that it has become habitual to me; and it is only the company of those I truly like, that I would prefer to the quiet indulgence of my own thoughts and reveries. I therefore pass much of my time alone through choice. I breakfast alone, when I read the papers; then pass the morning in my study, until summoned to my afternoon drive. This I usually take alone, amusing myself, as I before observed, with looking out upon the world. I return home in time to dress for dinner, which I take in company with Mr. Livingston, and occasionally a guest or two; and in the evening I take my quiet seat at the opera, where I need no company to help me enjoy the music. This is the

scheme of many of my days, though occasionally diversified by visits to my particular intimates, and evening gatherings at the French embassy, or at Mr. O'Shea's. My literary occupations have a great effect in reconciling me to a solitary life, and even in making it pleasant. * * * Besides, I am now at that time of life when the mind has a stock of recollections on which to employ itself; and though these may sometimes be of a melancholy nature, yet it is a "sweet-souled melancholy," mellowed and softened by the operation of time, and has no bitterness in it. My life has been a chequered one, crowded with incidents and personages, and full of shifting scenes and sudden transitions. All these I can summon up and cause to pass before me, and in this way can pass hours together in a kind of reverie. When I was young, my imagination was always in the advance, picturing out the future, and building castles in the air; now, memory comes in the place of imagination, and I look back over the region I have travelled. Thank God, the same plastic feeling, which used to deck all the future with the hues of fairyland, throws a soft coloring on the past, until the very roughest places, through which I struggled with many a heartache, lose all their asperity in the distance.

[*To the Same.*]

April 3d.— * * * This is my sixty-second birthday. I recollect the time when I did not wish to live to such an age, thinking it must be attended with infirmity, apathy of feeling, peevishness of temper, and all the other ills which conspire to "render age unlovely;" yet here my sixty-second birthday finds me in fine health, in the full enjoyment of all my faculties, with my sensibilities still fresh, and in such buxom activity that, on my return home yesterday from the Prado, I caught myself bounding up stairs three steps at a time, to the astonishment of the porter, and checked myself, recollecting that it was not the pace befitting a Minister and a man of my years. If I could only retain such health and good spirits, I should be content to live on to the age of Methuselah.

To-day I am to dine at the house of a rich neighbor, Mr. Arcos, who has a fine, joyous, musical family of young men, so that I anticipate a jovial birthday dinner, and am determined to be as young as any of the party.

You must not keep angling for me for your Swiss tour. I am not to be caught, even though you bait your hook with Mrs. E—— and her black velvet dress. I *have* visited Switzerland, though I may never have talked about it to you. In my young days I crossed St. Gothard, on my return from Italy. The road was not practicable for wheel carriages then, as now, so that I crossed on horseback, three days from the Italian valley of the Tecino, to the banks of the Lake of the Four Cantons; and a wild, picturesque journey it was: from the rich, umbrageous scenery of Italy, to the then terrific pass of the Devil's Bridge, and the dreary valley of Schoellenen. I traversed all of the four cantons, coasted by some of the scenes of the exploits of William Tell, visited Lucerne, Zurich, Basle, &c., and then struck off on my first visit to Paris. I well remember what a home feeling I had in Switzerland; what delight I had in again meeting with log houses among the mountains; what pretty girls I saw in every village. I am sure I should not see as many now, even though I have the advantage of looking through spectacles. Oh, days of my youth! how much younger and greener the world then was than now. And the women!—the world is full of old women now; they were all young in those times.

* * * Let me hear all about Kate's visit to Tom Thumb. I hope she may not be guilty of the same indiscretion as Mrs. E——. I rather think she will be inclined to *bang* the General.

[*To the Same.*]

May 24th.— * * * Yesterday we had a grand ceremony—the Queen going in state to close the *Cortes;* after which the *corps diplomatique* repaired to the palace to make a farewell visit to the Queen and her mother and sister, who depart this day for Barcelona.

* * * There is a complete breaking up of society here for the summer. The diplomatic corps disperses in every direction. Part will come together again at Barcelona. Even Mr. Livingston takes his departure for France in the course of a few days, so you see I shall be perfectly alone. If I can only exercise my pen, however, I shall be content.

The following extract of a letter to Mrs. Paris, dated August 9th, presents scenes and groups characteristic of Spain. There is something striking in the picture it gives of the loneliness of the vast landscape in the neighborhood of Madrid:

My evening drives, though lonely, are pleasant. You can have no idea of the neighborhood of Madrid from that of other cities. The moment you emerge from the gates, you enter upon a desert: vast wastes, as far as the eye can reach, of undulating, and, in part, hilly country, without trees or habitations, green in the early part of the year, and cultivated with grain, but burnt by the summer sun into a variety of browns, some of them rich though sombre. A long picturesque line of mountains closes the landscape to the west and north, on the summits of some of which the snow lingers even in midsummer. The road I generally take, though a main road, is very solitary. Now and then I meet a group of travellers on horseback, roughly clad, with muskets slung behind their saddles, and looking very much like the robbers they are armed against; or a line of muleteers from the distant provinces, with their mules hung with bells, and tricked out with worsted bobs and tassels; or a goatherd, driving his flock of goats home to the city for the night, to furnish milk for the inhabitants. Every group seems to accord with the wild, half-savage scenery around; and it is difficult to realize that such scenery and such groups should be in the vicinity of a populous and ancient capital. Some of the sunsets behind the Guadarrama mountains, shedding the last golden rays over this vast melancholy landscape, are really magnificent.

I have had much pleasure in walking on the Prado on bright moonlight nights. This is a noble walk within the walls of the city, and not far from my dwelling. It has alleys of stately trees, and is ornamented with fine fountains decorated with statuary and sculpture. The Prado is the great promenade of the city. One grand alley is called the saloon, and is particularly crowded. In the summer evenings there are groups of ladies and gentlemen seated in chairs, and holding their *tertulias*, or gossiping parties, until a late hour; but what most delights me, are the groups of children, attended by their parents or nurses, who gather about the fountains, take hands, and dance in rings to their own nursery songs. They are just the little beings for such a fairy moonlight scene. I have watched them night after night, and only wished I had some of my own little nieces or grandnieces to take part in the fairy ring. These are all the scenes and incidents that I can furnish you from my present solitary life.

I am looking soon for the return of the Albuquerques to Madrid, which will give me a family circle to resort to. Madame Albuquerque always calls me Uncle, and I endeavor to cheat myself into the idea that she is a niece; she certainly has the kindness and amiableness of one, and her children are most entertaining companions for me.

Your letter from the cottage brings with it all the recollections of the place: its trees and shrubs, its roses and honeysuckles and humming birds. I am glad to find that my old friend, the catbird, still builds and sings under the window. You speak of Vaney's barking, too; it was like suddenly hearing a well-known but long-forgotten voice, for it is a long time since any mention has been made of that most meritorious little dog.

* * * * * *

A short time after, we find he is about to send in his resignation, and has made a sudden transfer of his establishment to the Albuquerques'—an arrangement satisfactory to all parties, excepting, he remarks, "to my poor servants, who, at first, were quite in consternation."

[*To Mrs. Storrow.*]

MADRID, Sept. 6, 1845.

MY DEAR SARAH:

This is the country of revolutions, and one has just taken place in my own domains. I have made a transfer of my establishment (furniture, &c.) to the Albuquerques', with whom

I shall live *en famille* for the residue of my residence in Madrid, having the intention to send home my resignation, so as to be relieved from my post by the opening of spring, if not before. I retain a small part of the Apartment, and maintain the office of the Legation there. This arrangement suits us all admirably. The Albuquerques have a commodious, well-furnished house, ready provided for them, at a time when they were at their wits' end to find a habitation, and I am saved all the trouble, delay, and sacrifice of breaking up and selling off an establishment by piecemeal. In the mean time, being now relieved from the responsibilities of housekeeping, I have resolved upon making a brief visit to Paris. * * * I will return to Madrid, until regularly relieved from my post by a successor. When we return, Lorenzo undertakes the superintendence of the Albuquerques' household, in the same capacity that he has lived with me. The faithful Juana likewise remains as housekeeper and lady's maid; and my excellent cook retains his office, so that I shall have my old servants about me. At present, I am living delightfully in the Albuquerque family, and feel quite as if I were among relatives.

The "brief visit to Paris" which Mr. Irving was meditating, resulted, as we shall see, in a much longer absence from Madrid than was his purpose when he left.

It was on his journey to Bordeaux, at this time, on his way to the capital of France, that he was induced to go out of his route to visit the little town of Tonneins, rendered memorable to him as the scene where, long years before, he had played the part of the English prisoner of war. The reader may recollect this incident of his youthful days, as given in the fourth chapter of the first volume.

From Bordeaux he proceeded by sea to Nantes, then ascended the Loire in steamboat, "through very beautiful and historical scenery," and at Orleans took the railroad to Paris, where, he observes, "I arrived quite the worse for a fortnight of fatiguing travel." On the 1st of November he was expecting "to be able, in the course of a few days, to return for the last time to Madrid." On the 15th of the same month, he writes to me that he was still lingering in Paris, in hopes of seeing Mr. McLane, the American Minister at London, who talked of making a brief visit to the French capital, and wished to find him there. "He is very anxious," he writes, "about the state of our affairs with England. The Oregon question is becoming more and more difficult of adjustment." * * * "Much will depend upon the temper and language of the forthcoming Message of Mr. Polk."

On the 29th of December he writes to me, still at Paris:

I have deferred my return to Madrid, and am in the midst of preparations for a visit to England, where my friends think I may be of more service, during the present crisis, than in Spain. I shall remain in England three or four weeks, part of which I shall pass at Birmingham, and will then set out for Madrid, there to await the arrival of my successor. I send my resignation by this steamer.

The President's Message, though firm and unflinching on

the subject of the Oregon question, has not been of a tone to create any *flare-up* in England. I think he is justifiable in the view he takes of that question, and believe that the present Cabinet of Great Britain would be well disposed to entertain the proposition which was so haughtily rejected by Mr. Packenham. I still hope the matter may be settled by negotiation; but, should England provoke a war upon the question as it stands, I am clearly of opinion that we have the right on our side, and that the world will ultimately think so.

Immediately after the date of the foregoing letter, Mr. Irving proceeded to England, and, on the 3d of February, writes me as follows, from London:

MY DEAR PIERRE:

I have now been about a month in England, part of the time at Birmingham, and part in London. I came here under an invitation from Mr. McLane, and in the idea that I might be of more public service here, at this particular juncture, than I would be at Madrid. I think I have been of service through old habits of intimacy with people connected with the Government, and through the confidence they have in me, in inspiring more correct notions of the disposition and intentions of our Government, and in facilitating the diplomatic intercourse of Mr. McLane.

I have been closely occupied, during the greater part of my sojourn in England, in studying the Oregon question, and in preparing an article for publication, in the hope of placing our rights and our conduct in a proper light before the British public. I have not finished the article to my satisfaction, and circumstances have concurred to make it very doubtful whether I shall give it to the press.

A close and conscientious study of the case has convinced me of the superiority of our title to the whole of the territory, and of the fairness of the offers we have made for the sake of peace, and in consideration of the interests which have grown up in the country during the long period of the joint occupancy. British diplomatists have greatly erred in not closing with our proposition of the 49th parallel, with some additional items of accommodation. They should never have pushed so pertinaciously for the three additional degrees on the Pacific and the north bank of the Columbia. This was merely to protect the interests of the Hudson's Bay Company; but they might have been protected by some other arrangement involving no point of pride. The full possession of the Columbia River is a matter of importance in our eyes, as being one of the great outlets of our empire. By neglecting to close with our offer, and to negotiate upon the basis of the 49th parallel, the British diplomatists have left the question at the mercy of after influences, through the malignancy of the British press and the blustering of our candidates for popularity, to get up prejudice and passion on both sides, and to make diplomatic negotiation almost hopeless.

As I doubt whether I can do any further good here at present, I propose setting off for Paris in the course of a few days, thence to continue on to Madrid, where I shall await the arrival of my successor. I long to throw off diplomacy, and to return to my independent literary pursuits. My health is now excellent.

From London, Mr. Irving proceeded to Paris, to

take leave of his niece, Mrs. Storrow, who was soon to set off on a visit to the United States, and, on his departure, made a rapid journey day and night to Madrid, to await the arrival of his successor, who had not yet been nominated.

From Madrid he writes to Mrs. Paris, March 29th, after a long absence from the Court:

There have been several changes in the Cabinet here, which have caused great agitation in the political circles. Narvaez, who had been in eclipse for a short time, is restored to power, and is again at the head of the Government, with a Cabinet completely under his dictation. The sessions of the *Cortes* are suspended; a royal decree has completely gagged the press, and there is every appearance of absolute rule. * * * The question of the marriage of the young Queen becomes more and more embarrassing. Until it is settled, the affairs of Spain will always be in a precarious state, and the kingdom liable to convulsions.

I had letters from home, a few days since—one from the cottage, from my dear Kate, dated in February last. She had just heard of my having sent my resignation to Government, and now felt persuaded that I would soon return. She gives me until the month of June. I had hoped to be home before that time, but now I see no likelihood of it. My successor was not appointed at the middle of February. When appointed, it will take him some time to prepare for embarkation; then he will probably come by the way of England and France, and loiter by the way—especially at Paris, which is a kind of fitting-out place, to buy furniture, &c., &c. I watch the American papers anxiously for some notice on the subject.

To-morrow I shall have news by the steamer of the 1st March, and I hope it will bring me something definite on the subject. Now that I am in a manner half dismounted from my post, I am anxious to have done entirely with diplomatic business, and to be on my way home.

April 25th, he writes to Mrs. Paris, shortly after the precipitate banishment of Narvaez:

The day after to-morrow we have a grand *Besa manos* on the birthday of the Queen Mother. It will be the first grand Court ceremony since my return from Paris.

You will have heard of the late events in the Spanish Court—the downfall and banishment of Narvaez. It was considered a harsh and ungrateful act on the part of the sovereigns, and has added to the unpopularity of the Queen Mother. The changes and sudden transitions in the Spanish Court are something like those in the courts of the East. It only wants the bowstring to make the resemblance complete. I am getting tired of courts, however, altogether, and shall be right glad to throw off my diplomatic coat for the last time.

In one of his diplomatic despatches to Mr. Webster, before his retirement from the administration of President Tyler, in the spring of 1843, referring to the unparalleled number of changes that had taken place in the Spanish Cabinet within the preceding eight years, which, in the Department of State, in which the lowest number occurred, amounted "to two and a half ministers per annum," Mr. Irving remarks:

It gives a startling idea of the interruptions to which an extended negotiation with this Government must be subject. * * * This consumption of Ministers is appalling. * * * To carry on a negotiation with such transient functionaries, is like bargaining at the window of a railroad car: before you can get a reply to a proposition, the other party is out of sight.

CHAPTER XXII.

HISTORICAL EXTRACT FROM A DIPLOMATIC DESPATCH—HEARS OF THE APPOINTMENT OF A SUCCESSOR—HIS FEELING IN REGARD TO THE WAR WITH MEXICO—ALLUSION TO THE SETTLEMENT OF THE OREGON QUESTION—ARRIVAL OF GENERAL SAUNDERS—AUDIENCE OF LEAVE—RETURN TO SUNNYSIDE—THE ADDITION—PREPARING A COMPLETE EDITION OF HIS WORKS—LETTER TO GOUVERNEUR KEMBLE.

I CLOSE the Minister's narrative of the caprices of Spanish politics with the following extract from an official despatch to James Buchanan, Secretary of State, in which there had been allusion to a crisis of many days' continuance in completing the new Cabinet under Isturiz, as head of the State Department. The despatch is dated April 18th, 1846 :

While dissension has been prevalent at headquarters, an insurrection has broken out in Gallicia. Symptoms of this appeared during the last period of Narvaez' administration, and apprehensions were entertained that the Prince Don Enrique, who was at Corunna, would be induced to head it. Narvaez proceeded in the matter with his usual promptness. Military measures were taken to suppress the insurrection, and a royal command was issued to the Prince to leave the kingdom instantly, and choose some place in France for his residence, there to await royal orders, with the understanding that, should he absent himself from the place chosen, he would be stripped of all the honors and consideration of a royal prince of Spain; and, should he return to Spain contrary to the royal command, he would subject himself to prosecution before any tribunal in the kingdom. The Prince obeyed the royal command implicitly, and chose Bayonne as his place of exile. Scarce had he been there a few days, when Narvaez himself arrived there—a banished man! The public papers state that Narvaez, soon after his arrival, paid the Prince a visit of respect, arrayed in full uniform. The interview must have been a curious one. As has been well observed, there is so much of the comic in these sudden and violent changes and transitions in Spanish politics, that we should be disposed to laugh at them, only that they occur so rapidly we have not time to laugh. Accustomed as I have become to all kinds of contradictory moves, I should not be surprised to see Narvaez back here again before long, at the head of affairs. The Government, in its perplexed condition, with differences of opinion in the Cabinet, with an active and confident opposition gaining strength in the capital, and rumors of conspiracies in the provinces, begins to feel the want of Narvaez' energy, activity, and spirit of control. This is especially the case since it is found that, in Gallicia, some of the army have joined the insurgents. Every one of the leading personages in power attempts to shift off the odium of his precipitate banishment, and to hint a wish for his return. In the mean time, the arbitrary measures instituted under his ministry continue in force; and an attempt has been made to imitate his military rigor, by issuing a circular to the *Gefes Politicos*, or heads of municipalities throughout the kingdom, authorizing them to declare martial law in their respective jurisdictions on any appearance of popular disturbance. These rigorous measures, however, are considered as proofs of distrust and alarm on the part of Government, rather than of confidence and decision. A general uneasiness prevails throughout the community, and fearful forebodings of an approaching convulsion.

Soon after the date of the foregoing extract, Mr. Irving was informed, through the public papers, that Romulus M. Saunders, of North Carolina, had been appointed to the Spanish mission. His resignation had been transmitted in December, and he had been looking impatiently for tidings of the appointment of a successor.

At this time came the news of the breaking out of the war with Mexico—a result of the scheme of the annexation of Texas, which had been brought to a successful issue at the close of Mr. Tyler's administration, while John C. Calhoun was Secretary of State.

On the 24th of June, he writes me from Madrid, where he was still awaiting the uncertain arrival of his successor:

I regret exceedingly that we have got engaged in a war with Mexico. That power has been badly advised; she should have received Mr. Slidell, and the matters between us might have been amicably arranged. She has been induced to believe that certain foreign powers would back her, very probably; if so, she will find that, after all their tampering, they will leave her in the lurch. The situation in which our little army under General Taylor was placed, apparently cut off from his supplies, and surrounded by a superior force, gave me great uneasiness. I feared some humiliating blow, and saw that the English press was preparing to trumpet it forth to Europe with the customary insults and exaggerations. I feared, also, that a blow of the kind would tend to prolong the war, as we could not think of peace until we had completely obliterated the disgrace. When I read, therefore, the account of the gallant manner in which Taylor and his little army had acquitted themselves, and the generous manner in which they had treated their vanquished enemies, the tears absolutely started into my eyes, and a load was taken from my heart. I sincerely hope this brilliant victory will be followed up by magnanimous feeling on the part of our Government, and that the war may be brought to a speedy close on fair and honorable terms.

With kind recollections of England and the home feeling he had once enjoyed there, Mr. Irving had been much disturbed of late by noticing, in the Madrid *Gazette*, articles from English journals, in which all our acts and intentions in regard to the Oregon question and the disputes with Mexico were grossly misrepresented, and we were reviled as a people without principle or faith. As the *Gazette* was exclusively a Court paper, edited by persons about the Government, he took occasion to inquire of Mr. Isturiz, the Minister of State, whether these British calumnies were believed and countenanced by the cabinet. Mr. Isturiz assured him that he had not noticed the offensive articles, and that he would take care to have them excluded for the future.

In another letter, showing how much he deprecated the effect of these persevering attempts to debase the national name, he remarks: "A rancorous prejudice against us has been diligently inculcated of late years by the British press, and it is daily producing its fruits of bitterness."

"Bulwer," he once exclaimed to the British Minister at Madrid, in strong excitement on the same subject, "I should deplore exceedingly a war with England, for depend upon it, if we must come to blows, it will be serious work for both. You might break our head at first, but by Heaven! we would break your back in the end."

Late in July, in a letter to me, he has this allusion to the final adjustment of the Oregon embroilment:

> The settlement of the Oregon question is a vast event for our national credit and national prosperity. The war with Mexico will in all probability be wound up before long, and then our commercial affairs will have no external dangers to apprehend for a long series of years.
>
> I have reason to congratulate myself that, in a quiet way, I was enabled, while in England, to facilitate the frank and confiding intercourse of Mr. McLane and Lord Aberdeen, which has proved so beneficial to the settlement of this question; so that, though I did not publish the pamphlet I had prepared, my visit to England was not without its utility.

On the 25th of July, Mr. Irving informs me that General Saunders had arrived about three days before. "I, of course," he adds, "am busy preparing to pass the legation into his hands as soon as he has been accredited, which will probably be two or three days hence. I shall then take my departure almost immediately, having made all my travelling preparations." Soon after, he closes his diplomatic letters to Mrs. Paris with this account of his audience of leave.

A few evenings since, I had my audience of the Queen, to deliver the letter of the President announcing my recall. Ten o'clock was the hour appointed. Though sated with court ceremonies, I could not but feel a little sensitive on visiting the royal palace for the last time, and passing through its vast apartments but partially lighted up. I found the Queen in an inner cabinet, attended by the Minister of State and several ladies and gentlemen in waiting. I had prepared my speech in Spanish, which was to the following effect:

"MADAM:

"I have the honor to deliver into the hands of your Majesty a letter from the President of the United States, announcing my recall from the post of Envoy Extraordinary and Minister Plenipotentiary in this Court.

"I am charged by the President to express, on delivering this letter to your Majesty, his constant and earnest desire to maintain the amicable relations which so happily exist between the two countries.

"For my own part, I can assure your Majesty that I shall carry with me into private life the same ardent desire for the welfare of Spain, and the same deep interest in the fortunes and happiness of its youthful sovereign, which have actuated me during my official career; and I now take leave of your

Majesty, wishing you, from the bottom of my heart, a long and happy life, and a reign which may form a glorious epoch in the history of this country."

The following is as close a translation as I can make of the Queen's reply:

"It is with much regret that I receive the announcement of your recall from the post of Envoy Extraordinary and Minister Plenipotentiary of the United States near my person.

"Very gratifying to me are the wishes you express for the happiness of Spain. On that, I found the happiness which you desire for me personally, and the glory of my reign.

"You may take with you into private life the intimate conviction that your frank and loyal conduct has contributed to draw closer the amicable relations which exist between North America and the Spanish nation, and that your distinguished personal merits have gained in my heart the appreciation which you merit by more than one title."

This little speech reads stiff in translation, but it is very graceful and gracious in the original, and I have been congratulated repeatedly on receiving one so much out of the cold, commonplace style of diplomacy. In fact, my farewell interview with the whole of the royal family was extremely satisfactory. * * *

The Minister of State (Mr. Isturiz) has likewise been uncommonly cordial in his expressions of regret at my departure. In a word, from the different members of the Cabinet, and from my colleagues of the diplomatic corps, I have met with nothing but the most gratifying testimonials of esteem and good will in my parting interviews.

Thus closes my public career. At six o'clock this evening I set off from Madrid, in company with Mr. Weismuller, a connection of the Rothschilds, stationed at this capital, to post for France in a private carriage. My saddest parting will be with the Albuquerques, who seem to me more like relatives than friends. * * *

My intention is to push for England almost without stopping, so as to be ready to embark in one of the August steamers, should certain public business with which I may be intrusted by the Spanish Government render it necessary.

I regret that the late arrival of General Saunders at Madrid, and various concurring circumstances, should oblige me to give up all the farewell visits I had promised to pay to certain of my European friends, and should render my stay with our dear sister so brief as it must now be. I have promised them and myself, however, a supplementary visit to Europe after I have been home some time, and have got all my American affairs in order; when I will pass a few months in revisiting persons and places endeared to me by past pleasures and kindnesses.

This last purpose was never fulfilled. Mr. Irving had reached London by the middle of August, and early in September he bade adieu forever to European scenes, embarking in the steamer Cambria for Boston, where he arrived on the 18th of that month, after an absence from his native country of nearly four years and a half. The following afternoon he took steamboat at New York for Tarrytown, two miles north of Sunnyside.

"I long to be once more back at dear little Sunnyside, while I have yet strength and good spirits to enjoy the simple pleasures of the country, and to rally a happy family group once more about me. I grudge every year of absence that rolls by. To-morrow is my birthday. I shall then be sixty-two years old. The evening of life is fast drawing over me; still I hope to get back among my friends while there is yet a little sunshine left." So wrote the Minister from the midst of his court life at Madrid, April 2d, 1845. It was the 19th of September, 1846, when the impatient longing of his heart was gratified, and he found himself restored to his home for the thirteen years of happy life still remaining to him.

A month or two before his official mission closed at Madrid, he had dismissed a correspondent's suggestion that he should rent the cottage, in the following terms:

I have some Scotch blood in my veins, and a little of the feeling, with respect to my cottage, that a poor devil of a laird has for the stronghold that has sheltered his family. Nay, I believe it is the having such an object to work for, which spurs me on to combat and conquer difficulties; and if I succeed in weathering a series of hard times without striking my flag, I shall be largely indebted to my darling little Sunnyside for furnishing me the necessary stimulus. So no more talk of abandoning the cottage. In the words of Thomas the Rhymer—

> "Betide, betide, whate'er betide,
> Haig shall be Haig of Bemerside."

So far, indeed, from renting the cottage, his first concern was to build an addition to it, and enlarge its accommodations, which were quite too cramped for the number of its inmates. To Mrs. Storrow, who had now returned to Paris from a visit of some months to her native country, he writes, October 18th: "I am making preparations to commence, in the course of a day or two, the addition to the cottage. * * * I have a plan from Mr. Harvey which harmonizes with the rest of the building, and will not be expensive enough to ruin me."

While occupied with his new building, Mr. Irving was engaged, whenever he could find mood and leisure, in preparing a complete edition of his works, with corrections, alterations, and additions, with a view to make an arrangement for the whole, either by disposing of the copyrights, or by farming them out collectively for a term of years at a yearly consideration. It was important to him to get his literary property in train to yield an income, which had been unproductive ever since he embarked on his foreign mission. In the exigency of his official engagements, he was obliged to depart without having been able to make any arrangement with his Philadelphia publishers, Messrs. Lea & Blanchard, for a renewal of the old agreement for the exclusive publication of his works, or receiving from them any proposal by which he might continue to derive profit from them during his absence. They had probably grown timid during the long depression of the literary market, and did not feel confident that his works were capable of a renewed and active circulation. Their former contract comprised Knickerbocker's History of New York, the Sketch Book, Bracebridge Hall, Tales of a Traveller, the Life and Voyages of Columbus (excepting the Abridgment), the Companions of Columbus, the Conquest of Granada, and the Alhambra. Before he left, he sought to make a new arrangement with them, including his subsequent writings, at the rate of three thousand dollars a year. "You see," he writes to me from Sunnyside, on the 31st of December, 1846, in mentioning this particular, "I asked higher than the sum you proposed to ask; indeed, much higher than they could have afforded to give with advantage. I think, however, a similar arrangement for my works would be much more profitable at present than it would have been at that time." If Lea & Blanchard held back, other publishers, who believed his works might be made a source of emolument to him as well as to them, were pressing forward with liberal overtures. It was difficult for him, however, to bring himself resolutely to the task of preparing his works for a republication, while engaged in superintending the building of the new part of his house. "I was greatly disappointed at not seeing you at Christmas," he writes to me from Sunnyside, at the close of the year. "I wished much to talk to you about my literary affairs. I am growing a sad laggard in literature, and need some one to bolster me up occasionally. I am too ready to do anything else rather than write."

On the 6th of January, I wrote to Mr. Irving that the Screw Dock Company, in which he had an interest, had declared a *quarterly* dividend of five per cent., equivalent to twenty per cent. per annum, which it gave for a series of years; adding, that I had been called upon to pay out so much of late for him, it was quite cheering to have something coming in. I give his reply:

SUNNYSIDE, Jan. 6, 1847.

MY DEAR PIERRE:

* * * I am glad to hear you are receiving such a snug little bag of money from the Screw Dock. In faith, the Dock deserves its name. I fancy there must be a set of Jews at the windlasses to screw the ships so handsomely. Tell them to screw on, and spare not! These are building times, when all the world wants money.

Since I was so "flush of money on his account," he then proceeds to specify three outstanding debts which I could pay, and adds:

You now know the full extent of all my "indebtedness," excepting what relates to my new building, and to domestic expenses.

I know I am "burning the candle at both ends" this year, but it must be so until I get my house in order, after which expenses will return to their ordinary channel, and I trust my income will expand, as I hope to get my literary property in a productive train.

I give one or two further extracts, which afford glimpses of the tenor of his life and feelings for a few months after his return. At the date of the first, his old malady had seized again upon one of his ankles, and had become aggravated by his standing too much out of doors in cold and wet weather, superintending the new building.

[*To Mrs. Pierre M. Irving.*]

SUNNYSIDE, Feb. 14,

MY DEAR HELEN:

Your letter was like manna in the wilderness to me, finding me mewed up in this little warm oven of a house, where, if I remain much longer without getting out of doors occasionally, I shall grow quite rusty and crusty. Fortunately, I was troubled for two or three days with an inflammation in my eyes, which made me fear I was about to be blind; that has passed away, and you cannot think what a cause of self-gratulation it is to me to find that I am only lame. We have all abundant reason to be thankful for the dispensations of Providence, if we only knew when and why.

Still it is some little annoyance to me that I cannot get about and find some means of spending that sum of money which you tell me Pierre has been making for me. I think he takes advantage of my crippled condition, which prevents my going on with my improvements; and I fear, if I do not get in a disbursing condition soon, he will get the weather gage of me, and make me rich in spite of myself.

* * * * * *

Your account of Mrs. ———'s reception was quite animated. I cannot expect you to abstract yourself from so much social enjoyment, and come to sober little Sunnyside while the gay season lasts; therefore I retract all that I said in my last letter to Pierre about your making me a visit just now, and will not say a word more on the subject; not but that it would be an act of common humanity—to say nothing of natural affection.

He was still cut off from recreation out of doors, and confined to the house by his unlucky ankle, when he wrote the following, to the same correspondent:

SUNNYSIDE, March 12, 1847.

* * * * * *

We were in hopes, a day or two since, that we had got rid of winter. The frost was out of the ground, and the roads were beginning to settle; but cold weather has suddenly returned upon us, and everything is again frozen up. This keeps me back in the finishing of my new building, for I was on the point of putting the workmen upon it. I am impatient to complete the job. I want to get my study in order, and my books arranged. I feel rather cramped for room, now that I have resumed literary occupations, and am at the same time an invalid. Besides, the interior of my household wants some different arrangement, as you must be aware. * * * But the fact is, I am growing a confounded old fellow; I begin to be so studious of my convenience, and to have such a craving desire to be comfortable.

Give my love to all the household, and tell Pierre to make money for me as fast as possible, as my expenses will break out anew with the blossoms of spring, and will need all his *screwing* to keep pace with them.

Affectionately, your uncle,

WASHINGTON IRVING.

About the same time, he writes to his sister, Mrs. Paris:

I trust this teasing, obstinate malady may wear away as spring advances; at any rate, I shall be able, by and by, to get out on the grass and lounge under the trees. But what a change from my usual active habits! My great annoyance is not to be able to go about my place and see to getting things in order, and have them done to suit me. There is nothing like the eye of a master, however active and faithful may be the servants. I am anxious, also, to resume operations on my new building, and get it finished, that I may regulate my house and household, and establish myself more conveniently, feeling much the want of more accommodation in my study for my books and papers.

A few days later, he writes to me:

* * * I am getting on well with my delinquent ankle, and am able, now the snow is gone, to take a turn occasionally out of doors, and visit the garden and poultry yard, which is very refreshing. I hope, by the time Helen gets through her "spring arrangements," disposes of her bandbox and carpet bag, and comes up here, she will find me

> "once more able
> To stump about my farm and stable."

I expect the carpenters this morning, to resume operations on the new building, and I shall keep all hands at work until the job is finished

The following is in reply to a letter in which I had

informed him of two small remittances from the West, the offer at cost of an English saddle and bridle, and another *quarterly* dividend of five per cent. from the Screw Dock:

SUNNYSIDE, April 13, 1847.

MY DEAR PIERRE:

I was just setting off for town, this morning, to meet Mr. Prescott at dinner at Mr. Cary's, when a few drops of rain and the prognostications of the weatherwise made me draw back. I regret it now, as I hardly know when I shall be able to get away from superintending the arrangement of my grounds, house, &c.; and I long to have a "crack" with you.

* * * * * *

I cannot afford a new saddle to my new horse. I am getting my old saddle furbished up, which must serve until I can recover from the ruin brought upon me by the improvement of my house. You see, I am growing economical, and saving my candle now that I have burnt it down to an end.

* * * * * *

I am surprised and delighted at the windfall from Milwaukie, and shall now not despair of the sky's falling and our catching larks. Toledo, too, begins to crawl. There's life in a muscle! The screw, however, is the boy for my money. The dividends there are like the skimmings of the pots at Camacho's wedding.

For some weeks past he had been engaged in close literary application. "That you may not be frightened at my extravagance, and cut off supplies," says a letter to me, "I must tell you that I have lately been working up some old stuff which had lain for years lumbering like rubbish in one of my trunks, and which, I trust, will more than pay the expense of my new building."

I close the volume with the following allusion to the new addition, of which he speaks in a letter as forming one of the most striking and picturesque features of his little edifice. It is in reply to Gouverneur Kemble, who had banteringly asked him the meaning of the *pagoda*, which he had noticed in passing up the river in the boat:

MY DEAR KEMBLE:

I have long been looking out for your promised visit, but now your letter throws it quite into uncertainty. I should have come to you before this, for I long to take you once more by the hand; but I have been detained at home by building and repairing, and the necessity of fighting off, by baths and prescriptions, the return of a malady which beset me in Spain, and which endeavors to keep possession of one of my ankles. However, I trust to finish all my buildings and improvements before long, and then I shall endeavor to look in upon you at Cold Spring.

* * * * * *

As to the *pagoda* about which you speak, it is one of the most useful additions that ever was made to a house, besides being so ornamental. It gives me laundry, store rooms, pantries, servants' rooms, coal cellar, &c., &c., &c., converting what was once rather a make-shift little mansion into one of the most complete snuggeries in the country, as you will confess when you come to see and inspect it. The only part of it that is not adapted to some valuable purpose is the cupola, which has no bell in it, and is about as serviceable as the feather in one's cap; though, by the way, it has its purpose, for it supports a weathercock brought from Holland by Gill Davis (the King of Coney Island), who says he got it from a windmill which they were demolishing at the gate of Rotterdam, which windmill has been mentioned in Knickerbocker. I hope, therefore, I may be permitted to wear my feather unmolested.

Ever, my dear Kemble, affectionately yours,

WASHINGTON IRVING.

END OF VOLUME III.

www.ingramcontent.com/pod-product-compliance
Lightning Source LLC
LaVergne TN
LVHW020110110826
845151LV00001B/120

* 9 7 8 1 4 2 5 5 4 4 0 6 5 *